Burke and the French Revolution

BURKE

AND THE

FRENCH REVOLUTION

BICENTENNIAL ESSAYS

EDITED BY

STEVEN BLAKEMORE

THE UNIVERSITY OF GEORGIA PRESS / ATHENS & LONDON

© 1992 by the University of Georgia Press
Athens, Georgia 30602
All rights reserved
Designed by Louise M. Jones
Set in 10½/13 Fournier by Tseng Information Systems, Inc.
Printed and bound by Thomson-Shore Inc.
The paper in this book meets the guidelines for
permanence and durability of the Committee on
Production Guidelines for Book Longevity of the
Council on Library Resources.

Printed in the United States of America

96 95 94 93 92   C   5 4 3 2 1

Library of Congress Cataloging in Publication Data
Burke and the French Revolution : bicentennial essays /
edited by Steven Blakemore.
p.   cm.
Includes bibliographical references and index.
ISBN 0-8203-1370-X (alk. paper)
1. Burke, Edmund, 1729–1797—Views on French Revolution.
2. France—History—Revolution, 1789–1799.
3. Burke, Edmund, 1729–1797. Reflections on the French
Revolution.   I. Blakemore, Steven.
DC150.B9B87   1992
944.04—dc20   91-558
                                                    CIP

British Library Cataloging in Publication Data available

Contents

Editor's Note

Until recently there has been no authoritative edition of Burke's oeuvre. Fortunately, this is being addressed by Paul Langford and the other editors who are in the process of completing what will eventually be a twelve-volume edition of Burke's *Writings and Speeches* (Oxford: Clarendon Press, 1981–). Unfortunately, volume 8 of this edition (*The French Revolution, 1790–1794*) contains none of Burke's speeches dealing with the Revolution, and it lacks two of Burke's major antirevolutionary writings, *An Appeal from the New to the Old Whigs* (1791) and *Letters on a Regicide Peace*—the latter appearing after 1795. Consequently, the authors represented in the present volume have used standard editions of Burke's writings and speeches.

Editor's Introduction

When Edmund Burke responded to the French Revolution two centuries ago, both the Revolution and Burke seemed immediately to acquire oppositional mythic status, existing as Manichaean forms of energy. These antagonistic forces dialectically defined and delineated each other and practically everything else involved in the tumult. Consequently, Burke and the Revolution have become, for many, a paradoxical bloc. In a sense, Burke was subsumed by the Revolution, and the Revolution's contradictory, controversial "meaning" has become a constituted part of Burke's response so that today he is principally remembered for his antirevolutionary oeuvre. Likewise, the Revolution and what it does or does not represent is often posited against Burke, for admirers of the Revolution have been, in many ways, responding to Burke for two centuries.

In 1790 Burke was the first prominent public man to question critically the Revolution and its course. He was the first to argue that it constituted a new species of oppressive, expansionist power, and he hence analyzed what, to him, were the dark and esurient energies that propelled it aggressively into the hearts, minds, and countries of Europe. Because he was the first to raise substantial questions about the Revolution's fundamental essence—at a time when the Revolution was being celebrated in most of Europe with enthusiastic approval—its supporters felt impelled to reply to his initial critique, out of which flowed a series of sustained assaults on practically every aspect of the Revolution. Ever since Burke sounded what seemed to be one lone clarion call of alarm, the Revolution's significance has been debated in many of the terms formulated by both Burke and his revolutionary respondents.

Today the abiding interest in Burke and the Revolution is, I think, a general recognition that the Revolution still impinges on the modern mind—its echoes still resonate in the evolution of modern revolutionary movements—in the very language by which we still describe and debate democracy and despotism, revolution and counterrevolution. If

Burke and the Revolution have been accordingly mythologized by partisan ideology, it is because both seem to represent something intensely intrinsic to twentieth-century life. What this ambiguous "something" is varies according to the way the Revolution is thought of, but it is connected to a tacit sense that specific twentieth-century political systems, for good or bad, and the correspondent "life" they create are indirect products of the French Revolution.

One's view of the Revolution is thus often intertwined with approval or disapproval of Burke: both exist in complementary opposition, and if the Revolution still attracts or appalls, Burke is likewise still read with sympathy or aversion, because he crystallized an antirevolutionary *mentalité* that, like the Revolution, still tinctures our thinking about the issues and realities vivified by both. As Paine pointed out in *The Rights of Man*, oppositional "knowledge" cannot be "unknown"; consequently, both Burke and the Revolution have been incorporated into our thinking and feeling. They still speak to us across the centuries in two languages that are strikingly modern.

Burke's critique, of course, has never been successfully interpreted as a historical curiosity piece—a nostalgic defense of the ancien régime. If it were, Burke would merely interest us the way Sir Robert Filmer does—he would merely entertain us, instead of eliciting, like the Revolution itself, the hostile or supportive responses that continue to color our thinking about the world then and now.

Burke was alarmed, but he was not nostalgic about his beleaguered eighteenth-century "world." When the great iconoclastic power of the Revolution erupted into European consciousness, he realized that the inherited, traditional European world—a world he contended had evolved over 2,000 years—was forever changed. He recognized that this world had psychologically ceased to exist once the Revolution had changed man's sense of a continuous, correspondent past. By articulating his vision of the old European world, Burke intended to show what was lost and the attendant consequences of this loss. From this followed his analysis of the Revolution's genesis and its constituent parts—an analysis that culminated in his argument that the Revolution was the greatest assault on reality in the world's history.

Specifically, in his analysis of the revolutionaries' "paradoxical" thinking—thinking that deviates from traditional, inherited thought (see *Oxford English Dictionary*, meanings 1 and 2B), Burke formulated what can be characterized as a counterrevolutionary theory of repression and resemblance. He suggested that the revolutionaries' obsession with the evil past results in parodic replications of this past—a past that initially exists as a revolutionary caricature of the old repressive regime. By repressing, subsequently, all "counterrevolutionary" difference, they ironically and unwittingly energize and enact the very oppressive power they claim they are replacing. They resemble the fantasied monsters of the Old Regime, because their obsession with repressing its imaginary power reveals their secret fascination with power. They hence create ironically what was heretofore only imaginary.

To put this into modern terms, Burke describes a revolutionary system that is recognizably totalitarian, but his critique is directed, in part, at Enlightenment and revolutionary descriptions of the old order—descriptions that Burke believes are polemical caricatures of imaginary oppression. Burke suggests that the French revolutionaries were the first to act out on the world's stage their political fantasies of complete ideological and physical power (both Burke and the revolutionaries criticize each other for staged theatrical presentations at variance with "reality"). Thus, according to Burke, they reveal their latent fascination with the very power they criticize. For Burke the supreme irony is that the revolutionaries realize the oppressive Enlightenment "nightmare"—what was once unreal is forced unnaturally on the "natural" world by the ideology that empowers it. The Revolution turns, mutatis mutandis, into the monster it denies.

Since revolutionary power was, to Burke, entirely new and unprecedented, he contended that it had to be confronted with a correspondent energy—that revolutionary terror, the revolutionary "sublime," could be countered only by a new sublime form of countervailing force. Consequently, he insisted that the Revolution could not be defensively contained but had to be decisively destroyed through a total offensive war against the Jacobin state. This strategy of attack is reflected in his antirevolutionary oeuvre, where Burke wages a total textual war against the Revolution.

The revolutionaries, in turn, responded with sustained offensive assaults on Burke's texts and hence on Burke himself. It is the language of this war that still speaks to us across the centuries, reverberating in the texture of twentieth-century thought. Because Burke and the Revolution still confront each other, because they both represent contending kingdoms of power, they continue to challenge and provoke us today, and thus a reassessment of both seemed judiciously appropriate in light of the bicentennial.

The essays in this book stem from an open invitation for submissions published in assorted academic and scholastic journals. While the specific subject was Burke and the Revolution, the contributors were free to explore any aspect, using any methodology they chose. One of the fruitful results is an endeavor to rehistoricize Burke—to return to the contextual circumstances—to the tumultuous revolutionary world he wrote against.

Since Burke is often discussed as if his ideas were platonic forms, unsullied by the dross of time, the contributors endeavor to return Burke to history as it presences itself in the texts they question and probe. Likewise, the authors tacitly crystallize their own historical positions out of which Burke and the Revolution still war in and with the language of contemporary thought. Indeed, two centuries after the most astonishing revolution in modern history, we continue to absorb and to be absorbed by both.

Chronology
of Important Dates

1729   Edmund Burke born (Dublin, 12 January [New Style]).

c. 1735–c. 1740   EB lives with relatives of his mother in Ballyduff, County Cork.

1741–44   EB attends Abraham Shackleton's boarding school at Ballitore, thirty miles from Dublin.

1744–49   EB educated at Trinity College, Dublin.

1748   Montesquieu publishes *De l'Esprit des Lois*.

1750   EB begins study for the bar at Middle Temple, London; studies abandoned by 1755; interests largely literary.

1756   EB's *A Vindication of Natural Society* published.

1757   EB marries Jane Mary Nugent (1734–1812), daughter of Irish Catholic doctor; publishes *A Philosophic Enquiry into the Origin of Our Ideas of the Sublime and Beautiful*; contracts to write *An Abridgement of English History* (published posthumously). The elder Pitt becomes secretary of state of England under George II.

1758   EB contracts to edit the *Annual Register*; birth of his sons Richard (February 1758–94) and Christopher (December, died in infancy).

1759–64   EB becomes private secretary to William Gerard Hamilton, who, as Irish chief secretary, twice employs EB in Ireland (1761–62, 1763–64).

1760   Accession of George III.

1762   Rousseau's *Du contrat social* and *Emile* published.

1762–65   Ministries of Lord Bute and George Grenville; Stamp Act
                enacted, 1765.

1763   Treaty of Paris ends Seven Years' (French and Indian) War.

1764   EB joins Sir Joshua Reynolds, Samuel Johnson, and others in
                founding "The Club." John Wilkes expelled from Commons;
                riots in London. EB breaks with William Gerard Hamilton.

1765   EB private secretary to the marquis of Rockingham; member
                of Parliament for Wendover (reelected 1768). First
                Rockingham ministry (1765–66); Stamp Act repealed;
                Declaratory Act "declares" British *right* to tax colonies.

1766–68   Elder Pitt (Lord Chatham) chief minister, but collapses;
                Townshend duties on tea, glass, paper, etc., 1767.

1768   EB borrows money to buy estate at Beaconsfield
                ("Gregories," "Butler's Court"). Further Wilkes riots.

1769   EB indirectly but damagingly involved, with his brother
                Richard, William Burke, and Lord Verney, in heavy losses in
                East India stock. *Letters* of "Junius" published.

1770   EB publishes *Thoughts on the Cause of the Present Discontents*
                and becomes parliamentary agent for the colony of
                New York.

1772   Warren Hastings becomes governor of Bengal.

1773   EB visits France with his son. Lord North's (East India)
                Regulating Act opposed by EB and the Rockingham Whigs.
                Boston Tea Party, followed by the "Intolerable Acts" in
                Massachusetts.

1774   EB's *Speech on American Taxation*. First Continental Congress
                in America. EB elected MP for Bristol. Warren Hastings
                becomes governor general in India. Accession of Louis XVI.

1775   EB's *Speech on Conciliation with America*. Battles of Lexington
                and Concord.

1776	American Declaration of Independence.
1777	British surrender at Saratoga.
1778	France enters War of American Independence.
1779	EB in trouble with his Bristol constituents.
1780	EB loses Bristol seat, largely due to his views on America and support for free trade and religious tolerance for Ireland. Elected MP for Malton. Gordon riots.
1781	EB becomes leading member of Commons Select Committee on Indian Affairs. British surrender at Yorktown signals early end of American war.
1782	EB becomes paymaster general in second Rockingham ministry, which lasts only three months. Death of Rockingham; Shelburne becomes prime minister; EB resigns his post.
1783	*Ninth Select Committee Report* on Indian affairs. Shelburne defeated; Fox-North coalition ministry; EB again paymaster (eight months), his last public office, which he loses when the ministry falls (December).
1784	General election confirms defeat of Whigs. The Younger Pitt prime minister for the rest of EB's life, and beyond. Death of Samuel Johnson.
1785	EB's *Speech on the Nabob of Arcot's Debts*. Select Committee publishes *Eleventh Report*.
1787	Constitution of United States of America drafted; ratified 1788. House of Commons votes to impeach Warren Hastings. Meeting of the Notables in France; fall of Calonne.
1788	EB opens Hastings impeachment proceedings in Westminster Hall; supports abolition of slave trade.
1788–89	Illness and temporary madness of George III. EB at odds with his party during Regency crisis.

1789   French States General meets (May); becomes National
                Assembly (June); Bastille stormed (July); decrees abolishing
                feudal rights (August); the "October Days"; church property
                nationalized (November). EB begins his "Paris letter" to
                Charles-Jean-François Depont.

1790   Civil Constitution of the Clergy in France (July). EB
                publishes *Reflections on the Revolution in France.*

1791   EB breaks publicly with Fox and a majority of the Whigs
                over the French Revolution (May). French royal family's
                abortive flight to Varennes (June). Thomas Paine replies to
                EB's *Reflections* in *The Rights of Man* (1791–92). EB publishes
                *A Letter to a Member of the National Assembly, An Appeal from
                the New to the Old Whigs,* and *Thoughts on French Affairs.*

1792   France at war with Austria (April). Attack on Tuileries
                (August). French armies overrun Belgium, Rhineland, Nice,
                Savoy. September massacres in Paris. EB active on behalf of
                French refugee clergy in England.

1793   Execution of Louis XVI (January) and of Marie Antoinette
                (October). National Convention declares war on England
                (February). Revolt in la Vendée. Reign of Terror in France
                (1793–94).

1794   EB's final speech in the Hastings impeachment; he ends his
                parliamentary career; deaths of his brother and his son.

1795   Hastings acquitted. EB begins *Letters on a Regicide Peace.* Rule
                of the Directory begins in France (November).

1796   EB publishes *Letter to a Noble Lord, Thoughts on Scarcity,* and
                two of the letters later published in *Letters on a Regicide Peace.*
                Founds school for émigré boys at Penn in Buckinghamshire.

1797   EB dies (9 July); buried at Beaconsfield.

Burke and the French Revolution

ONE

————⟨◉⟩————

Burke's Tragic Muse: Sarah Siddons and the "Feminization" of the *Reflections*

Christopher Reid

We ne'er can pity what we ne'er can share

Nicholas Rowe, Prologue to *The Fair Penitent* (1703)

In a celebrated passage in *Reflections on the Revolution in France*, Edmund Burke allows the polemic to pause for a moment in order to explain and justify his melancholy response to the fall of the ancien régime.[1] Beginning with the apparently guileless assertion that "it is *natural*" that he should be affected as he is, he goes on to compare the feelings excited in him by the events of October 1789 to the moral and emotional effects of the tragic drama and concludes, "Some tears might be drawn from me, if such a spectacle were exhibited on the stage." In developing this analogy, Burke refers fleetingly but intriguingly to his own experience of tragedy in performance, as he recalls "the tears that Garrick formerly, or that Siddons not long since, have extorted from me." The passage as a whole has excited very different kinds of attention. For Burke's opponents of the 1790s, and most prominently for Thomas Paine, it was confirmation of the empty theatricality and emotional display which, according to their strictures, disfigured the discourse of the *Reflections*. Recent commentary on the passage has placed it more positively within a complex but coherent pattern of images which, according to one interpretation, provides the key to Burke's whole conception of politics.[2]

Paine's contempt for the "weeping effect" of Burke's "tragic paint-ings" is a useful point of departure because in expressing it he alerts us, albeit through caricature, to a specifically Restoration and eighteenth-century idea of tragedy in which pathos is the defining element.[3] It will be my argument here that this historically specific conception of the genre informs the ideological world of the *Reflections* and shapes its status as a text. It lies behind some of that work's most memorable con-figurations: its highlighting of the distress of a woman of high rank and its elevation of the family as a symbol of the attachments and obliga-tions of civil society. Furthermore, it clarifies the rhetorical status of the *Reflections* as a mode of performance which, by positioning the reader in a situation of spectacle, works on the sympathies in order to produce intense emotional effects. And finally, through its rapprochement with bourgeois manners and the associated "feminization" of its values, the tragedy of the period acquired a complex social meaning in which the *Reflections* is deeply implicated.

Siddons and Distressed Womanhood

In order to develop this argument, it will be necessary to consider something of the theory and practice of Restoration and eighteenth-century tragedy, including the rhetoric of tragic performance as Burke would have witnessed it. The theatrical presence and style of Sarah Siddons (1755–1831), to whose powers of emotional arousal Burke, as we have seen, pays a passing tribute in the *Reflections*, will be given particular attention in my account. The greatest tragic actress of her generation, she would have been for Burke, in the decade leading up to the publication of the *Reflections*, the most striking dramatic representa-tion of the female distress which is generally regarded as its rhetorical centerpiece. Beyond the brief allusion in the *Reflections*, evidence from other sources supports the suggestion that Burke regularly attended her performances. In her own *Reminiscences*, for instance, Siddons re-calls with pride some of the luminaries who saw her plays: "Sir Joshua [Reynolds] often honoured me by his presence at The Theatre. . . . He always sat in the Orchestra, and in that place were to be seen (O glori-ous constellation!) Burke, Gibbon, Sheridan, Windham, and, 'though last not least,' the illustrious Fox . . . and these great men would often visit my Dressing Room after the Play, to make thier [*sic*] bows and

honour me with thier applauses."[4] While it is not always easy to deter-
mine with precision particular performances at which Burke may have
been present, we do know from contemporary accounts that he saw her
as Zara in *The Mourning Bride*, as Lady Macbeth, as Elwina in Hannah
More's *Percy*, and in the title role of Robert Jephson's *Julia; Or, The Italian
Lover*.[5] The strong probability is that during the period of "Siddons-
mania" which followed her triumphant return to Drury Lane in 1782
Burke saw her perform many of the roles in which she enraptured polite
society. From a review of such roles, of the kinds of drama in which
she appeared, and from contemporary impressions of her style as an
actress, there emerges a powerful image of the suffering female virtue
to which Burke was to pay homage in his portrait of Marie Antoinette.

Although she occasionally played comic parts, Siddons is generally
thought to have lacked Garrick's extraordinary versatility, and it was
exclusively as a tragic actress that she achieved her astonishing success.
Her repertoire in the 1780s included a number of Shakespearean roles,
some of them eighteenth-century adaptations, but she was for the most
part engaged to play in Restoration and eighteenth-century tragedies,
many of them now half-forgotten.[6] Despite the relative neglect into
which it has fallen, the main contours of the tragic literature of that
period are well enough known. The emergence of the female protagonist as the dramatic focus, usually in the role of a victim, is one of its
most prominent features. This development is associated with a change
in emotional expectation, whereby a pitying response takes precedence
over the Aristotelian duality of pity and fear. A third and related characteristic which deserves mention here is the use of scenes of pathos for
the formal expression of correct moral sentiments.

The history of these developments, and especially of their social significance, is a complex one. The elements I have identified appear with
varying degrees of emphasis in the plays in which Siddons performed,
and which Burke would have known, from the heroic dramas of Dryden,
to the pathetic tragedies of Thomas Southerne, Thomas Otway, and
Nicholas Rowe, to the explicitly bourgeois tragedies of George Lillo
and Edward Moore, and to the melodramas which passed for tragedy
in the later eighteenth century. But the tendency toward what may be
described, in accordance with the gender categories of the time, as a
"feminization" of response is marked, even in the most academic attempts at the tragic drama. A mid-century example, William Mason's

Elfrida, A Dramatic Poem. Written on the Model of the Antient Greek Tragedy
(1752), may serve as an illustration. The play is prefaced by a series
of letters in which Mason explains how he has attempted to adapt the
"antient method" so as to conform to "the genius of our times." He
insists that "the three great Unities" have been strictly observed, but
this neoclassical rigor is qualified by his willingness "to follow the modern masters in those respects wherein they had not so faultily deviated
from their predecessors." Thus, in particular, "a story was chosen, in
which the tender, rather than the noble passions were predominant, and
in which even love had the principal share. Characters too were drawn
as nearly approaching to private ones, as Tragic dignity would permit;
and affections rais'd rather from the impulse of common humanity, than
the distresses of royalty, and the fate of kingdoms."[7]

In Mason's account of these innovations in the tragic drama, there is
an important connection between the kinds of emotion sought and the
spheres of life to be represented. In addition to following "the modern
masters" in their preference for "tender" passions rather than "noble"
ones—a division of the emotions which follows from stock ideas of
gender—he is able to acquiesce in their choice of the private dimension of character rather than "the fate of kingdoms" as an appropriate
realm for tragedy. As Mason develops this second point, the emphasis
shifts slightly but significantly from a distinction between general conditions of life ("private" as opposed to "public") to a more specifically
social reference to matters of rank ("the distresses of royalty"). His
play *Elfrida*, to which his remarks are prefaced, and in which Siddons,
at royal command, played the title role in 1785, exemplifies this common ambiguity. While his decision to appeal to "the impulse of common
humanity" may appear to suggest a resolution to extend the social range
of tragedy, the cast of *Elfrida* is in fact largely composed of characters
of high rank. On the other hand, the promised tender and private elements are abundantly supplied by a plot which turns on elevated trials
of love in which Elfrida, daughter of the Duke of Devonshire, is the
virtuous object of desire. Elsewhere in eighteenth-century drama there
are, of course, examples of tragedy in which the status of the leading
characters is explicitly bourgeois: the plays of Lillo and Moore project
a genuinely new tragic voice in which prose is preferred as the medium
appropriate to the bourgeois content. More generally, however, the pattern is closer to Mason's, where the rejection of the court as the locus of
the tragic action indicates a diminishing interest in the "public" dimen-

sion of characters' lives without necessarily requiring a transformation of the social milieu. The important stress falls on the *private* nature of an action with which, it is contended, and as a direct consequence of that privateness, the audience will be able to sympathize, whatever the rank of the participants.

Perhaps the most important element in this literary history was the breaking of the link between tragedy and the state. The royal protagonist was either displaced altogether or presented in an essentially domestic role.

> No princes here lost royalty bemoan,
> But you shall meet with sorrows like your own,

Rowe promises the audience in his prologue to *The Fair Penitent*, and this substitution of "private woes" for the supposed preoccupations of "the great" became a stock theme of such prologues throughout the century. Rowe's domestication of the tragic response is apparent, much later, in the prologue Edward Malone provided for Robert Jephson's *Julia*, a tragedy for which Burke apparently expressed some approval on its opening night in 1787:[8]

> From Thespis' days to this enlighten'd hour,
> The stage has shewn the dire abuse of power;
> What mighty mischief from ambition springs;
> The fate of heroes, and the fall of kings.
> But these high themes, howe'er adorn'd by art,
> Have seldom gain'd the passes of the heart:
> Calm we behold the pompous mimick woe,
> Unmov'd by sorrows we can never know.
> Far other feelings in the soul arise,
> When private griefs arrest our ears and eyes;
> When the false friend, and blameless, suffering wife,
> Reflect the image of domestick life:
> And still more wide the sympathy, more keen,
> When to each breast responsive is the scene;
> And the fine cords that *every* heart intwine,
> Dilated, vibrate with the glowing line.

Malone is more attentive to the physiology of sympathy than Rowe, whose prologue predates most of the theoretical literature on sensibility, but his argument is otherwise much the same. Their common aim, to gain "the passes of the heart" through a spectacle of private woe, was one which Burke sought to achieve in some of the most celebrated scenes in the *Reflections*.

Burke's selection of the suffering queen as the principal object of his lament is consistent with the developments I have described. The literary history of Restoration and eighteenth-century tragedy throws much light on that celebrated portrait. In an important essay, Laura Brown has shown how the emergence of the "defenseless woman" as protagonist coincides with a major transition in the form of tragedy: "The serious drama of the early Restoration is distinctively, notoriously aristocratic; that of the eighteenth century is sentimental, moral, and implicitly or explicitly bourgeois. Between these two formal and ideological poles stands the female protagonist."[9] The mode of "pathetic tragedy" in which this protagonist appears is therefore in effect a compromise between conceptions of tragedy which are shaped by quite different values. Brown's subtle reading of this history allows for varying degrees of emphasis and stages of development within the transitional form, from the early examples of works by John Dryden and Nathaniel Lee, which "retain the trappings of heroic form" but present characters "whose dramatic significance is defined by their pathetic situation rather than their aristocratic merit," to Rowe, in whose "she-tragedies" she finds a new current of the "didactic ethical assertion" which characterizes the explicitly bourgeois drama of Lillo.[10]

Sarah Siddons, the foremost personator of female distress on the late-eighteenth-century stage, appeared in many tragedies of the "affective" or "pathetic" type described by Brown. From an examination of the defining features of the roles she performed in the 1780s, there emerges a certain congruence between the Siddonian projection of suffering womanhood and Burke's representation of the fallen queen of France. His portrayal of Marie Antoinette falls into two contrasting parts (*Refl.* 148–49). In the first, based on reports he has heard, she appears in her present character as a queen, wife, and mother, displaying a fortitude appropriate to her rank, amid the violence and humiliation of the "October Days" (5–6 October 1789). In the second, based on personal recollection, she is pictured in her former splendor as a seventeen-year-old dauphiness, as yet untouched by the world. For the most part, it was in the first of these roles that Siddons, born in the same year as the French queen, was cast. If she could be said to have had a typical part it was that of a virtuous matron, often separated from her husband by force of circumstance and exposed to the threats of violent, lustful, and ambitious men. Even when she did not appear as a figure of exemplary virtue, her role was usually in some sense that of a victim: as Calista in Rowe's *The Fair Penitent*, for example, or, more decisively, in the title role of his *Tragedy of Jane Shore* (1714), the pity she excited as one brought low both by her own weakness and by the ill usage of heartless men outweighed the disapproval provoked by her misconduct. In this respect, her most celebrated role, that of Lady Macbeth, was not her most typical, though interestingly, in an analysis written after her retirement from the stage, she drew attention to the essentially "feminine nature" of that character, finding in her a delicate sensibility temporarily repressed by ambition.[11]

The pathetic tragedies which provided Siddons with most of her parts are preoccupied with shattered households and threatened personal ties. In these plays, the action turns on the complex and sometimes contradictory domestic relations which enmesh the female protagonist, and which constitute both her glory and her burden. In Arthur Murphy's *The Grecian Daughter* (1772), the protagonist is both a wife and a mother, but as the title indicates, it is the filial role that is stressed, though in a way which reveals the interconnectedness of women's functions within the household. In the play's defining moment, Euphrasia—the "Grecian Daughter" of the title—relieves her father, the captive king of Sicily who is expiring from hunger and thirst, by the most "natural" means within her power. A spectator on the sentimental scene applauds her

> Wonder-working virtue!
> The father foster'd at his daughter's breast!—
> O! filial piety!—The milk design'd
> For her own offspring, on the parent's lip
> Allays the parching fever.[12]

In other plays, the pathos is occasioned by a drama of choice, as the Siddons figure is forced to sever one kind of relation in order to preserve another (as in Hannah Cowley's *The Fate of Sparta; Or, The Rival Kings* [1788]), or to contemplate compromising her ideals of chastity in order to save a threatened child (Hall Hartson's *The Countess of Salisbury* [1767] and Bertie Greatheed's *The Regent* [1788]). Contemporary reports repeatedly remark on the emotional intensity with which Siddons realized these domestic roles. Although the dramatic material with which she had to work was often unworthy of her talents, the sentimental possibilities of a character such as Lady Randolph, whose overwhelming love for her long-lost son forms the troubling emotional core of John Home's celebrated tragedy *Douglas* (1756), are still evident. The importance of this maternal aspect of her stage character was neatly and sentimentally confirmed when her eight-year-old son appeared alongside her at Drury Lane, playing Isabella's son (to Siddons's Isabella) in the performance of Southerne's *The Fatal Marriage*, which signaled the beginning of her success in London.[13]

In Siddons's repertoire of the 1780s, the main elements of a system of female virtue can be discerned. To employ categories suggested by Burke in his *Philosophical Enquiry into the Origin of Our Ideas of the Sublime and Beautiful* (1757), the "feminine" qualities of tenderness and compassion are modified, but not superseded, by the "masculine" traits of fortitude, justice, and a dedication to duty. For although the female protagonist remained essentially isolated and exposed, some display of internal moral resources, lifting the spectacle above that of merely passive suffering, was thought necessary if truly tragic emotions were to be aroused. It was on these grounds that a witness to Siddons's interpretation of the role of Jane Shore in the mid-1780s expressed some dissatisfaction with the part, while acknowledging the powerful verisimilitude of her performance: "I absolutely thought her the creature perishing through want . . . shocked at the sight, I could not avoid turning from the suffering object; I was disgusted at the idea, that an event affecting our mortal frame only, should be capable of producing greater misery than the most poignant anguish of the mind.—We wish to have something exalted in the distress to interest us, and there is nothing of that kind in the famishing Shore, whose sufferings have no immediate reference to any but herself."[14] The "something exalted" which this commentator desired is just what Siddons exhibited in her more typical roles. Characteristically, Siddonian woman, while denied access to the apparatus of male power, was nonetheless an emblem of active as well as suffering virtue. Euphrasia, melting with compassion at the "spectacle of woe" presented by her father, asserts herself not only as his nurse but ultimately as his champion when she dispatches his adversary with a blow from a concealed dagger.

It was in roles of exalted distress, to which her dignified bearing and commanding presence on stage were particularly suited, that Siddons most deeply impressed her audiences. As Queen Katharine in her brother's adaptation of Shakespeare's *Henry VIII*, for example, the powerful feelings of pity she excited were significantly qualified by awe, a combination of emotions to which Katharine herself draws attention in her stately address to Wolsey:

> Sir,
> I am about to weep: but, thinking that
> We are a queen, (or long have dream'd so,) certain,
> The daughter of a king, my drops of tears
> I'll turn to sparks of fire,— [15]

The fortitude displayed here, as in Burke's account of the conduct of Marie Antoinette, is explicitly an attribute of rank. In view of her particular strengths as a tragic actress—her ability to inspire awe as well as to arouse compassion—it is not surprising that Siddons should have been especially noted for her portrayal of queens (including, in the 1780s, Margaret of Anjou and Mary, Queen of Scots, as well as Queen Katharine) and of women otherwise of high station.[16] Her friend, Hester Lynch Thrale, apparently concurred when the following observations concerning her range as an actress were put to her: "She so constantly acted the character of great personages in affliction, that, on the whole, she had a mournful visage, and an awful tone of voice, very detrimental to the success of her comic attempts; and indeed unfriendly to her efforts in the less impassioned scenes of tragedy; or when she played merely genteel women in middle life."[17] And in an agreeably understated account in her own *Reminiscences* of her reception by the royal family on her first visit to Buckingham House, she recalls being told that "Her Majesty had expressd [*sic*] herself surprised to find me so collected in so new a position, and that I had conducted myself as if I had been used to a Court," and she reminds us, by way of explanation, that "at any rate, I had frequently personated Queens."[18]

I suggested a little earlier that there is a certain congruence between Burke's idealized description of Marie Antoinette and the essential attributes of Siddonian woman. The main elements of that correspondence are now in place. In the famous paragraphs devoted to the events of 5 and 6 October 1789, Burke applies the stereotypes and conventions of pathetic and domestic tragedy to a scene of specifically royal distress

(*Refl.* 141–50). Already within the space of a few lines he has three times pictured Louis XVI, following his involuntary removal from Versailles to the Tuileries, as a "captive king" (*Refl.* 139). In his account of the October Days, he extends this familiar emblem of fallen greatness into a group portrait, as the "royal captives" are led on their forced march to Paris and the converted "Bastile for kings" which awaits them. Notoriously, however, the main emphasis of the passage falls on the figure of the defenseless queen. "Beauty in distress is much the most affecting beauty," declared the young Burke in his *Philosophical Enquiry*, and it was a principle to which he returned in fashioning the portrait of Marie Antoinette.[19] Her beauty as he had witnessed it in 1773 is still strong in Burke's recollection as he describes with indignation the present distress of "this persecuted woman" who has been forced "to fly almost naked" (*Refl.* 141) from the scene of outrage. In bringing to our view what is for him the very essence of the feminine, Burke also discloses to us the humanizing private face of royalty. For it is as a wife and a mother, as well as a queen and a daughter of a queen, that Marie Antoinette ornaments the pages of the *Reflections*. Escaping from the "ruffians and assassins" at her door, she seeks refuge "at the feet of a king and husband" (*Refl.* 142) who together with the "royal infants," of whose presence in the palace Burke is careful to remind us, completes the nucleus of this abused family.

Yet vulnerability is not the only quality attributed to Marie Antoinette in Burke's description: in paying his tribute, he gives almost equal prominence to the other and more active side of Siddonian woman. He is able to congratulate the queen for displaying the fortitude of one who "feels with the dignity of a Roman matron," who "in the last extremity . . . will save herself from the last disgrace; and . . . if she must fall . . . will fall by no ignoble hand" (*Refl.* 148). There is something insistently allusive and even iconographical about this part of the description. It is the product of a culture steeped in theatrical images of female distress. Siddons appeared in a number of roles which in some way involve the convention of suicide—threatened, if not ultimately performed—as a response to what is perceived as "disgrace." In February 1789, she first played Volumnia, arguably Shakespeare's most memorable portrait of female fortitude, in the adaptation of *Coriolanus* by her brother, John Philip Kemble. His understanding of the play is indicated by the alternative title of *The Roman Matron* which he assigns to it. As this subtitle promises, and in conformity with the feminization of eighteenth-century tragedy, as well as in deference to Siddons's reputation, the role of Volumnia, striking enough in the original, is further accentuated. In adapting the tragedy, Kemble drew not only on Shakespeare but also on James Thomson's *Coriolanus* of 1749. It was Thomson's version that provided Volumnia's stately rebuke to her hitherto intransigent son in the final act:

> Let us no more before the Volscian people
> Expose ourselves a spectacle of shame.
> Hear me, proud man! I have
> A heart as stout as thine. I came not hither,
> To be sent back rejected, baffled, sham'd,
> Hateful to Rome, because I am thy mother:
> A Roman matron knows, in such extremes,
> What part to take.[20]

And the verbal threat is confirmed by gesture, as the Roman Matron draws out her dagger.

As an orator, Burke seems to have been particularly alert to the persuasive emotional possibilities of this kind of rhetoric of performance.[21] The portrait of Marie Antoinette suggests that this skill did not desert him when he chose to reach his audience through the medium of the written word. Much of the description is conceived in accordance with the system of actions and gestures which constituted the visual language of the tragic actress. We can see something of this, I think, in Burke's reference to an instrument of suicide when he laments that the queen "should ever be obliged to carry the sharp antidote against disgrace concealed in [her] bosom" (*Refl.* 149). According to his Victorian editor, E. J. Payne, Burke is here "alluding to the queen's carrying poison about with her."[22] I suspect, however, that most readers, taking their cue from the first word of the phrase "sharp antidote," understand it in more immediately visual terms as imaging a dagger.[23] In Burke's own audience, the phrase would have excited strong cultural associations with the contemporary stage. In particular, it would have called to mind the tragic tableaux in which the figure of Siddonian woman, threatened, like Marie Antoinette, with violation, prepared to defend her honor.

The *Reflections* as Performance

If, as I have suggested, Burke's presentation of the crisis of the October Days conforms to the central conventions of pathetic tragedy, then it follows that the response he seeks to arouse in his readers is one in which pity will predominate. In a famous exchange of letters with Philip Francis, who had read an early draft of portions of the *Reflections*, Burke sought to demonstrate the authenticity of the feelings expressed in his lament for the fallen queen by declaring that he had himself shed tears as he composed it (*Corr.* 6: 85–92). In the *Reflections* itself, as we have seen, he imagines the tears that a dramatic exhibition of fallen greatness might draw from him and goes on to speak exclusively of tears when he acknowledges his susceptibility to the tragic arts of David Garrick and Siddons. The model of tragedy which Burke seems to have in mind here is a Restoration and eighteenth-century one in which our feelings are cultivated rather than purged. The spectacle of suffering elicits tears which, as the tokens of a virtuous and benevolent heart, we can indulge with pleasure. In the very same passage, however, Burke clearly refers to an Aristotelian conception of tragedy as a model for our response to calamities such as the fall of kings. Hence he notes, "In events like these our passions instruct our reason. . . . We are alarmed into reflection; our minds (as it has long since been observed) are purified by terrour and pity; our weak unthinking pride is humbled, under the dispensations of a mysterious wisdom" (*Refl.* 157). With its criteria of purgation and the restoration of a proper balance of emotions within the logical context of a coherently structured plot, the Aristotelian model to which Burke here alludes seems at odds with the pathetic conventions which shape his response to the October Days.

The important discussion of the psychological effects of tragedy which Burke included in his *Philosophical Enquiry* is worth recalling here. At the heart of Burke's explanation is the faculty of sympathy which he describes as "a sort of substitution, by which we are put into the place of another man, and affected in many respects as he is affected" (*PE* 44). It is from this premise of the involuntary actions of sympathy that Burke develops one of the most striking features of his analysis: the exaltation of emotional over rational elements in the tragic response. The mixed passions of delight and uneasiness which we feel when con-templating both "real" and "fictitious" distresses operate "antecedent to any reasoning, by an instinct that works us to its own purposes, without our concurrence" (*PE* 46). The delight with which we observe scenes of misery is not without a moral outcome. Indeed, Burke suggests that this "delight" is providentially ordained precisely in order that we should seek out such scenes, and by so doing be induced to feel the painful uneasiness with which delight becomes mixed, and which "prompts us to relieve ourselves in relieving others" (*PE* 46). This desirable moral outcome, however, is produced entirely at the level of the passions— arising, as Burke puts it, "from the mechanical structure of our bodies, or from the natural frame and constitution of our minds" (*PE* 45)— rather than through the judgment of the spectator.

This analysis has important consequences for Burke's conception of tragedy. For what interests him above all in the tragic drama is the psychological effect on the spectator of a sympathetic engagement with a suffering character. The Aristotelian concern with the working through of an entire tragic *action,* and the rational as well as emotional demands which this makes on an audience, is of little importance in Burke's account. In his celebrated argument that instances of actual suffering are always more compelling than their fictitious representations, the example he provides—the execution of "a state criminal of high rank" (*PE* 47)—itself illustrates his understanding of tragedy in terms of moments of spectacle. In W. P. Albrecht's study of the relation between theories of tragedy and ideas of the sublime, Burke is seen as a pivotal figure in a development which assigns "importance to the immediate emotional response rather than to the fable."[24] As we have seen, this emphasis on the affective capacities of tragedy does not imply a repudiation of its moral dimension. Rather, moral inferences are displaced from the audience's experience of a complete action to its appreciation of the intensity of the dramatic moment: "As strong excitement gained ground as the important ingredient in tragedy, plot was depreciated until what was valued most was not a closely knit sequence of events but a series of moments with emotional impact and moral force. The need for sympathetic identification made character more important than action."[25]

Some of the consequences of this preference can be seen in the dramatic writing of the period. Even in plays where a neoclassical doctrine of the dramatic unities is officially in force, the formal tendency is toward the highlighting of emotional tableaux, with the action performing a largely secondary and supportive function. Increasingly the role of the spectator is that of a consumer of emotion and moral sentiment. A comparable, though perhaps even more pronounced development can be traced in the eighteenth-century novel, from *Clarissa*, with its formal principle of instructive and affective moments of sentiment taking precedence over the concatenation of plot, to the deliberately fractured narratives of Sterne and Mackenzie, where those moments are foregrounded and stylized as sentimental tableaux. And one might see the *Reflections* itself as participating unevenly in this literary history, shifting ground as it does from the conventions of rational argument, which characterize the political discourse of the eighteenth-century parliamentary establishment, to its use of focused moments of distress as a means of engaging the sympathetic emotions of the reader.

This unevenness is an important aspect of the textual character of the *Reflections*. Its discourse works at a number of different registers, and consequently it would be untrue to suggest that the passage on the October Days is typical of its method. But while not typical, it may nonetheless be decisive in its literary manner and ideological appeal. In seeking to engage the reader's sympathies, the passage not only is shaped by the conventions of pathetic tragedy but also enacts them. It is as if Burke were somehow seeking to transform the written text into a spoken one, to assert the orator's sincere and passionate presence, and to communicate an impression of the moment of delivery.[26]

As a mode of performance, Burke's effusive method is consistent with the essentially rhetorical conception of language which he elucidates in the *Philosophical Enquiry*. As we shall see, in its emotional intensity and effect it is also comparable to the style of acting associated with Sarah Siddons. In the final section of the *Philosophical Enquiry*, entitled "How WORDS influence the passions," Burke addresses himself to the use of language in "eloquence and poetry," but much of what he says would be equally applicable to the art of acting. In order to succeed, "the speaker"—and significantly it is to a "speaker" rather than a "writer" that he refers—must "call in to his aid those modes of speech that mark a strong and lively feeling in himself" (*PE* 175). This confirms his earlier statement that the business of "poetry and rhetoric" is "to affect rather by sympathy than imitation; to display rather the effect of things on the mind of the speaker or of others, than to present a clear idea of the things themselves" (*PE* 172). Developing this argument, Burke divides words into two categories: "clear" expressions, which address them-selves to the understanding and therefore he would presumably regard as appropriate to philosophical and scientific discourse, and "strong" expressions, which address themselves to the passions and therefore be-long to poetry and eloquence. As he elaborates on the properties of this second class of words, the kinship between the poetic, rhetorical, and histrionic arts becomes clear: "Now, as there is a moving tone of voice, an impassioned countenance, an agitated gesture, which affect indepen-dently of the things about which they are exerted, so there are words, and certain dispositions of words, which being peculiarly devoted to passionate subjects, and always used by those who are under the influ-ence of any passion; they touch and move us more than those which far more clearly and distinctly express the subject matter. We yield to sympathy, what we refuse to description" (*PE* 175).

As James T. Boulton has pointed out, the principles of discourse which Burke defines here are put into practice in the "apostrophe" to Marie Antoinette.[27] By adopting "those modes of speech which mark a strong and lively feeling in himself," he applies himself directly to the sympathies of his readers. For Burke, as for other eighteenth-century writers, sympathy is not a specialized faculty, confined in its operations to certain aesthetic events. On the contrary, it is, as he reminds us re-peatedly in the *Reflections*, the very condition of moral being. There is, then, an important link between Burke's conception of the effects of eloquence (and consequently of acting) and the more general conduct of moral relations. In the *Philosophical Enquiry*, he describes the process by which sentiments are transferred from breast to breast as "the conta-gion of our passions." By means of a "strong" expression, "we catch a fire already kindled in another, which probably might never have been struck out by the object described" (*PE* 175–76). David Hume makes use of the same metaphor in his *Treatise of Human Nature* (1739–40), in which sympathy is the principle of social being, when he remarks, "The passions are so contagious, that they pass with the greatest facility from one person to another, and produce correspondent movements in all human breasts."[28] When Burke pronounces his feelings on hearing of the humiliations suffered by Marie Antoinette, we are not required to exercise our reason in order to form an opinion. Such a response would be to deny our humanity, in the manner of those cold-hearted rationalists of the school of the rights of man who "have perverted in themselves, and in those that attend to them, all the well-placed sympathies of the human breast" (*Refl.* 130). Burke's insistence in the *Reflections* on the unimpeachable naturalness and rightness of his feelings about the events in France depends upon this notion of a sympathy which, by allowing a communication of sentiments, provides for the instantaneous conviction of moral truth. The theater is held up as a model for this process. For in the theater, unlike dissenting churches, the audience has not closed off its natural sympathies. It offers a genuine test of the truth of moral sentiment, a test of its communicability through sympathy, for dramatists "must apply themselves to the moral constitution of the heart" (*Refl.* 158). In the theater, Burke assures us, evil will be detected through "the first intuitive glance, without any elaborate process of reasoning" (*Refl.* 159).[29]

This demand for the immediate engagement of the audience's sympathies led, in the second half of the eighteenth century, to the development of a style of acting characterized by emotional intensity. In assessing the merits of the French actress Claire Josèphe Clairon, Garrick criticized her want of "those instantaneous feelings, that life-blood, that keen sensibility, that bursts at once from genius, and, like electric fire, shoots through the veins, marrow, bones and all, of every spectator."[30] This was not, by all accounts, a fault with which Sarah Siddons could have been charged. In his *Memoirs of Mrs. Siddons* (1827), James Boaden recalls the overpowering impression she made on her audience when she appeared in the title role of Rowe's *Tragedy of Jane Shore*: "I well remember (how is it possible I should ever forget?) the *sobs,* the *shrieks,* among the tenderer part of her audiences; or those *tears,* which manhood, at first, struggled to repress, but at length grew proud of indulging. We then, indeed, knew all the LUXURY of grief; but the nerves of so many a gentle being gave way before the intensity of such appeals; and fainting fits long and frequently alarmed the decorum of the house, filled almost to suffocation." By such means, we are told, Siddons inspired in her spectators "the sympathetic emotions of virtue."[31]

Boaden's account of this memorable performance could stand, almost without alteration, as a commentary on some of the more spectacular episodes in the impeachment of Warren Hastings. In delivering his impassioned denunciation of the depredations and physical abuse inflicted on the people of India, Burke engaged in a mode of discourse which may be characterized as histrionic in the strict sense.[32] He endeavored to reach his audience by much the same means, and to move them in much the same way, as did the great performers on the late-eighteenth-century stage. Reports of the notorious third day (17 February 1788) of Burke's opening speech at the impeachment bear witness to the emotional effect his horrified narration had on members of the fashionable audience. Assembled at Westminster Hall, the highest court in the land, in social composition this audience was probably not dissimilar to that which would attend command performances at Drury Lane.[33] Among those reportedly listening to Burke's speech was Sarah Siddons, at whose performances Burke had confessedly wept. She, in turn, was similarly moved by his, finding that "every illusion of the stage paled into insignificance before the realities which Burke had conjured up before her eyes." Burke's "recitation of Hastings's crimes," we are told, "proved too much for some of the ladies. Mrs. Sheridan had to be carried out in a faint."[34] The same fate apparently befell Siddons herself a few months later when Sheridan delivered his famous speech on the sufferings of the Begums of Oude.[35]

Burke's *Reflections* and other counterrevolutionary writings bear the unmistakable imprint of this histrionic style. With its emotional insistence and pathetic imagery, the portrait of Marie Antoinette appealed to sensibilities which were being fed by performers such as Siddons on the Georgian stage. In this way, Burke makes his defense of tradition in accordance with contemporary tastes. From this synthesis, I would suggest, his most famous text derives both its peculiarity and its rhetorical strength.

The Modernity of the *Reflections*

In his demand that tragic drama should provide the spectator with an intensely emotional experience, Burke was not implicitly favoring pity over fear as a source of aesthetic pleasure. Indeed, in the *Philosophical Enquiry*, with its appreciation of the awe-inspiring power of the sublime, the reverse, if anything, is the case. Yet in the most memorable passage in the *Reflections*, pity is the emotion Burke most wishes to communicate to his readers. Accused by Philip Francis of "pure foppery," he casts himself unrepentantly as an anguished Man of Feeling. Burke's assumption and defense of this stance raise important questions about the historical status and function of the *Reflections*. To what extent, for example, may it be characterized as a "sentimental" work? And if, at some of its most critical moments, this is indeed its manner, what then is the ideological meaning of this "feminized" mode of discourse?

The *Reflections* proceeds, and makes its point, by way of contrasts as much as through chains of reasoning. In the contrast which is at the core of the work, the whole weight of British tradition is thrown against the callow and confused innovation of revolutionary France. It is as a classic conservative defense of traditional forms of government, and more broadly of traditional social practices and institutions, that the *Reflections* has long been read, valued, and understood. It may seem strange, then, that the author of one of the shrewdest and earliest replies to the work should have found something irritatingly and even discreditably *fashionable* in Burke's literary manner. In her *Vindication of the Rights of Men* (1790), Mary Wollstonecraft ridicules Burke's pamphlet as a farrago of fashionable feelings and attitudes. She compares his work to a piece of modish chinoiserie, denounces his "gothic notions of beauty," and objects to the frequency with which he "advert[s] to a sentimental jargon."[36] The *Reflections*, she argues, is the product of a shallow, mechanical, and artificial sensibility; as such, it is likely to find an audience among the circles of enervated women which gather in polite society: "Even the Ladies, Sir, may repeat your sprightly sallies, and retail in theatrical attitudes many of your sentimental exclamations. Sensibility is the *manie* of the day, and compassion the virtue which is to cover a multitude of vices, whilst justice is left to mourn in sullen silence, and balance truth in vain."[37] Wollstonecraft's astute, though unsystematic, critique anticipates Paine's in associating Burke's emotional manner with the conventions of the contemporary stage. Her insights into the configurations of gender which mark the *Reflections*, however, give her reply a special quality and importance.[38] Wollstonecraft's profound meditations on the meaning and value of sensibility were central to her life and work. From this perspective, she is able to accuse Burke, the doughty upholder of the ancient constitution, of making a modish appeal to contemporary taste.

Naturally enough both Wollstonecraft and Paine focus on the lament for Marie Antoinette in order to support their critique of the theatricality of the *Reflections*. There is, however, an element of polemical oversimplification, and perhaps even of caricature, in their strictures. For a number of reasons, the *Reflections* cannot be described as a "sentimental" work *tout court.* The histrionic mode of pathetic tragedy is not sustained beyond the account of the October Days, although intermittently Burke continues to issue strong emotional appeals to his readers. His stance varies from that of a Man of Feeling, at the one extreme, to that of a sagacious elder statesman at the other. The *Reflections* is equally irregular in terms of the modes of discourse which it introduces: the traditions of Augustan satire and the procedures of political economy are represented as fully, and almost as conspicuously, as the language of tragic lament. Furthermore, as I have suggested, the image of distressed womanhood which Burke projects in the *Reflections* is not as uncomplicatedly passive as some of the stereotypes of sentimentalism might lead one to expect.

In some of his writings, in fact, Burke uses the commonplaces of sentimental literature as instruments of mockery, at least insofar as they are applied to men. Included among the essays published in the Dublin periodical *The Reformer,* which appeared in the year Burke graduated from Trinity College and are usually attributed to him, is a review of a production in 1748 of Benjamin Hoadley's sentimental comedy *The Suspicious Husband.* "The Ladies, and Gentlemen likest to Ladies, cry'd it up as an excellent Performance," is the young Burke's wry comment.[39] More than forty years later, he was to renew this ridicule of "effeminacy"—the very foppishness of which he himself stood accused—as part of his counterrevolutionary campaign. Looking forward in his *Remarks on the Policy of the Allies* (1793) to the defeat of the Jacobin republic and the establishment of an interim government in France, he makes it clear that the necessary authority cannot be expected from "a shewy, superficial, trifling, intriguing court, guided by cabals of ladies, or of men like ladies."[40] In the *Letters on a Regicide Peace* (1796–97), he dismisses the suggestion that in the face of calamity the national character has degenerated fatally into "effeminacy," yet it is exactly according to this stereotype that the administration of Pitt and its diplomatic representatives are denounced for maintaining contact with the "Regicide" republic. Again and again they are stigmatized for their "unmanly" political conduct. Thus we are told, in Letter 1, that the speech from the throne which opened the parliamentary session of 1795 "threw out oglings and glances of tenderness. Lest this coquetting should seem too cold and ambiguous, without waiting for its effect, the violent passion for a relation to the regicides, produced a direct message from the crown."[41] The collapse of political authority is such, Burke insists, that "we have nothing left but the last resource of female weakness, of helpless infancy, of doting decrepitude,—wailing and lamentation. We cannot even utter a sentiment of vigour."[42]

Ridicule of this sort, however, is not inconsistent with the feminized stance of the lament for Marie Antoinette. Indeed, there is a distinct political logic in Burke's ideas of gender. When he denounces "effeminacy," it is with reference to the public authority of the state. When he celebrates the "feminine" principles of love and sensibility, it is with reference to the conciliatory relations of civil society.[43] In this way, Burke's writing is significantly—but also intricately and unevenly—involved in what Terry Eagleton has characterized as "a deep-seated 'feminization' of values throughout the eighteenth century," which, he argues, "is closely allied with the emergence of the bourgeoisie."[44] As Eagleton demonstrates in his briskly entertaining account, this feminization was undertaken less on women's terms than in the interests of certain classes of men. By the 1750s, he remarks, "the barbarous values of militarism, naked dominance and male *hauteur*, badges of a predatory public aristocracy, have been mollified by the fashionable virtues of uxoriousness, sensibility, civility, and *tendresse*."[45] Although Eagleton does not mention Burke by name, this reads very much like a description of the cultural order the passing of which Burke mourns in the *Reflections*. For the function of what Burke there calls a "mixed system of opinion and sentiment" is to manage and legitimize a liaison between otherwise contending classes. The lineaments of aristocratic power are softened and made more comely through a coloring of "feminine" values. This system of opinion, Burke tells us, "without confounding ranks . . . produced a noble equality, and handed it down through all the gradations of social life." It "mitigated kings into companions, and raised private men to be fellows with kings. Without force, or opposition, it subdued the fierceness of pride and power; it obliged sovereigns to submit to the soft collar of social esteem." By such means, power was domesticated and made "gentle" (*Refl.* 150–51).

The sentimental discourse of the *Reflections* is Burke's tribute to this "feminine" principle which permeates the whole sphere of manners. "Manners," he tells us (in the first of the *Letters on a Regicide Peace*) in one of his most revealing statements, "are of more importance than laws" (*Works* 8: 172). Political power, that is to say, can only on very rare occasions (such as a military threat to the state) be exercised in an unmediated or "naked" form. More commonly it has to be legitimized and transmitted through a system of "manners" or cultural values. In the *Reflections*, that system is embodied in the figure of Marie Antoinette. Drawing on the conventions of pathetic tragedy, Burke pictures her as a vulnerable and tenderhearted mother, an image which is in stark contrast to the one widely disseminated in France, where she was popularly portrayed as a supercilious and dissolute Austrian princess. Louis XVI, constitutionally if not temperamentally an autocrat, is honored as a mild-mannered father of his people. Little is said in the *Reflections* of the political identity and functions of the French king. We rarely catch a glimpse of the public face of royalty; its fetishized domestic face is more important. As Boulton has shown, Burke's tribute to the French royal family is the culmination of a whole network of images in which the traditional order is represented in terms of sacred family bonds.[46]

Burke could in fact be quite unsentimental about monarchy when he chose. Less than a year before the calamity of the October Days, he delivered a series of astonishing speeches as the House of Commons grappled with the constitutional crisis caused by the king's mental disorder. The king's incapacity presented the Portland Whigs with the opportunity to argue for the installation of the politically sympathetic Prince of Wales as Regent. In a notorious remark, which Burke's opponents of the 1790s did not allow him to forget, he asked the Commons to "recollect that they were talking of a sick king, of a monarch smitten by the hand of Omnipotence, and that the Almighty had hurled him from his throne."[47] In another debate, he speculated on the possible progress of the king's malady and spoke quite openly of the violent and grotesque acts to which such insanity was likely to lead. Responding to the protests of other members, who saw his speech as an outrageous breach of decorum, he justified himself on the grounds that in such affairs "delicacy" must be sacrificed to truth.[48]

In the *Reflections*, the importance of delicacy—of keeping the sanctifying veils in place—is reasserted. Burke perceived the example of France as a threat to the system of social and political compromises which he understood to be the historical essence of Whiggism. In defining the spirit of the British constitution, he often directs us back to its obscurely ancient origins, but his more specific and significant point of reference is the constitutional settlement of 1688. This settlement secured an alliance between a politically dominant landowning class and a commercially powerful bourgeoisie. It provided the rationale for Burke's own political role as a strategist and thinker from a professional background who had become attached to an essentially aristocratic parliamentary group. The events in France, and, more immediately, the encouragement they gave to dissenters and radicals at home, appeared to put this system at risk. What Burke saw as a bourgeois revolution in France was, in his view, a repetition, albeit on a grander scale, of the detestable Puritan experiment of the 1640s, an error which the triumph of 1688 had expunged.

Burke came to believe that the unity of the royal family, whose differences he had not long since sought to exploit, might prove an important factor in the struggle against "the progress of French arms and principles" (*Corr.* 7: 292). In this belief, he may well have been correct. It has recently been argued that one of the consequences for Britain of the upheavals in France was a growth of national feeling, exemplified by the phenomenon of a newly popular monarchy. Attitudes toward George III's predecessors, and to George III himself in the first half of his reign, had been less cordial. Indeed, as one historian has put it, "Ever since the passing of that immediate euphoria which greeted the Restoration, no English or British monarch other than perhaps Anne had achieved more than partial or transient popularity; no sovereign at all had been able to act as an unquestioned cynosure for national sentiment."[49] From the late 1780s, however, the social appeal of George III was greatly extended. In advancing this process, his spotless "domestic reputation," which secured considerable middle-class approval for the monarchy, was as important as his attention to public ceremonial. In this way, "the royal *family* and not just the monarch . . . acquired increasing currency and popularity in this period."[50] As another writer has recently remarked, in the person of George III the monarchy had undergone a process of social "modernization."[51]

Paradoxical as it may appear, it is in this context, I think, that Burke's account of the October Days, and, more broadly, the project of the *Reflections* as a whole should be seen. For a work which sets such store by tradition, the *Reflections* is stylistically and ideologically a surprisingly "modern" text. Its assimilation of the conventions of contemporary tragic performance is an important instance of this. Other and related stylistic elements, such as the pronounced and fashionable Gothicism which Wollstonecraft derides, suggest that Burke's age of chivalry may have been a relatively recent creation. In its powerful assertion of private and "feminine" values, the *Reflections* contributes to an embourgeoisement—a consolidation—of aristocratic life. One of the most striking features of the work, and indeed of Burke's other counterrevolutionary writings, is its intense aestheticizing of politics.[52] Political institutions are transformed through Burke's potent use of metaphor into objects of taste, admiration, and attachment. As Burke himself puts it, "To make us love our country, our country ought to be lovely" (*Refl.* 152). Although his audience was, in social composition, relatively narrow, what he asked of it was an extraordinary inclusiveness of response. While in France, Jacobinism proceeded to refashion the culture as well as the polity of the nation, Burke countered by creating a political discourse which turned existing institutions into objects of intense emotional regard. Nowhere is this more true than in his images of the French monarchy. "We ne'er can pity what we ne'er can share," Rowe had concluded in his prologue to *The Fair Penitent*, thinking of the inaccessibility to ordinary sympathies of the fates of kings. In the *Reflections* and, more especially, in the lament for Marie Antoinette, Burke forged a discourse which would permit that impossible sharing to take place. Adapting the conventions of domestic tragedy, and thereby highlighting the private dimension of royal distress rather than the griefs of pomp which cannot stir us from our detachment, he found a way of reclaiming the fall of the great from its apparent remoteness.

Notes

1. Edmund Burke, *Reflections on the Revolution in France* (hereafter cited as *Refl.*), in *The Works of the Right Honourable Edmund Burke*, 16 vols. (London: F. and C. Rivington, 1803–27) 5: 156–59 (hereafter cited as *Works*).

2. See Paul Hindson and Tim Gray, *Burke's Dramatic Theory of Politics* (Aldershot: Avebury, 1988). Important earlier discussions include Peter H. Melvin, "Burke on Theatricality and Revolution," *Journal of the History of Ideas* 36 (1975): 447–68, and James T. Boulton, *The Language of Politics in the Age of Wilkes and Burke* (London: Routledge and Kegan Paul, 1963) 142–46, a work to which my own contribution is generally indebted.

3. Thomas Paine, *The Rights of Man*, ed. Henry Collins (Harmondsworth: Penguin, 1969) 71–72.

4. *The Reminiscences of Sarah Kemble Siddons, 1773–85*, ed. William Van Lennep (Cambridge: Harvard UP, 1942) 19.

5. See, respectively, *The Correspondence of Edmund Burke*, ed. Thomas W. Copeland et al., 10 vols. (Cambridge: Cambridge UP; Chicago: U of Chicago P, 1958–78) 9: 433 (hereafter cited as *Corr.*); Roger Manvell, *Sarah Siddons: Portrait of an Actress* (London: Heinemann, 1970) 122; William Roberts, *Memoirs of the Life and Correspondence of Mrs. Hannah More*, 3d ed., 4 vols. (London: R. B. Seeley and W. Burnside, 1835) 2: 54; and *Life and Letters of Sir Gilbert Elliot, First Earl of Minto*, 3 vols. (London: Longmans, Green, 1874) 1: 154. Donald C. Bryant, *Edmund Burke and His Literary Friends* (St. Louis: Washington UP, 1939) contains much valuable information concerning Burke's relations with contemporary playwrights and performers.

6. Full details of Siddons's repertory at Drury Lane are given in Manvell 353–55. Further information concerning casts and performances can be found in *The London Stage, 1660–1800*, part 5, ed. Charles B. Hogan (Carbondale: Southern Illinois UP, 1968).

7. William Mason, *Elfrida, A Dramatic Poem. Written on the Model of the Antient Greek Tragedy* (London: J. and P. Knapton, 1752) i–ii.

8. "I went home with Burke and Windham, and Walker King supped with us, and we criticised Burke out of his admiration for his countryman's (Jephson's) performance" (*Life and Letters of Sir Gilbert Elliot* 1: 154).

9. Laura Brown, "The Defenseless Woman and the Development of English Tragedy," *Studies in English Literature* 22.3 (1982): 429–43 (430).

10. Brown 432, 435.

11. For Siddons's "Remarks on the Character of Lady Macbeth," see Thomas Campbell, *Life of Mrs. Siddons*, 2 vols. (London: Effingham Wilson, 1834) 2: 10–39.

12. Arthur Murphy, *The Grecian Daughter. A Tragedy. Marked with the Variations in the Manager's Book at the Theatre-Royal in Drury Lane* (London: W. Lowndes and S. Bladon, 1787) 24. Here, and elsewhere, I refer where possible to editions based on acting copies of the 1780s. Although Burke no doubt knew of the classical episode of Xanthippe and Cimon on which the scene in *The Grecian Daughter* is based, he may have had Murphy's play in mind when he paid tribute to the productivity of America in his *Speech on Conciliation with the Colonies* (1775): "For some time past, the old world has been fed from the new. The scarcity which you have felt would have been a desolating famine, if this child of your old age, with a true filial piety, with a Roman charity, had not put the full breast of its youthful exuberance to the mouth of its exhausted parent" (*Works* 3: 45). Murphy, whose play was first performed in 1772, was one of Burke's oldest London friends. Bryant cites Burke's early biographer, Robert Bisset, to the effect that he "had great pleasure in beholding, as well as in reading, the dramatic performances of his friend and countryman" and mentions in this context his appreciation of "the representation of filial affection in *The Grecian Daughter*" (207).

13. Campbell 1: 156 cites the *Morning Post* of 10 Oct. 1782: "Yesterday, in the rehearsal of the *Fatal Marriage*, the boy, observing his mother in the agonies of the dying scene, took the fiction for reality, and burst into a flood of tears, a circumstance which struck the feelings of the company in a singular manner."

14. *The Beauties of Mrs. Siddons: Or, A Review of her Performances . . . in Letters from a Lady of Distinction to her Friend in the Country* (London: J. Strahan, 1786) 48.

15. *King Henry the Eighth, a Historical Play, Revised by J. P. Kemble* (London, 1804) 33.

16. In Thomas Francklin, *The Earl of Warwick* (1767), and John St. John, *Mary Queen of Scots, A Tragedy* (1789).

17. *Piozziana; Or, Recollections of the late Mrs. Piozzi* (London: Edward Moxon, 1833) 85.

18. Siddons, *Reminiscences* 22.

19. Edmund Burke, *A Philosophical Enquiry into the Origin of Our Ideas of the Sublime and Beautiful*, ed. James T. Boulton (London: Routledge and Kegan Paul, 1958) 110 (hereafter cited as *PE*).

20. *Coriolanus; or, The Roman Matron. A Tragedy. Altered from Shakespeare. Printed exactly conformable to the representation at the Theatre Royal, Drury-Lane* (London: J. Christie, 1789) 75.

21. See, for instance, the account of his celebrated "dagger scene" in a debate on the Aliens bill (Dec. 1792) in *The Parliamentary History of England, from the Earliest Period to the Year 1803*, ed. William Cobbett, 36 vols. (London: R. Bagshaw and Longman, 1806–20), vol. 30, col. 189.

22. *Burke: Select Works*, ed. E. J. Payne, 3 vols. (Oxford: Clarendon Press, 1898) 2: 337.

23. This is, for example, Paul Fussell's reading in his *The Rhetorical World of Augustan Humanism: Ethics and Imagery from Swift to Burke* (Oxford: Clarendon Press, 1965) 225.

24. William P. Albrecht, *The Sublime Pleasures of Tragedy: A Study of Critical Theory from Dennis to Keats* (Lawrence: UP of Kansas, 1975) 46.

25. Albrecht 8.

26. See Peter Hughes, "Originality and Allusion in the Writings of Edmund Burke," *Centrum* 4.1 (1976): 32–43, where it is argued that in the *Reflections* "discourse turns into event" and "rhetorical statement turns into perlocutionary act" (32).

27. Boulton 130–31.

28. David Hume, *A Treatise of Human Nature*, ed. L. A. Selby-Bigge, 2d ed., rev. P. H. Nidditch (Oxford: Clarendon Press, 1978) 605. For an important recent account of the place of sympathy in the ethics of Hume and Adam Smith, see John Mullan, *Sentiment and Sociability: The Language of Feeling in the Eighteenth Century* (Oxford: Clarendon Press, 1988) 18–56.

29. For a detailed consideration of the influence of the paradigm of the the-

ater on the fiction, aesthetics, and moral philosophy of the period, see David Marshall, *The Figure of Theater: Shaftesbury, Defoe, Adam Smith, and George Eliot* (New York: Columbia UP, 1986).

30. David Garrick, cited in Earl R. Wasserman, "The Sympathetic Imagination in Eighteenth-Century Theories of Acting," *Journal of English and Germanic Philology* 46 (1947): 264–72 (269). For a more recent view of the importance of ideas of sympathy in the acting of the period, see Leigh Woods, *Garrick Claims the Stage: Acting as Social Emblem in Eighteenth-Century England* (Westport: Greenwood P, 1984).

31. James Boaden, *Memoirs of Mrs. Siddons. Interspersed with Anecdotes of Authors and Actors*, 2 vols. (London: Henry Colburn, 1827) 1: 327. Commenting on this passage in his Introduction to *Plays by George Colman the Younger and Thomas Morton* (Cambridge: Cambridge UP, 1983), Barry Sutcliffe remarks, "According to strict Aristotelian definition, terror and pity should properly be produced by tragic action, whereas the pity evoked by Sarah Siddons seems to have been achieved by means of a portrayal of the human predicament in such a way as to have induced powerful and spontaneous sympathetic emotions in her audiences" (41).

32. On this point, see Hughes 41.

33. According to Michael R. Booth, "Throughout the last half of the eighteenth century the patent theatres were largely the preserve of the aristocratic, the fashionable, the educated, the gentry, and the middle-class tradesmen" (*The Revels History of Drama in English*, vol. 6: *1750–1880* (London: Methuen, 1975) 7.

34. Sir Philip Magnus, *Edmund Burke: A Life* (London: John Murray, 1939) 170–71.

35. Magnus 171.

36. Mary Wollstonecraft, *A Vindication of the Rights of Men, In a Letter to the Right Honourable Edmund Burke*, 2d ed. (London: J. Johnson, 1790) 7, 10, 68.

37. Wollstonecraft 5.

38. On this question, see Ronald Paulson's analysis of the *Vindication* in his *Representations of Revolution (1789–1820)* (New Haven: Yale UP, 1983) 79–87.

39. *The Reformer*, no. 10 (31 March 1748), quoted in A. P. I. Samuels, *The Early Life, Correspondence, and Writings of the Rt. Hon. Edmund Burke* (Cambridge: Cambridge UP, 1923) 321.

40. Edmund Burke, *Remarks on the Policy of the Allies*, in *Works* 7: 186.

41. Edmund Burke, *Letters on a Regicide Peace*, in *Works* 8: 106.

42. Burke, *Letters on a Regicide Peace*, 296–97, Letter 3.

43. See Neal Wood's pioneering account in "The Aesthetic Dimension of Burke's Political Thought," *Journal of British Studies* 4 (1964): 41–64.

44. Terry Eagleton, *The Rape of Clarissa: Writing, Sexuality, and Class Struggle in Samuel Richardson* (Oxford: Basil Blackwell, 1982) 14.

45. Eagleton 15.

46. Boulton 112–13.

47. *The Speeches of the Right Honourable Edmund Burke, in the House of Commons, and in Westminster Hall*, 4 vols. (London: Longman; J. Ridgway, 1816) 3: 409. Wollstonecraft's criticism of these speeches in her *Vindication* 56–62 is especially astringent.

48. Burke, *Speeches* 3: 418–19.

49. Linda Colley, "The Apotheosis of George III: Loyalty, Royalty, and the British Nation, 1760–1820," *Past and Present*, no. 102 (1984): 94–129 (95).

50. Colley 124–25.

51. Tom Nairn, *The Enchanted Glass: Britain and Its Monarchy* (London: Radius, 1988) 163–74.

52. For an approach to this phenomenon, see R. T. Allen, "The State and Civil Society as Objects of Aesthetic Appreciation," *British Journal of Aesthetics* 16 (1976): 237–42.

TWO

Theater and Countertheater in Burke's
Reflections on the Revolution in France

Frans De Bruyn

"I shall not live to behold the unravelling of the intricate plot which saddens and perplexes the awful drama of Providence now acting on the moral theatre of the world," wrote Edmund Burke in the opening paragraphs of his *Letters on a Regicide Peace*, his last great polemic on the French Revolution. The metaphor invoked here of revolution as grand, tragic theater must be the most sustained, if not the most pervasive, leitmotiv running through the outpouring of letters, pamphlets, speeches, and treatises that the events in France provoked from Burke's fevered pen. In his earliest recorded comment on the Revolution, he wrote to Lord Charlemont on 9 August 1789 of his "astonishment at the wonderful Spectacle, which is exhibited in a Neighbouring and rival Country—what Spectators and what actors."[1] The perception that all the political world's a stage is certainly not new with Burke, nor is it a point of novelty to observe, as Thomas Paine had been quick to note in 1791, that the theatrical metaphor is central to Burke's histrionic interpretation of revolutionary events. James T. Boulton voices the consensus of interpretive opinion with his argument that the theatrical references in *Reflections on the Revolution in France* are intended "to arouse the emotional fervour normally associated with serious drama and to suggest that the proper state of mind for observers of the French Revolution is that appropriate to watching a tragedy."[2]

Boulton's thesis is unexceptionable, as far as it goes, but its perspective by no means exhausts the extraordinary range and complexity of Burke's theatrical allusions in his writings on the French Revolution. Taking Boulton's statement as his starting point, Peter H. Melvin argues that Burke is not simply advancing his own conception of the political uses of drama but also drawing attention, with characteristic insight, to the Jacobins' revolutionary political artistry, particularly their radical, totalizing conception of revolution as theater: "The whole of revolutionary society was to become a vast theatre; everyone was to become an actor, a dissembler, except the Jacobins themselves."[3] As Burke himself states in the *Regicide Peace* tracts, "All sorts of shows and exhibitions, calculated to inflame and vitiate the imagination and pervert the moral sense, have been contrived."[4] The purpose of these public spectacles, which, Burke charged, included public rituals of denunciation—sons calling for the execution of their parents and parents denouncing their children as "Royalists" or "Constitutionalists"—was to purify and revolutionize French society through the coercive power of terror and mutual suspicion. Whatever their inward beliefs, citizens would be driven to enact a show of revolutionary zeal: "Anxiety which provoked mere conformity would finally produce febrile activity on behalf of the Revolution."[5] Equally important, the theatrical rituals of the ancien régime, those public spectacles designed to enforce symbolically the authority of the existing order, were being replaced systematically by new ceremonies and observances. Thus, for a time the pomp and panoply of the Roman Catholic Church gave way to the rationalistic Cult of the Supreme Being; in Burke's inimitable words, "They institute impious, blasphemous, indecent theatric rites, in honor of their vitiated, perverted reason, and erect altars to the personification of their own corrupted and bloody republic."[6]

Reflections on the Revolution in France, however, was written in the opening months of the Revolution, long before the concerted theatricality of the revolutionary government became apparent. Unless one wishes to credit Burke with a proleptic insight into the development of revolutionary ideology and behavior, another explanation must be sought for the pervasive presence of the theatrical metaphor in the *Reflections*—not simply as an extended allusion embedded in the text but as an integral, architectonic element in its design. The event that occasioned the *Reflections*, Dr. Richard Price's sermon at the Old Jewry commemorating the Glorious Revolution, furnishes a decisive clue. Burke's reading of

Price's published sermon, *A Discourse on the Love of Our Country*, with its appended congratulatory correspondence between the Revolution Society and the French National Assembly, alerted him suddenly to the danger that the principles promulgated by the French Revolution posed to the domestic politics and social equilibrium of England. This primary concern, the risk of the revolutionary infection spreading from France to England (to borrow a favorite Burkean image), decisively influenced the shape of his argument in the *Reflections*, which, though ostensibly addressed to a French correspondent, is directed in the first instance to an English readership.

Thus, with his primary audience in mind, he is careful to address his readers in the sometimes arcane forms of eighteenth-century British political discourse. In particular, he draws attention to what might be called a "discourse of the crowd," employing emerging forms of mass political protest in late-eighteenth-century England as a fundamental structural element in his treatise. Burke dwells at length on what E. P. Thompson has aptly labeled the countertheater of the crowd, which answered with its own symbolism the studied theatrical style of official authority, with its coronations, levees, and lord mayor's days, and which opposed its own calendar of political observances to the official calendar of political celebrations and commemorations in Hanoverian England.[7] The central dramatic plot of the *Reflections*, the October 1789 march upon Versailles, which forms the emotional climax of Burke's treatise, cannot be understood fully unless it is read in the context of the ritualized language of late-eighteenth-century English "insurrectionary" behavior. Not only does he assimilate the novel and the unknown (the dizzying spectacle in France) to the known and familiar (civil affrays like the Wilkite disturbances and the Gordon Riots), but he also invokes potent English political myths dating from the Civil War and the Glorious Revolution in a violent struggle to establish the interpretive boundaries that will govern the English response to events in France. Burke finds himself locked in a conflict with the Revolution's well-wishers, both moderates and radicals, for interpretive authority. Whose "reading" of the Revolution and whose appropriation of the symbols and rituals of English political discourse are to prevail?

I

The most celebrated and enduring of the many responses to Burke's *Reflections* is Thomas Paine's *Rights of Man* (1791). That Paine's reply deserves its high reputation is evident in the incisiveness with which he defines the clash of interpretive discourses in the debate that the *Reflections* has triggered: "I cannot consider Mr. Burke's book in scarcely any other light than a dramatic performance; and he must, I think, have considered it in the same light himself, by the poetical liberties he has taken of omitting some facts, distorting others, and making the whole machinery bend to produce a stage effect. Of this kind is his account of the expedition to Versailles. . . . It suits his purpose to exhibit the consequences without their causes. It is one of the arts of the drama to do so." To Burke's tragic scenes, Paine seeks to counterpose truth: fact opposes fiction in this passage, and life confronts art. In a fundamental sense, he sees no interpretive clash at all between his and Burke's accounts of the Revolution but only the opposition of reality to quixotic delusion. "Mr. Burke should recollect that he is writing History, and not *Plays*; and that his readers will expect truth, and not the spouting rant of high-toned exclamation." Paine does not pause to reflect that history writing is as much a narrative or dramatic art as the writing of plays, an insight that Burke instinctively grasped. By assigning appropriate "facts" and "causes" to explain the "consequences" that Burke melodramatically dwells upon, Paine ineluctably commits himself to his own narrative or version of events. He cannot do otherwise, for the effort to understand discrete historical events inevitably involves him in the articulation of a plot or story. Defending his sequence of explanation as more accurate and comprehensive than Burke's, Paine argues, "If the crimes of men were exhibited with their sufferings, stage effect would sometimes be lost, and the audience would be inclined to approve where it was intended they should commiserate."[8] True enough, one is inclined to respond, but then the audience would be viewing or reading a different play, as Paine clearly intends they should.

The dramatic scenes that Burke places at the center of his *Reflections* exploit a powerful double perspective, offering two simultaneous versions of the march on the king and queen at Versailles. One of these is the familiar tragic plot: the violent assault upon Marie Antoinette, followed by the via dolorosa of the royal family's forced return to Paris—

Burke's "Jacobean tragedy," as Ronald Paulson terms it.[9] The other is the same sequence of events with the revolutionary crowd placed in the foreground, not unlike, in a sense, the foregrounding of Satan in the opening books of *Paradise Lost*. Though he views the crowd close up, Burke is clearly observing its behavior disapprovingly from above, very much in the manner Alexander Pope surveys the antics of the dunces in his *Dunciad*. Pope's poem invokes a discursive hierarchy in which serious, elevated discourse is assimilated to the genres of tragedy and epic and is contrasted with the inferior, impure discourse of the dunces, which is grotesque, burlesque, and bathetic. Pope and Burke are caught up in an elaborate rhetoric of exclusion, associating their cultural and political enemies with the grotesque, low elements of the street and carnival—an outdoor, urban culture, both repellent and fascinating, that was progressively repudiated and displaced in the eighteenth century by the more "rational" and respectable pleasures of the coffee house, salon, and spa. At the same time, however, the visionary force that fires them both and energizes their writing paradoxically draws its power from precisely those subterranean elements that their impassioned discourse seeks to exorcise and exclude. As Peter Stallybrass and Allon White have noted with reference to Pope, "Whilst Augustan poetry witnesses an unprecedented labour of transduction in which it battled against the Smithfield Muse to cleanse the cultural sphere of impure and messy semiotic matter, it also fed voraciously and incessantly from that very material." [10]

The emotional intensity and texture of authenticity that Burke communicates in his descriptions of crucial, dramatic revolutionary events—despite his having been witness to none of them—originates specifically in his experience of the Wilkite disturbances and the Gordon Riots in London, the latter disorders a scant ten years in the past at the time of the French Revolution. Indeed, Burke recalls Lord George Gordon in the *Reflections*, drawing an explicit parallel between the English "mob . . . which pulled down all our prisons" and the Parisians who stormed the Bastille in July 1789.[11] During the Gordon Riots of 1780, Burke had experienced firsthand the fury of the mob, whipped up into an anti-Catholic frenzy; as an outspoken supporter of the Catholic Relief Act (1778), he had become a direct target of the rioters. Though soldiers were dispatched to protect his London house, from which books and pictures had been prudently removed, Burke himself refused to be intimidated by the crowd and went out deliberately, as he writes, "in the street amidst this wild assembly into whose hands I delivered myself informing them who I was."[12]

A report of the parliamentary debates following the riots (19 or 20 June 1780) records briefly Burke's impressions of what he had seen:

> He went into a full account of the late riots; expatiated on the inhumanity of the mob; said that Mr. Langdale, with twelve children, had suffered to the amount of 50,000l. . . . The inhumanity of fanatics, he said, was such, that after the destruction of the school near the city, a petition had been presented, desiring that the poor man, who owned it, might not have a lease of the land again to build another. . . . [H]e quoted, in a facetious manner, the names of several women—not being able to read and write themselves, these monsters were desirous of preventing others from receiving education. . . . Mr. Burke stated, in a very long speech, the means taken to bring about all the mischief; he said it had happened by the zeal of wicked and abandoned men, who had gone about industriously misleading poor, ignorant, and deluded people.[13]

Though this account offers little more than the barest summary of Burke's speech, it highlights a number of elements that were to figure prominently in his subsequent descriptions of the Parisian mob.

His appeal to the emotions of his auditors through affecting personal anecdotes, his exaggerated characterization of the rioters as base, inhumane, "wicked and abandoned" fanatics and monsters, his singling out of the women participants as latter-day furies, and his recognition of a symbolic selectiveness in the crowd's choice of victims—all these elements in his analysis of the Gordon Riots recur conspicuously in the famous narrative of the march on Versailles. The Parisians invading the palace are transformed into a "band of cruel ruffians and assassins, reeking with . . . blood," and they leave in their destructive wake a scene "swimming in blood, polluted by massacre and strewed with scattered limbs and mutilated carcases." Burke's account continues: "Two . . . gentlemen of birth and family who composed the king's body guard . . . with all the parade of an execution of justice, were cruelly and publickly dragged to the block, and beheaded in the great court of the palace. Their heads were stuck upon spears, and led the procession; whilst the royal captives who followed in the train were slowly moved along, amidst the horrid yells, and shrilling screams, and fanatic dances, and infamous contumelies, and all the unutterable abominations of the furies of hell, in the abused shape of the vilest of women" (*Refl.* 164–65). Even a cursory comparison with contemporary accounts reveals how freely Burke has embellished the facts; what he clearly hoped, however, was to furnish an account that would ring imaginatively true for his audience.[14] This he accomplishes by attributing to the Parisian throng precisely those characteristics that distinguished, at least in the estimation of the English elite, the behavior of London crowds. Standing at one remove from the French Revolution, Burke offers his readers an English fiction because English political realities are his primary subject.

To understand fully the discourse of the crowd that informs Burke's crowded, bloody scene, one must revive imaginatively a sense of the ceremonial and theatric splendor with which official authority clothed itself in the period—the rituals and symbolism of the courts, the church, and the crown. The example of Tyburn, the awful rites of public execution, conveniently illustrates both the pageantry with which government and law exercised their power and the means by which the crowd subversively undercut such awe-inspiring spectacles.

In his *Enquiry into the Causes of the Late Increase of Robbers* (1751), Henry Fielding draws attention to the self-conscious theatricality of the rites by which justice is executed, arguing that executions should be performed like a well-written tragedy, in which a "Murder behind the Scenes, if the Poet knows how to manage it, will affect the Audience with greater Terror than if it was acted before their Eyes."[15] (Here he directly anticipates Burke's doctrine of sublime obscurity in his *Philosophical Enquiry into the Origin of Our Ideas of the Sublime and Beautiful*.) Fielding is not advocating that executions be carried out in private but is simply inveighing against the prevailing carnival atmosphere on hanging days, which often transformed malefactors into antiheroes or even martyrs to the rigors of justice. Thus, Fielding insists that an atmosphere of dramatic solemnity must be maintained—if necessary, by artifice: "The Execution should be in the highest degree solemn. It is not the Essence of the Thing itself, but the Dress and Apparatus of it, which makes an Impression on the Mind, especially on the Minds of the Multitude to whom Beauty in Rags is never a desirable, nor Deformity in Embroidery a disagreeable Object." As a successful dramatist, Fielding might be expected to display a keen awareness of the administration of justice as a supremely dramatic enactment, but his analysis is nonetheless striking in its emphasis on the external trappings of spectacle and show as the crucial elements in the maintenance of order and authority. Burke is of the same mind, arguing that the fomenters of the Gordon Riots should be punished with the greatest possible dramatic solemnity: "*six*, at the very utmost . . . ought to be brought out and put to death on one and the same day, in six different places, and in the most solemn manner that can be devised."[16]

The symbolism of this official theater was not lost on the crowd, which often staged its own plebeian countertheater or crowd rituals parodically mimicking the actions of its "betters." Thus, as John Brewer reports, "On April Fool's day 1771, effigies of the Princess Dowager, Lord Bute, the Speaker of the House of Commons and the two Fox brothers were placed in two carts preceded by a hearse, and taken through the streets of London to the properly constituted execution place of all traitors, Tower Hill, where they were decapitated by a chimney sweep who also doubled as the officiating minister; they were then unceremoniously burnt. . . . Here was ritual retribution on a parallel with that actually exacted during the Revolution in France."[17] The crowd's actions accurately mimic the solemnities of a public execution: "the ritual of authority became the rites of the mob." This deliberate act of mimesis—the appropriation of the trappings of authority by a subordinate group to enact *their* conception of justice—disturbed and obsessed the authorities, as is evident in the single-mindedness with which they pursued and seized the standards, trophies, and symbols of the crowd during popular protests. The reason for this preoccupation with trappings and external appearances is not difficult to fathom.

Brewer, for instance, cites the astute observation of Adam Ferguson in his *Essay on the History of Civil Society* that any civil order organized on the basis of hierarchy and subordination depends heavily on public ritual to mark subtle gradations of status and power:

> The object of every rank is precedency, and every order may display its advantages to their full extent. The sovereign himself owes great part of his authority to the sounding titles and dazzling equipage which he exhibits in public. The subordinate ranks lay claim to importance by a like exhibition, and for that purpose carry in every instant the ensigns of their birth, or the ornaments of their fortune. What else could mark out to the individual the relation in which he stands to his fellow-subjects, or dis-

tinguish the numberless ranks that fill up the interval between the state
of the sovereign and that of the peasant? Or what else could, in states
of a great extent, preserve any appearance of order, among members
disunited by ambition and interest, and destined to form a community,
without the sense of any common concern? [18]

Without the official theater of state—coronations, state openings of
parliament, court levees, lord mayor's days—individuals would lack
a collective focus, a point of cynosure, upon which to fix a sense of
community and common enterprise. With the advent of an increasingly
rootless, atomized, capitalist social order, "disunited by ambition and
interest," these rites of state seem to Burke more crucial than ever; at
the very moment that subordination comes increasingly under pressure,
its indispensability as an instrument of social control becomes more and
more apparent. "The magistrate must have his reverence, the laws their
authority," he argues. "The body of the people must not find the principles of natural subordination by art rooted out of their minds. They
must respect that property of which they cannot partake" (*Refl.* 372).
The keen consciousness of rank and the forms of deference and differen-
tiation in the period ensured that parodies of official theater from below
were often viewed with gravity and alarm rather than amusement. It
is one thing to adopt a parodic discourse from above, as Pope does in
his mock-heroic poems, but quite another to do so from the déclassé
perspective of the dunces.

A similar obsession with countertheatrical symbolism can be detected
in Burke's description of the Parisian crowd at Versailles. He dwells on
the throng's trophies, the two "heads . . . stuck upon spears" leading
the procession, which bring to mind the grisly and monitory spectacle
of the traitors' heads that were customarily left grinning and festering
on Temple Bar. The marchers on Versailles perform a consummate act
of countertheater, "all the *parade* of an execution of justice" (my emphasis), which is all the more terrifying to Burke because it has begun
to literalize what had previously been a purely symbolic discourse (as
in the mock executions described above by Brewer). Though often destructive in their effects, the English rituals of political protest—"effigy
burning; the hanging of a boot from a gallows; the illumination of win-
dows (or the breaking of those without illumination); the untiling of
a house"—tended to circumscribe and channel promiscuous violence,

directing it at specific targets.[19] With the French revolutionaries, these rituals took a demonic turn, escalating crowd violence to a new level of intensity and ferocity.

Burke strains for a comparison sufficiently sensational to convey his sense of the monstrous injury and indignity visited upon the royal family as they were triumphantly escorted back to Paris on 6 October 1789: "It was . . . a spectacle more resembling a procession of American savages, entering into Onondaga, after some of their murders called victories, and leading into hovels hung round with scalps, their captives, overpowered with the scoffs and buffets of women as ferocious as themselves, much more than it resembled the triumphal pomp of a civilized martial nation" (*Refl.* 159). The contrast between theater and countertheater is made explicit here: the "triumphal pomp of a civilized martial nation" (a phrase of exquisite, if unintentional, irony) is set against the savage spectacle of the Parisian mob, whose symbols are no longer a boot or an effigy but the bloody scalps of their victims. Burke seeks to counter the obvious symbolic force of the triumphal return to Paris by transmuting the context or discursive field within which its symbolism can become intelligible. Like Swift, who subverts Puritan claims to divine afflatus by explaining the "operation of the spirit" in the mechanical terms of pseudoscientific discourse, conflating inspiration and libido, Burke undercuts the corporate and political legitimacy of the Parisian crowd's actions by reducing them to a context of anarchic savagery—that of a presocial, Hobbesian state of nature. The protests of the crowd are thus drained of any political significance and can be read only as acts of blind, irrational violence. Burke vehemently denies any coherence or intelligibility to the crowd's countertheatrical discourse, even as he affirms the official theater of France's "triumphal pomp"—its coercive military might.

II

The ritual of official theater in eighteenth-century Britain was closely tied up with calendrical observances—anniversaries of important historical events—whose celebration or commemoration had great symbolic and ideological significance. In the urbanized and increasingly politicized atmosphere of Georgian England, the time-honored dates of the agricultural year (May Day, Plough Monday, Twelfth Night, etc.)

were displaced by celebrations of the nation's political landmarks: the reigning monarch's birthday; the birthday and accession of Charles II, marking the Restoration (29 May); the date of the Hanoverian succession (1 August); the birthday of William III and the occasion of his landing at Torbay, celebrated as the anniversary of the Glorious Revolution (4 November); and Guy Fawkes' Day (5 November). These holidays together constituted a Hanoverian political calendar designed, as John Brewer remarks, "to inculcate loyal values in the populace, and to emphasize and encourage the growth of a national political consensus."[20] On a number of occasions, however, particularly in the first half of the century, the calendar became a focus for ideological conflict, with Whigs and Tories, Hanoverians and Jacobites celebrating rival Hanoverian and Stuart anniversaries with processions, effigy burnings, oaths, toasts, and commemorative sermons. Thus, for example, Jacobite attempts to burn William III in effigy on 4 November 1715 were broken up by Whig supporters, who in turn organized pope-burning processions and anniversary celebrations of their own as demonstrations of loyalty to George I.[21]

By mid-century, with the question of the royal succession no longer in dispute, the dates of the political calendar were celebrated in a spirit of general unanimity. But with the emergence of this public consensus, the calendar and its rituals of observance, like other symbols of official authority, became in their turn the targets of parody and mock imitation. The radical movement that coalesced around John Wilkes in the 1760s created a "countercalendar" of celebrations parodying the established cycle of birthdays and anniversaries: "Wilkes's birthday, the anniversary of the St. George Fields Massacre, the numerous Middlesex elections, the release of Wilkes from the King's Bench, each of these occasions was feted not merely as a celebration but as a means of impinging upon the popular political conscience in a way that the government had employed for over a generation."[22] The demonstrations that marked these countercelebrations were generally orchestrated by that most distinctive and characteristic eighteenth-century institution, the club.

The proliferation of local clubs, lodges, and societies in the period served a wide variety of purposes—economic, social, political, literary, and intellectual. Through their pooling of financial, intellectual, and organizational resources, these voluntary associations conferred a degree of independence upon their members from traditional economic and political relationships of clientage and aristocratic patronage. Radical leaders like Wilkes found in the clubs a ready source of financial and political support, which they shrewdly exploited. Unlike the loyalist societies or "mug-house" clubs of the early Hanoverian years, which were organized by the Whig gentry to inculcate loyalty to the new regime, the later associations provided an organizational foundation for independent political thought and initiative.

The symbolism and discursive activity organized around the political calendar and the clubs forms a salient, though often overlooked, constituent of the historical context within which the *Reflections* was conceived and within which it becomes fully intelligible. Recent studies of the *Reflections* have often treated it as fundamentally a work of political theory abstracted from the historical process of which it is a part. Such an approach offers certain methodological advantages but runs the distinct danger of distorting the work's contingent, paradoxical complexity or reducing it to (and reifying) its explicitly ideological dimension—thereby harnessing the text to the service of a narrow political doctrine. Thus, as Alfred Cobban wrote in 1960, "Burke has escaped from the more foolish jibes of the left in Britain, only to fall a victim to the uncritical adulation of the right in America. . . . These attempts to condemn or applaud the ideas or annex the name and reputation of Burke, like any other attempt to exploit the past to the advantage of transient political interests, are not history."[23]

But the purpose in reviving the political culture in which Burke and the *Reflections* were immersed is not to provide a kind of scenic historic landscape or backdrop against which his work is picturesquely situated. The aim, rather, is to "historicize" Burke's treatise—to remind ourselves, as Michael McKeon observes of literary texts in general, that the text "partakes of historical process: that it is a strenuous and exacting labor of discourse that seems thereby to detach itself from its historical medium, but that bears within its own composition the distinguishing marks of its continuity with the world it has ostensibly left behind."[24] The *Reflections* has been spectacularly successful in rising above the intellectual fray, as indicated by its status as a classic of political philosophy and of modern conservatism, but when it is resituated in the historical discourse of its time, its tone of magisterial authority gives way to one of strenuous striving and debate—a debate immersed in the contemporary, historically specific discourse symbolized by the Hanoverian calendar.

The opening pages of the *Reflections* establish the real ground on which this initial battle in the propaganda war over the French Revolution is to be fought. The event that Burke identifies as having occasioned his treatise is one so typical and commonplace as to be almost without noteworthiness, the annual meeting of the Revolution Society on 4 November 1789: "I find, upon enquiry, that on the anniversary of the Revolution in 1688, a club of dissenters, but of what denomination I know not, have long had the custom of hearing a sermon in one of their churches; and that afterwards they spent the day cheerfully, as other clubs do, at the tavern" (*Refl.* 87). Burke admits that there is, on the face of things, "nothing" here to which he can reasonably "take exception"; he even acknowledges that he has "the honor to belong to more clubs than one, in which the constitution of this kingdom and the principles of the glorious Revolution, are held in high reverence" (*Refl.* 88, 85–86). But having implicitly recognized the important role of clubs like the Revolution Society as voices and molders of public opinion, he proceeds to repudiate and exclude what he implicitly affirms. He sets out not only to dispel any impression that the Revolution Society acts "in some sort of corporate capacity, acknowledged by the laws of this kingdom, and authorized to speak the sense of some part of it" (*Refl.* 88), but also to deny its legitimacy as a political voice in any capacity whatsoever, public or private.

In his vehement exclusion of the Revolution Society and its activities from the realm of legitimate political discourse, Burke betrays a profound anxiety about the power of countertheatrical symbolism. He fears that the Hanoverian political calendar is about to be appropriated, or even displaced, by a revolutionary ideology with its own commemorative festivals, as he notes with dismay in *Thoughts on French Affairs* (1791): "The appointment of festive anniversaries has ever in the sense of mankind been held the best method of keeping alive the spirit of any institution. We have one settled in London; and at the last of them, that of the 14th of July, the strong discountenance of government, the unfavorable time of the year, and the then uncertainty of the disposition of foreign powers, did not hinder the meeting of at least nine hundred people, with good coats on their backs, who could afford to pay half a guinea a head to show their zeal for the new principles."[25] Not only Bastille Day, but also the fifth and sixth of October, the exultant return of the people of Paris with their king and queen, might well become a "festive anniversary" in a revolutionary calendar: hence, Burke's eagerness to characterize the events of those two days as a "horrid, atrocious, and afflicting spectacle" (*Refl.* 159) rather than a triumphal procession. But try as he might to exclude this popular discourse and dismiss its proponents as outside the limits of rationality and respectability, he is nonetheless forced to acknowledge the presence among this "rabble" of many individuals with a considerable stake in their country—"with good coats on their backs" and guineas in their pockets.

Burke also fears a revival of the ideological conflict that the dates of the political calendar had occasioned in the early Hanoverian period. Dr. Price's commemorative sermon sets forth a revisionist view of the Glorious Revolution which threatens, in Burke's view, to make 4 November a celebration of political ideals that are potentially revolutionary in scope. The question at issue is what kind of narrative will be fashioned out of the facts of history; in a nation deeply imbued with the habit of defining itself in terms of its past, what version of that past, what memory, is to prevail? "In history a great volume is unrolled for our instruction," affirms Burke, but its value very much depends on *how* it is appropriated, as he immediately warns: "It may, in the perversion, serve for a magazine, furnishing offensive and defensive weapons for parties in church and state, and supplying the means of keeping alive, or reviving dissensions and animosities, and adding fuel to civil fury" (*Refl.* 247). This danger is evident in the revolutionary typology Price has created by illegitimately juxtaposing three historical dates: the execution of Charles I, the Glorious Revolution, and the recent events in France—"confounding all the three together" (*Refl.* 100), as Burke puts it. First, he accuses Price and his followers of turning the annual celebration of the Glorious Revolution into a subversive affirmation of radical democratic principles (thereby resituating 4 November as a ground of partisan conflict, which it had so frequently been earlier in the century, rather than as the confirmation of political consensus that it subsequently became). Second, he suspects them of transforming another holiday, the anniversary of Charles's execution on 30 January, from a day of solemn commemoration into one of unseemly celebration. Finally, to complete their revised political calendar, they include

Bastille Day as a holiday appropriate to be observed by freedom-loving
Englishmen.

In a speech before the House of Commons on 11 May 1792, Burke
offers his scenario of the consequences that will follow from such observances; dissenters and radicals, he predicts, "met to commemorate
the 14th of July, shall seize on the Tower of London and the magazines
it contains, murder the governor, and the Mayor of London, seize upon
the king's person, drive out the House of Lords, occupy your gallery,
and thence, as from an high tribunal, dictate to you."[26] Here the countertheater of the crowd, the mock ceremonial of the street, ceases to be
a symbolic gesture and threatens suddenly to become a genuine social
explosion; the dreamlike visions of Pope's *Dunciad*, in which the carnivalesque, populist entertainments of the Smithfield muses invade the
precincts of Westminster, threaten to become a demonic, nightmarish
reality—as has already happened in France, where the National Assembly has dwindled into "a profane burlesque" performing a "farce
of deliberation": "They act like the comedians of a fair before a riotous audience; they act amidst the tumultuous cries of a mixed mob of
ferocious men, and of women lost to shame, who, according to their
insolent fancies, direct, control, applaud, explode them; and sometimes
mix and take their seats amongst them; domineering over them with
a strange mixture of servile petulance and proud, presumptuous authority" (*Refl.* 161). The symbolic inversion alluded to in this passage—
the *mundus inversus*, or "world upside-down," topos in which traditional
hierarchies of parent and child, husband and wife, master and servant
are overturned—has burst its symbolic bounds and, in the process of
literalization, has been transformed into a truly revolutionary action.

A central question in modern studies of the countertheatrical and
the carnivalesque has been whether such parodic behavior represents a
genuine mode of subversion or simply serves as a social "safety valve,"
perhaps even as a reinforcement of the existing order. If Burke seemed
inclined to something like the latter view in his assessments of the
Gordon Riots, he swings decisively to the former in his appraisal of
the events of 1789. The example of France has charged the symbolic,
wish-fulfilling fantasies of countertheater with prophetic energy: "The
most wonderful things are brought about in many instances by means
the most absurd and ridiculous . . . and apparently, by the most contemptible instruments" (*Refl.* 92). Accordingly, popular demonstrations

can no longer be regarded as harmless releases of energy but must be repressed as subversive enactments of radical change.

III

To speak of "inversion" or a "world upside-down" motif is to adopt the point of view of the dominant political and cultural group in society, which naturally views alternative forms of expression as culturally worthless and politically illegitimate. Thus, from Burke's perspective, the "famous sermon of the Old Jewry" can be nothing else than a farcical dramatic performance—a farrago of "plots, massacres, [and] assassinations" to satisfy a depraved, bloodthirsty audience: "A cheap, bloodless reformation, a guiltless liberty, appear flat and vapid to their taste. There must be a great change of scene; there must be a magnificent stage effect; there must be a grand spectacle to rouse the imagination, grown torpid with the lazy enjoyment of sixty years' security. . . . The Preacher found them all in the French Revolution" (*Refl.* 156). Burke sounds here a familiar Scriblerian note, linking political upheaval with decadence in literary and cultural standards—a decline symbolized by the bathetic taste of Dr. Price's audience for cheap sensation and "grand spectacle." Here, as with Pope's powerful prophecy of universal darkness in *The Dunciad*, something of a conscious act of imagination is required to shake oneself free of Burke's compelling vision and to view circumstances for a moment from the dunces' perspective. Yet, that perspective is involuntarily inscribed in Burke's text, and the same events that he by turns regards as farcical or tragic assume the shape of apocalyptic comedy when they are seen through the eyes of his political opponents. The opposition between these two literary paradigms, played out in the pages of the *Reflections*, constitutes the structural core of the work: the familiar political and cultural symbolism of theater and countertheater supplies not only the content but also the fundamental form of Burke's polemic.

The elements that compose both these dramas, comic and tragic, are borrowings, as Ronald Paulson notes, from the Swiftean metaphors of radical dissent in *A Tale of a Tub*, a text inspired or, perhaps more accurately, haunted by the memory of the English Civil War:

> Burke's argument is determined less by logic than by a Swiftean chain
> of association that links Richard Price's Revolutionary Society speech

(which set him off) with the dissenters, their incendiary sermons, illumination and zeal, divine afflatus, the regicide Reverend Hugh Peters,
memories of the Civil War, and the "leading in triumph" of King
Charles I. The last becomes the type of (or analogue for) the conveyance
of Louis XVI to Paris by the crowd, with (to complete the parallel with
Charles I) the element of predictability or prophecy in the inevitable
execution that lies ahead.[27]

The comic version of these events is revealed in a lengthy passage from
Price's sermon which Burke cites to illustrate his contention that the
preacher's discourse amounts to nothing more than melodramatic farce,
the comedy "of a fair before a riotous audience."

Burke chooses as his text the peroration of Price's sermon, in which
the latter alludes to the Nunc Dimittis of Simeon and applies it to the
French Revolution: "I could almost say, *Lord, now lettest thou thy servant
depart in peace, for mine eyes have seen thy salvation.* . . . I have lived to see
Thirty Millions of People, indignant and resolute, spurning at slavery, and
demanding liberty with an irresistible voice. *Their King led in triumph,
and an arbitrary monarch surrendering himself to his subjects*" (*Refl.* 157). The
events of the Revolution and particularly of 5–6 October 1789 strike
Dr. Price as a divine, apocalyptic comedy, which draws its archetypal
shape and inspiration, as the allusion to Simeon suggests, from the story
of the birth of Christ, who has come to earth to overthrow tyranny and
redeem and transform human society. The irreconcilability of the two
men's political visions is dramatized in the clash of their discourse: the
same events that Burke denounces as "Theban and Thracian orgies"
are, he exclaims in horror, compared by Price "with the entrance into
the world of the Prince of Peace . . . announced by the voice of angels
to the quiet innocence of shepherds" (*Refl.* 165).

Burke unwittingly underscores the apocalyptic appeal of Price's discourse by describing the preacher, in what is clearly intended to be
a derisive comparison with the towering biblical figure of Moses, as
"viewing from the Pisgah of his pulpit, the free, moral, happy, flourish-
ing, and glorious state of France, as in a bird's-eye landscape of a promised land" (*Refl.* 157). Inscribed in Burke's heavy irony and powerfully
undercutting it is the potent comic narrative—a "divine comedy"—
of the Israelites' release from bondage in Egypt and their journey to
the Promised Land. The more he gives it a voice, the more this barely

submerged subplot, or countercurrent, to his argument grows in force, especially at this early stage in the propaganda war when public opinion had not hardened and become polarized. As James Mackintosh, one of Burke's most eloquent critics, notes in *Vindiciae Gallicae* (1791), "[Burke] affects to despise those whom he appears to dread. His anger exalts those whom his ridicule would vilify." James Boulton points out a parallel with Pope's treatment of the dunces in his *Dunciad*, which threatened, as Swift had warned, to confer immortality upon those he wished to consign to oblivion.[28] Similarly, the visionary optimism of Price and his followers, which Burke had sought to dismiss as the "importunate chink" of the "meagre, hopping . . . insects of the hour" (*Refl.* 181) glows with an unprecedented prominence and credibility in the reflected heat of his denunciatory passion.

A conspicuous feature of Price's revolutionary "comedy" (as, indeed, of all eighteenth-century political countertheater) is inversion, the world turned upside-down: a king is enslaved and slaves are made kings, or, in the words of another well-wisher to the Revolution quoted by Burke, "*A King [is] dragged in submissive triumph by his conquering subjects*" (*Refl.* 157n). In a truly apocalyptic world, such reversals are permanent features of the landscape: the first have come last, the last are first, and the lion lies down with the lamb. But inversion is a much more powerful device in contexts where hierarchies and power structures retain their force: hence, its durability as "a central and ancient principle" of all comedy.[29] The typical comic plot, as Northrop Frye has noted, involves a generational conflict in which the desires of the younger characters are resisted by paternal or otherwise entrenched interests; the resolution of this opposition "causes a new society to crystallize" around the resourceful protagonists. In this connection, Burke's persistent characterization of the French Revolution as the usurpation of paternal authority and age by youthful, insolent parvenus recapitulates the classic conventions of comedy, "with its clever children, wives, and servants pitted against dim-witted fathers, pedants, husbands, and masters."[30]

But the same events that, when seen from below, project a comic shape are tragic in their outlines when viewed from above. Thus, Burke identifies himself in his writings on the Revolution with the perspective of King Lear—age and authority beset by insolent youth, evil virility, and ruthless ambition. (When he turned on his political foes in the House of Commons, who ridiculed the vehemence of his opposition to the French Revolution, it was the words of Lear [3.6.61–62] that he revealingly quoted: "The little dogs and all Tray, Blanch, and Sweetheart, see, they bark at me!") Perhaps the most striking illustration of this altered perspective is Burke's accusation in *A Letter to a Member of the National Assembly* (1791) that the French legislature is promoting the subversion of the family and the overthrow of paternal authority: "the females of the first families in France may become an easy prey to dancing-masters, fiddlers, pattern-drawers, friseurs, and valets-de-chambre, and other active citizens of that description, who, having the entry into your houses, and being half domesticated by their situation, may be blended with you by regular and irregular relations." A situation that in another context might furnish the scenario for a farcical opera bouffe here poses a fundamental threat to the social order; the Assembly "propagate principles by which every servant may think it, if not his duty, at least his privilege, to betray his master."[31] Burke's expressed fears for the first families of France recapitulate, in a slightly different key, the pattern of events narrated in the *Reflections*, where the revolutionary mob shatters the domestic tranquillity of France's first family. But the demonic turn that these events have taken signals that this is no opera bouffe: the traditional reconciliation of opposing forces with which comedy concludes is shattered by a revolutionary conception of comedy which promises to make permanent the inversions of hierarchy that traditional comedy provisionally enacts. From Burke's perspective, such a theatrical representation can only be tragic in its final outcome.

Accordingly, the bitter end, rather than the joyous beginning, of Christ's earthly life furnishes the paradigm for Burke's reading of the events of 5–6 October. Dr. Price's "leading in triumph"—now "the most horrid, atrocious, and afflicting spectacle, that perhaps ever was exhibited to the pity and indignation of mankind" (*Refl.* 159)—becomes a latter-day via dolorosa, with the king and queen of France retracing Christ's steps to their own Calvary: "After they had been made to taste, drop by drop, more than the bitterness of death, in the slow torture of a journey of twelve miles, protracted to six hours, they were, under a guard, composed of those very soldiers who had thus conducted them through this famous triumph, lodged in one of the old palaces of Paris now converted into a Bastile for kings" (*Refl.* 165). Recalling Christ's agony in the Garden of Gethsemane, Burke describes the king as taking "the cup of human misery full to the brim" and drinking it "to the dregs" (*Refl.* 163). Moreover, echoes of Restoration and eighteenth-century sentimental tragedy reverberate in the events Burke recounts: the violent assault, amounting to rape, upon the queen; her escape "to seek refuge at the feet of a king and husband"; and the "unprovoked, unresisted, promiscuous slaughter" of the king's loyal retainers (*Refl.* 164). To complete this sensational, sentimental drama, he casts Marie Antoinette as a tragic heroine who bears up under her sufferings, humiliation, and captivity "with the dignity of a Roman matron," that is, "in a manner suited to her rank and race, and becoming the offspring of a sovereign distinguished for her piety and her courage." In the final extremity, avers Burke, "she will save herself from the last disgrace" and die like a Roman: "if she must fall, she will fall by no ignoble hand" (*Refl.* 169).

This contention of discourses between Price and Burke cannot be regarded merely as a rhetorical clash or an opposition of generic archetypes but must be understood as a deeply historicized conflict: the form that each chooses for his discourse is profoundly determined by historical circumstance. Burke acknowledges this when he seeks to account for Price's seemingly inexplicable "fit of unguarded transport" in his sermon: "I allow this prophet to break forth into hymns of joy and thanksgiving on an event which appears like the precursor of the Millenium, and the projected fifth monarch" (*Refl.* 166). In referring to the fifth monarchy, Burke alludes to the last of the five empires foreseen by the prophet Daniel in his apocalyptic interpretation of King Nebuchadnezzar's dream (Dan. 2.44); during the English Revolution, the chiliastic sect known as the Fifth Monarchy Men, together with other millenarians, identified this fifth kingdom with the new era heralded by the execution of Charles I. Burke thus traces Price's apocalyptic language back to the momentous days of Charles's trial and execution, citing a passage in a sermon delivered at Whitehall after the trial had commenced, in which the preacher, the radical independent divine Hugh Peters, greets the imminent deposition of the king with the same words of Simeon that echo in Price's sermon some 140 years later (*Refl.* 157–58).

Moreover, Burke charges, Price's ecstatic description of the French king "led in triumph" by his people constitutes a kind of plagiarism of the symbolically charged actions of the Rev. Hugh Peters who, according to a witness at his trial for high treason in 1660, triumphantly led the procession bringing Charles I to his first day in court. Burke quotes the

testimony of Thomas Walkeley in the *State Trials*: "I saw his Majesty in
his Coach with Six Horses, and *Peters*, like Bishop *Almoner*, riding before
the King triumphing."[32]

Finally, he might have pointed to another of Peters's sermons,
preached before the House of Commons a month before the trial, which
takes up the same typology of the Exodus that is later ironically invoked in the *Reflections*: "the subject of his Sermon was, *Moses leading the
Israelites out of Egypt,* which he applied to the Leaders of this *Army* whose
design is *to lead the people out of Aegyptian bondage: But how must this be
done?* . . . *This Army must root up Monarchy, not only here, but in* France,
*and other Kingdoms round about; this is to bring you out of Aegypt: This Army
is that Corner stone cut out of the Mountain, which must dash the powers of the
earth to pieces.*"[33] In Burke's eyes, Price is a plagiarist of history: his narrative "only follows a precedent" (*Refl.* 158), drawing out unwelcome
parallels between the French Revolution and the English Civil War. His
mimicking of Peters's millenarian sermon is indeed striking, though the
texts and tropes of Protestant apocalyptic discourse were so pervasive
as to constitute a fertile and extensive intertextual field. Nonetheless, in
an earlier sermon, Price had hailed the advent of a more enlightened
and progressive age in language that links him directly with his Puritan forebear: "The stone which was cut out of the mountain, without
human force, is hereafter to fill the whole earth, and the kingdom of the
Messiah to become universal. . . . A disdain of the restraints imposed by
tyrants on human reason prevails."[34]

By establishing the regicide Peters as the "precursor" (*Refl.* 158) or
originator of Price's discourse, Burke imposes on the latter's unfinished
comic narrative an inevitable, if as yet unacted, tragic conclusion: "The
actual murder of the king and queen, and their child, was wanting to
the other auspicious circumstances of this 'beautiful day.' . . . A groupe
of regicide and sacrilegious slaughter, was indeed boldly sketched, but
it was only sketched. It unhappily was left unfinished, in this great
history-piece of the massacre of innocents" (*Refl.* 166). But in accusing
the dissenters of reviving the dreadful apparition of regicide, he projects
onto his opponents his own most deep-seated nightmare of historical
memory; and if Price's sermon betrays him as nothing more than an imi-
tator, a thrall to a false pattern of history, Burke's tragic version of events
is scarcely more original. The via dolorosa that Louis XVI traverses in
Burke's account of his return from Versailles to Paris echoes the pattern
that Charles's contemporaries saw in his trial and execution. One writer

after another emphasized the king's last days as a Christ-like passion and martyrdom: "After Sentence, the King being hurried from their Bar, as he passed down the stairs, The common Souldiers . . . scoffed at him, casting the smoak of their stinking Tobacco in his face. . . . But one more insolent than the rest, defiled his venerable Face with his spittle, for his Majestie was observed with much patience to wipe it off with his Handkerchief, and as he passed, hearing them crie out Justice, Justice, *Poor soules* (said he) *for a peece of money, they would do so for their Commanders.*"[35] The ritual humiliations associated with Christ's Passion—scoffing and spitting—and Judas's betrayal of his master for thirty pieces of silver are recalled in this passage; other accounts stigmatized the king's persecutors as latter-day Pharisees and Pilates, and memorialized the scaffold at Whitehall as the king's Calvary. The parallels with the Passion story are almost irresistible: the death of King Charles, and now the "persecution" of Louis XVI, assume the contours of what Herbert Lindenberger calls a "martyr play, [which,] whether about a saint, a monarch, or simply some exemplary individual, can never completely escape being an imitation of Christ."[36]

Hugh Peters is accorded a prominent role in this *"Passion-Tragedie,"* as it was frequently called. The prosecutor at Peters's trial identified him as "the Person that stirred up the Soldiery below to cry for Justice" and portrayed him as a "Principle Actor in this sad Tragedy."[37] The language of Peters's accuser echoes another prominent strain in the discourse that Royalist writers had established to commemorate their martyr-king: Charles's suffering and death as heroic tragedy. Thus, the High Court of Justice at Westminster Hall, where the king was tried, is called a "Bloody Theatre" and the scaffold on which he mounted is described in similar terms as "the Theatre of his Murther."[38] Andrew Marvell sets the scene, with typical restraint, in his "Horatian Ode":

> That thence the royal actor borne,
> The tragic scaffold might adorn;
> > While round the armed bands
> > Did clap their bloody hands.

Richard Perrinchiefe's *Life of Charles I* exploits this discourse much more shamelessly (as does Burke, with more skill, in the *Reflections*):

> The *King*, after He had finished his Supplications, was through the *Banqueting*-house brought to the Scaffold, which was dress'd to terrour,

for it was all hung with Black. . . . But it prevailed not to affright Him
whose Soul was already panting after another Life. And therefore he
entred this ignominious and gastly Theatre with the same minde as He
used to carry to His Throne, shewing no fear of death. . . . *He that had*
nothing Common or Ordinary in His Life and Fortune is almost profaned by a
Vulgar pen. The attempt, I confess, admits no apology but this, That it was fit
that Posterity, when they read His Works . . . should also be told that His Actions
were as Heroick as his Writings, and His Life more Elegant than His Style.[39]

The overwrought, hagiographic tone of this passage reverberates in the
famous "purple prose"—the celebrated (or notorious) apostrophe to
Marie Antoinette and the lament for the passing of the age of chivalry—
that suddenly bursts forth from Burke's pen in response to Price's comic
optimism (Conor Cruise O'Brien shrewdly calls this his "Jacobite" manner).[40] All readers of the *Reflections*, beginning with Thomas Paine, have
recognized these great set pieces as the climax of the text, determining
the shape of everything that precedes and follows. In his vehemence
to exorcise and banish Dr. Price's comic visions, Burke reaches deeply
into his historic memory to uncover a language and form that can adequately voice his response to an event that had shaken him to the very
core of his being.

IV

By resituating the *Reflections* in its historical medium and political context, we come to recognize, as Burke himself did, how thoroughly historicized his treatise is—how inextricably it is bound up in the historical
process. His very choice of tragedy as the fundamental literary form for
his political discourse signals his awareness that the historical changes
he is witnessing in France may render tragedy obsolete, just as the
heroic forms of classical epic had become increasingly remote and problematic in the eighteenth century. With the final passing of the age of
chivalry, the social conditions that underpin the traditional conception
of tragedy will be swept away: "On [the new] scheme of things a king
is but a man; a queen is but a woman; a woman is but an animal; and
an animal not of the highest order. . . . Regicide, and parricide, and
sacrilege are but fictions of superstition, corrupting jurisprudence by
destroying its simplicity. The murder of a king, or a queen, or a bishop,
or a father, are only common homicide" (*Refl.* 171). If kings, queens,

and bishops no longer retain so much as a symbolic preeminence over their peoples; if, as Price affirms, "the dominion of kings [is] changed for the dominion of laws, and the dominion of priests giv[es] way to the dominion of reason and conscience," then tragedy, at least of the kind conceived by Aristotle and Shakespeare, is no longer available as a mode of literary discourse.

The tragic idiom that apotheosized Charles I sounds a note of extravagance and "romance" when applied to Louis XVI and Marie Antoinette, as even some of Burke's friends, among them Philip Francis, pointed out to him. "In my opinion all that you say of the Queen is pure foppery," wrote Francis to Burke on 19 February 1790. Not unexpectedly, Thomas Paine offers the most memorable dismissal of Burke's heroical-sentimental flights: "He pities the plumage, but forgets the dying bird. . . . His hero or heroine must be a tragedy-victim expiring in show, and not the real prisoner of misery, sliding into death in the silence of a dungeon."[41] Without detracting from the undeniable rhetorical power and skill of Burke's central tragic narrative, these two readers express their unease at the almost mock-heroic disparity of form and subject matter in his description of the royal family. Their very perception of this ironic gap (in contrast with the acceptability of the same discourse a century and a half earlier) points to fundamental shifts in social and political awareness which inevitably resonate in the changing relations of literary genres to one another—the emergence of new forms and the internal transformations of preexisting kinds.

The depth of Burke's commitment to his version of events and the ideological significance of that commitment can be measured by the theoretical discussion of tragedy—one of his most extensive and revealing explorations of the subject—that follows upon his narrative of the queen's humiliation. As if conscious that his manner of proceeding requires some explanation, Burke apologizes for having "dwelt too long on the atrocious spectacle of the sixth of October" (*Refl.* 175) and launches into a vigorous defense of his response to the Revolution. Posing himself the question "Why do I feel so differently from the Reverend Dr. Price?" he replies, at some length:

For this plain reason—because it is *natural* I should; because we are so made as to be affected at such spectacles with melancholy sentiments upon the unstable condition of mortal prosperity, and the tremendous uncertainty of human greatness; because in those natural feelings we learn

great lessons; because in events like these our passions instruct our reason; because when kings are hurl'd from their thrones by the Supreme
Director of this great drama, and become the objects of insult to the base,
and of pity to the good, we behold such disasters in the moral, as we
should behold a miracle in the physical order of things. We are alarmed
into reflexion; our minds (as it has long since been observed) are purified
by terror and pity; our weak, unthinking pride is humbled, under the
dispensations of a mysterious wisdom. (*Refl.* 175)

With a nod to Aristotle's doctrine of catharsis, Burke unfolds a theory
of tragedy in the midst of his political treatise, a move not so unusual,
perhaps, in a period still heavily committed to didactic theories of literature and unaccustomed to making sharp distinctions between literature
and other fields of polite letters. Indeed, tragedy was regarded throughout the eighteenth century as a profoundly political genre, both in its
topical and historical content.

Joseph Addison's *Spectator* contributions provide a context for Burke's
fiercely political conception of tragedy. In *Spectator* 219, the reader
is offered, as Ronald Paulson has noted, two "alternative models of
providential design."[42] On the one hand, "Men in Scripture are called
Strangers and Sojourners upon Earth, and Life is a *Pilgrimage*," but on the
other, as Epictetus suggests, the world is very much like "a Theatre,
where every one has a Part allotted to him." Addison professes himself
inclined to the latter metaphor, "which is," he states, "very beautiful,
and wonderfully proper to incline us to be satisfyed with the Post in
which Providence has placed us." Our great responsibility is "to excell
in the Part which is given us. If it be an improper one the Fault is not
in us, but in him who has *cast* our several Parts, and is the great Dis-
poser of the Drama."[43] To describe life as a pilgrimage is to emphasize
one's beginning and one's end—a genetic and teleological metaphor.
By contrast, Epictetus's theatrical analogy stresses life's arbitrariness,
inscrutability, and uncertainty. Addison's preference for thinking of life
as a spectacle or scene rather than a journey is revealing in a number
of ways. As Paulson observes, "For Addison, the theatrical scene seems
necessary to replace the determinedly teleological pilgrimage with a
series of provisional structures, roles, and scenes, which are more appropriate to man's life in society."[44] Addison's conservative commitment
to an essentially static, hierarchical social order is clearly in evidence,

as is (perhaps less obviously) England's traumatic collective memory of its destructive Civil War, in which the roles that Englishmen were called upon to play were fiercely contested.

Addison's conception of life as theater is equally congenial to Burke, who likewise emphasizes the inscrutability of the "Supreme Director of this great drama" and the necessity of submission to the incalculable ways of providence—"the dispensations of a mysterious wisdom." The feelings a person experiences upon witnessing a sudden reversal of fortune yield intuitive insights, chiefly the awareness that human greatness is dangerous and uncertain. Such lessons clearly have the effect of enforcing submission to existing social and political structures: the existing social order is explicitly linked to the eternal disposition of things. As the earl of Shaftesbury had put it earlier in the century, "The genius of [tragedy] consists in the lively representation of the disorders and mastery of the great; to the end that the people and those of a lower condition may be taught the better to content themselves with privacy, enjoy their safer state, and prize the equality and justice of their guardian laws."[45] Tragedy promotes social harmony by enforcing the lessons and underscoring the benefits of the social contract.

Harvey Mansfield has argued that this is precisely the function of tragedy in Burke's political discourse: the experience of tragedy and the fall of great heroes (which Burke deliberately reproduces in his central narrative in the *Reflections*), by reminding individuals of the benefits of civil security, serve as a "reenactment" of the original social contract, when the individual gave up the right "to assert his own cause." Lessons such as these seem uppermost in Burke's mind when he revives the problem of tragedy in the context of his impeachment proceedings against Warren Hastings: "It is wisely provided in the constitution of our heart, that we should interest ourselves in the fate of great personages. They are therefore made everywhere the objects of tragedy, which addresses itself directly to our passions and our feelings. And why? Because men of great rank, men of great hereditary authority, cannot fall without a horrible crash upon all about them. Such towers cannot tumble without ruining their dependent cottages." Glossing Burke's remarks, Mansfield comments, "The result of the realization that human greatness is uncertain is a natural feeling of awe; it makes men content with the little things that they have and eager to conserve that much. Love of finite things begins with the demonstration that love of great-

ness brings disaster. Tragedy, in Burke's theory, teaches the lesson that
is taught by the natural right of self-preservation, in Hobbes's theory—
the lesson that human vanity must be conquered to make human society
possible."[46]

Burke's insistence on inculcating a doctrine of "tragic submission"
in his account of events in France is closely bound up with his deeply
ambivalent attitude toward history. Though committed, as has already
been noted, to a traditional, humanistic conception of history as "a great
improver of the understanding," he fears that its reservoir of precepts
has been irretrievably contaminated by modernity with its doctrinally
and theoretically driven conflicts. Bruce James Smith describes the consequences that have followed from this fragmentation of tradition: "Abstract theory had become 'armed doctrine' by insinuating itself into
history and thus entering the realm of possibility. . . . Tradition had
spoken with one voice, but the discovery of history had made the past
problematic. Radicals and dissenters now had 'predecessors.' History
was full of rebellious, even regicidal, 'precept.' The past had become a
place of terror."[47] The ineradicable historical fact that Burke accuses the
dissenters of reviving (and to which he himself compulsively adverted)
is, of course, the execution of Charles I, but in France other historical
images were being conjured up for equally revolutionary purposes. The
"infamous massacre of St. Bartholomew" (*Refl.* 249) was performed on
the Parisian stage in order to sharpen the ideological instincts and sanguinary impulses of its audience: "In this tragic farce they produced the
cardinal of Lorraine in his robes of function, ordering general slaughter.
Was this spectacle intended to make the Parisians abhor persecution,
and loathe the effusion of blood?—No, it was to teach them to perse-
cute their own pastors; it was to excite them, by raising a disgust and
horror of their clergy, to an alacrity in hunting [them] down to destruction" (*Refl.* 249). This revolutionary appropriation of history in the form
of political theater catches Burke on the horns of a dilemma: though
he wishes to erase horrors such as these from the rolls of history, he
cannot give up the past, which alone stands in the way of "unbridled
innovation" and social disintegration.

Smith argues that Burke's way out of this dilemma is to obliterate
historical difference through an appeal to custom: "if we are to save
the future, we must hide the fact that the present is not like the past."
Henceforth, history is to be studied as the origin of "habit" rather than

as a source of "precept"—"an exercise to strengthen the mind, as furnishing materials to enlarge and enrich it, not as a repertory of cases and precedents for a lawyer."[48] Historians must "stand upon that elevation of reason, which places centuries under our eye, and brings things to the true point of comparison, which obscures little names, and effaces the colours of little parties, and to which nothing can ascend but the spirit and moral quality of human actions" (*Refl.* 250). One means of ensuring that the right lessons are learned in the study of history is to distance oneself from the welter of facts and events in order to discern the true shape, the recurrent pattern lying behind them. Thus, the tragic outline of Charles I's capture and execution in the 1640s repeats itself in the unfolding struggle of the French Revolution. Though the dramatis personae and the contingent circumstances undergo change, the essential character of the historical narrative stands unaltered. The fall of kings will always prove to be tragic, a persuasion that dictates Burke's choice of narrative form in the *Reflections* and explains its proleptic intensity—its prophetic anticipation, almost three years before the event, of Louis XVI's execution.

By contrast, the narrative structure of pilgrimage or the journey insists on the process of change and throws the audience's attention forward to its final outcome. Thus, the end of the journey in John Bunyan's famous pilgrimage narrative, *Pilgrim's Progress*, brings Christian to the gates of the Celestial City, the new Jerusalem foretold in the Book of Revelation. The word "progress" in Bunyan's title conveys the primary sense of a journey but the completion of the title—*from This World to That Which Is to Come*—imparts to the term, as Raymond Williams argues, a significant new shade of meaning: "a sense of a manifest destiny and *future* . . . [which] was soon to be secularized and given a wholly new content."[49] The prophetic typology of the Book of Revelation, which had inspired the Puritan radicals of the seventeenth century, was increasingly recognized in the eighteenth century as finding its fulfilling antitype in the gathering momentum of progress, a secular heaven-on-earth prognosticated by the linear, forward movement of history toward social and political improvement. The title of Richard Price's millenarian sermon *The Evidence for a Future Period of Improvement in the State of Mankind*, delivered at the Old Jewry in April 1787, testifies to his belief in the irresistible momentum and irreversibility of enlightened progress.

Burke was by no means an enemy of the idea of progress, but his metaphors of change—such as his celebrated characterization of the British political system as a perpetual cycle of "decay, fall, renovation, and progression" (*Refl.* 120)—continue to associate change with the cyclical rhythms of nature. Though he recognizes the inevitability of change, he seeks to minimize its corrosive influence by arguing for the preservation of the old and a reversion to or renovation of the past in the promulgation of the new. His obsessive concern to portray the French Revolution as a tragedy reflects, as Ronald Paulson notes, this desire to manage change: "The basic mythos of tragedy or comedy, with the dichotomies of youth and age, birth-death, and rise-decline, has always been used by man to keep mutability under control. Progress was one deviation from this basic metaphor, and for that reason ominous."[50] Burke was among the first to recognize that the French Revolution was not a revolution in the traditional sense of a return to a point of origin or to ancient liberties but rather an irreversible rising movement generated from below. The circular motion implied in the older definition recalls the venerable metaphor of the Wheel of Fortune, which figured so largely in medieval and Renaissance conceptions of tragedy; this language of fortune was shared, as J. G. A. Pocock has argued (*The Machiavellian Moment*, 1975), by political writers of the seventeenth and eighteenth centuries, who continued to see some version of the Machiavellian opposition between virtue and fortune or virtue and corruption as the fundamental tension of human social existence. The countertheater of the Revolution proclaims the final overthrow of this essentially tragic conception of history: a "revolution in sentiments, manners, and moral opinions" (*Refl.* 175) will ensure the onward march of virtue and the realization of a Rousseauian vision of human perfectibility.

V

In *A Letter to a Member of the National Assembly* (1791), Burke identifies the social and moral doctrines of Rousseau as the theoretical driving force behind the countertheater of the French Revolution: "Under this philosophic instructor in *the ethics of vanity,* they have attempted in France a regeneration of the moral constitution of man. Statesmen like your present rulers exist by everything which is spurious, fictitious, and false,—by everything which takes the man from his house, and sets him on a stage,—which makes him up an artificial creature, with painted, theatric sentiments, fit to be seen by the glare of candle-light, and formed to be contemplated at a due distance."[51] Rousseau's sentimentalism, together with his utopian faith that humanity's natural goodness will reassert itself with the transformation of the institutions that constrain and corrupt it, provides the basis for a theater that celebrates the overthrow of false social and political establishments and the emancipation of the previously repressed human soul.

But the emotional release expressed in the countertheatrical demonstrations of the French Revolution strikes Burke as contrived and spurious: the theory of human character and motivation that undergirds this revolutionary countertheater is both factitious and fictitious. Such a charge of false artificiality sounds a slightly jarring note, coming as it does from a writer who affirms in one of his most famous aphorisms that "Art is man's nature." Indeed, he acknowledges the indispensable artifice, role-playing, and theatricality of the old order—the fiction of an "age of chivalry" with its "pleasing illusions, which made power gentle, and obedience liberal," an age costumed in the "decent drapery of life . . . furnished by the wardrobe of a moral imagination." This elaborate ceremonial is now to be "exploded as a ridiculous, absurd, and antiquated fashion" (*Refl.* 170–71), a formulation that, in its essentials, reverses back upon himself the charge he levels against his opponents in the above-quoted *Letter.*

But Burke anticipates the contradiction in which he threatens to entangle himself by arguing, in effect, for a distinction between theatrical "art" and countertheatrical "artifice." The former differs from the latter in its emotional authenticity, which can be tested only with reference to an external standard, namely, the intuitive, feeling response to real-life experience. Thus, in response to the humiliations allegedly visited upon Louis XVI, he exclaims, "Some tears might be drawn from me, if such a spectacle were exhibited on the stage. I should be truly ashamed of finding in myself that superficial, theatric sense of painted distress, whilst I could exult over it in real life. With such a perverted mind, I could never venture to shew my face at a tragedy" (*Refl.* 175). The theater functions for Burke as a moral touchstone. If a tragic drama can elicit tears from a spectator, the same response should be forthcoming in real life.

In contrast, the artificial countertheater of Dr. Price and the French revolutionaries displays a profound "dissociation of sensibility"—an estrangement of thought from feeling—which carries in its wake a confusion of moral ends and means:

> Poets, who have to deal with an audience not yet graduated in the school of the rights of men, and who must apply themselves to the moral constitution of the heart, would not dare to produce such a triumph as a matter of exultation. . . . They would reject [the odious maxims of a Machiavellian policy] on the modern, as they once did on the antient stage, where they could not bear even the hypothetical proposition of such wickedness in the mouth of a personated tyrant, though suitable to the character he sustained. No theatric audience in Athens would bear what has been borne, in the midst of the real tragedy of this triumphal day; a principal actor weighing, as it were in scales hung in a shop of horrors,—so much actual crime against so much contingent advantage,—and after putting in and out weights, declaring that the balance was on the side of the advantages. (*Refl.* 176)

The "artifice" that Burke complains of—the "painted" sentiments and distresses of the revolutionary stage—arises, in his opinion, from a fatal separation between abstract ideas, such as the conception of "rights of man," and concrete actions and circumstances, such as "the cruel and insulting triumph of Paris, and of Dr Price" over the king (*Refl.* 177).

In order to realize the former, the Revolution must stifle and suppress any sympathy arising in the case of the latter. If Louis XVI should in fact be innocent of any personal crimes, he must nonetheless undergo ritual humiliation—his rights must be violated—because of his symbolic importance as the chief representative of a corrupt regime. In Burke's terms, revolutionary countertheater deliberately distorts and perverts the "natural feelings" of its audience so as to inculcate in their place abstract, counterintuitive beliefs. Thus, for instance, the National Assembly endorses a new, revolutionary morality by promulgating "false and theatric" ceremonies in honor of Rousseau, "[who] exhaust[ed] the stores of his powerful rhetoric in the expression of universal benevolence, whilst his heart was incapable of harboring one spark of common parental affection. Benevolence to the whole species, and want of feeling for every individual . . . form the character of the new philosophy."[52]

Burke unfolds a curiously literal-minded theory of tragedy in his *Reflections*, one that virtually ignores the distinction between tragic events in real life and dramatic tragedy as an *imitation* of reality. This denial of aesthetic distance is already apparent in his earliest consideration of the effects of tragic representations on a theater audience. Thus, in *A Philosophical Enquiry into . . . the Sublime and Beautiful* (1757), he makes the following point: "I imagine we shall be much mistaken if we attribute any considerable part of our satisfaction in tragedy to a consideration that tragedy is a deceit, and its representations no realities. The nearer it approaches the reality, and the further it removes us from all idea of fiction, the more perfect is its power."[53] His view here closely echoes that of his friend Samuel Johnson, who always insisted that even fiction must be governed by rigid standards of truth and probability. The inescapable inference to be drawn from this intimate linking of art and life is that tragedy, for Burke, embodies or enacts fundamental, irreducible truths about the nature of reality.

This, rather than the formal and mimetic qualities of tragic representations, constitutes the real source of its power, as he argues in *A Philosophical Enquiry*:

> Chuse a day on which to represent the most sublime and affecting tragedy we have . . . spare no cost upon the scenes and decorations; unite the greatest efforts of poetry, painting and music; and when you have collected your audience, just at the moment when their minds are erect with expectation, let it be reported that a state criminal of high rank is on the point of being executed in the adjoining square; in a moment the emptiness of the theatre would demonstrate the comparative weakness of the imitative arts, and proclaim the triumph of the real sympathy.[54]

Burke's emphasis on tragedy as an emotional, rather than aesthetic, experience explains why he can regard the execution of a high-born personage as the quintessential tragic moment. That he should see such an event as the closest "real-life" analogue to the theatrical performance of tragedy is telling; it signals the extent to which his conception of tragedy in the *Reflections* is colored by ideology, that is, by the assumption that certain social and political structures—in this instance, a hierarchical, aristocratic society—are the natural order of things. "We fear God," he affirms, "we look up with awe to kings; with affection to parliaments; with duty to magistrates; with reverence to priests; and with respect to nobility . . . [because] it is *natural* to be [so] affected; because all other feelings are false and spurious" (*Refl.* 182). In short, as Michael Freeman mordantly observes, "it is natural to be conservative, unnatural to be radical."[55]

But if Burke seeks to distinguish between political theater and countertheater, art and artifice, on the basis of "natural feelings," his argument is attacked on precisely the same grounds by Thomas Paine and Mary Wollstonecraft. The public execution that stirs deep feelings of terror and pity in Burke arouses only fear and loathing in Paine. "Who does not remember the execution of Damien, torn to pieces by horses?" he asks. "The effect of those cruel spectacles exhibited to the populace, is to destroy tenderness, or to excite revenge." The example of the attempted regicide Robert Francis Damiens, who attacked Louis XV in 1757 and was put to death by *écartèlement* after suffering unspeakable tortures, is alluded to in Burke's *Philosophical Enquiry* (39). Damiens's fate excited great interest in England and may have been one of several instances (the execution of Lord Lovat in 1747 being another) that prompted Burke's reference to the rites of execution in his discussion of tragic sympathy. But the sublime terror that is meant to inculcate salutary lessons at such events strikes Paine as a "base and false idea of governing men."[56] This flat rejection of Burke's position forms part of a larger refutation of the latter's tragic narrative in the *Reflections*.

Burke's condemnation of the Parisians' revolutionary countertheater had centered, as Paine notes, on the bloody moment after the return to Paris from Versailles when several of the king's officials were beheaded and their heads carried about upon spikes: "it is upon this mode of punishment that Mr Burke builds a great part of his tragic scene." In reply, Paine inquires blandly as to the inspiration for the crowd's sanguinary countertheatrical demonstration: "They learn it from the governments they live under, and retaliate the punishments they have been accustomed to behold. The heads stuck upon spikes, which remained for years upon Temple-bar, differed nothing in the horror of the scene from those carried about upon spikes at Paris: yet this was done by the English government."[57] The theatrical rituals by which official authority awed the populace and kept it in check have been turned back on the ruling elite with a vengeance.

If, as E. P. Thompson has argued in the case of eighteenth-century English countertheater, "there is a sense in which rulers and crowd needed each other, watched each other, performed theatre and counter-

theatre in each other's auditorium, moderated each other's political behavior," this "active and reciprocal relation," this balance between ruler
and ruled, had been altogether overthrown in France: "A vast mass of
mankind are degradedly thrown into the background of the human picture, to bring forward with greater glare, the puppet-show of state and
aristocracy."[58] The result is a sudden irruption of destructive violence
into the countertheatrical discourse of revolutionary France, a savage
redressing of the balance. Whereas plebeian crowd rituals had previously only *mimicked* official actions, they now moved from mimesis to
literal enactment, thus ironically fulfilling Burke's criterion for dramatic
intensity by abandoning fiction in favor of a grisly reality. Yet, in some
sense, the crowd's behavior remained symbolic, even though it had
spilled over into direct action, in that the violence was limited, as Paine
points out, to a few carefully chosen targets, among them the governor
of the Bastille and the mayor of Paris: "It is to the honour of the National
Assembly, and the city of Paris, that during such a tremendous scene of
arms and confusion . . . they have been able . . . to restrain so much."[59]

Both Paine and Wollstonecraft attack Burke's conception of theater
at its theoretical foundations, namely, its insistence that a certain class
of feelings is authentic, while all others are unnatural and spurious.
Paine argues that the rites of official theater may arouse unwelcome
and unexpected emotions, feelings very different from the anticipated
responses of sublime awe, astonishment, and terror. Referring to the
custom of mounting traitors' heads on Temple Bar, he writes, "It may
perhaps be said, that it signifies nothing to a man what is done to him
after he is dead; but it signifies much to the living: it either tortures their
feelings, or hardens their hearts; and in either case, it instructs them
how to punish when power falls into their hands."[60] For her part, Wollstonecraft insists that in his analysis of the French Revolution as a regal
tragedy, Burke has deliberately banished an entire world of objects and
experiences from the purview of his compassion and sympathy:

> A *gentleman* of lively imagination must borrow some drapery from fancy
> before he can love or pity a *man*.—Misery, to reach your heart, I perceive,
> must have its cap and bells; your tears are reserved . . . for the decla-
> mation of the theatre, or for the downfall of queens, whose rank alters
> the nature of folly, and throws a graceful veil over vices that degrade

humanity; whilst the distress of many industrious mothers, whose *help-mates* have been torn from them, and the hungry cry of helpless babes, were vulgar sorrows that could not move your commiseration, though they might extort an alms.[61]

Though more impressionistic, Wollstonecraft's refutation of Burke is in some respects more shrewd than Paine's. She recognizes the fundamental subjectivity of his appeals to a universal standard of intuitive moral sensibility, and she correctly locates the source of his doctrine of "natural feelings" in his ideological convictions: "your respect for rank has swallowed up the common feelings of humanity." Moreover, she attacks the basis for his affective analysis of the theater's moral power—its status as a "school of moral sentiments" (*Refl.* 176)—by questioning the value of an intuitive response to scenes of distress. Such responses, she argues, engender moral self-complacency without inciting the individual to virtuous action: "the being who is not spurred on to any virtuous act, still thinks itself of consequence, and boasts of its feelings. Why? Because the sight of distress, or an affecting narrative, made its blood flow with more velocity, and the heart, literally speaking, beat with sympathetic emotion. We ought to beware of confounding mechanical instinctive sensations with emotions that reason deepens, and justly terms the feelings of *humanity*. This word discriminates the active exertions of virtue from the vague declamation of sensibility."[62] Her insistence on rational judgment as an essential part of the act of moral and aesthetic apprehension entails not only a thorough revision of Burke's conception of official theater and his affective narrative of political events, but also a rejection, ultimately, of political theater of any kind as an inadequate, misleading mode of political discourse.

Perhaps Wollstonecraft's most penetrating insight into the tragic theater of the *Reflections* is her recognition of its intimate connection with Burke's celebrated theory of aesthetic response, outlined in his *Philosophical Enquiry*. In that early treatise, Burke had distinguished sharply between the experience of sublimity and the apprehension of beauty, arguing for the superior intensity of the former—which turns on pain and danger and is characterized by terror, awe, and astonishment—over the latter—which is actuated by pleasure and is distinguished by responses of love, tenderness, and affection. Wollstonecraft observes that this is not simply a philosophical distinction but also a hierarchical one:

in valuing sublimity over beauty, Burke esteems heroism over tenderness, tragedy over comedy, masculinity over femininity, and the "exalted
qualities [of] fortitude, justice, wisdom, and truth" over compassion,
kindness, and liberality.[63]

This hierarchy has a crucial political dimension as well, as is obvious
in Burke's association of the sublime emotions with the institutions of
the ancien régime: *fear* of God, *awe* toward kings, *duty* to magistrates,
reverence to priests, and *respect* to nobility. Wollstonecraft objects that this
privileging of certain feelings, experiences, and institutions over others
excludes and devalues the aspirations of the greater part of humanity—
specifically women. She thus accusingly addresses Burke: "You have
clearly proved that one half of the human species, at least, have not
souls; and that Nature, by making women *little, smooth, delicate, fair* crea-
tures, never designed that they should exercise their reason. . . . The
affection they excite . . . should not be tinctured with the respect which
moral virtues inspire, lest pain should be blended with pleasure, and
admiration disturb the soft intimacy of love."[64] Similarly, by denying
any sublime dignity to the feelings that the countertheatrical rituals of
the crowd seek to express, by dismissing them as "a servile, licentious,
and abandoned insolence, to be our low sport for a few holidays" (*Refl.*
183), Burke marginalizes and belittles the genuine grievances expressed
through this inarticulate, often inchoate symbolic discourse.

Burke's self-conscious aestheticization of official theater opens up a
theme whose profound implications cannot be explored here. The language of taste, as many of Burke's readers have noted, plays a central
role in the *Reflections*: the "barbarous philosophy" of the French revolutionaries, he insists, is "destitute of all taste and elegance" (*Refl.* 171).
The term "taste," as Christopher Reid notes, links the social or political
and aesthetic spheres, for "taste is the social ratification of the individual
aesthetic response."[65] And this convergence of the individual with the
community is celebrated in the ritual of official theater, which finds its
apotheosis in Burke's ecstatic paean to the state as an object of religious
worship:

> They who are convinced of this his [God's] will, which is the law of laws
> and the sovereign of sovereigns, cannot think it reprehensible, that this
> our corporate fealty and homage, that this our recognition of a signiory
> paramount, I had almost said this oblation of the state itself, as a worthy

offering on the high altar of universal praise, should be performed as all
publick solemn acts are performed, in buildings, in musick, in decoration,
in speech, in the dignity of persons, according to the customs of mankind,
taught by their nature; that is, with modest splendour, with unassuming
state, with mild majesty and sober pomp. (*Refl.* 196–97)

Burke has moved far beyond the crude didacticism or overt intimidation
of eighteenth-century rites of justice or ceremonies of royal pomp.

In this passage, he celebrates official theater as offering the partici-
pant an experience of transcendence, of an eternal order which ratifies
the existing order and the individual's place in it. The stability of society
crucially depends on this affirmation, for the fundamental characteristic of the social order is inequality, a reality that can be defended only
within the larger perspective of divine justice. Thus, the people "must
labour to obtain what by labour can be obtained; and when they find,
as they commonly do, the success disproportioned to the endeavour,
they must be taught their consolation in the final proportions of eternal justice" (*Refl.* 372). This consolation is taught through the tragic
doctrine of poetic justice—the widespread conviction in the eighteenth
century that, as a reflection of divine justice, the good (in any dramatic
representation) should be rewarded and the evil punished. Through the
observance of this critical principle, the enforcement of submission to
existing social and political hierarchies and to the mysterious dispensations of providence is overtly integrated into the formal structure of
tragic drama. Burke's choice of tragedy as the central narrative pattern
of his *Reflections*, therefore, signals his awareness of its ideological and
didactic potency on behalf of the counterrevolutionary cause that he
espouses. The narrative structure of his treatise is nothing less, finally,
than the formal embodiment of his passionate argument.

Notes

1. Edmund Burke, *Letters on a Regicide Peace*, in *The Works of the Right Hon-
orable Edmund Burke*, 12 vols. (Boston: Little, Brown 1881) 5: 233 (hereafter
cited as *Works*; all references are to this edition unless otherwise stated); *The
Correspondence of Edmund Burke*, ed. Thomas W. Copeland et al., 10 vols. (Cambridge: Cambridge UP; Chicago: U of Chicago P, 1958–78) 6: 10 (hereafter
cited as *Corr.*).

2. James T. Boulton, *The Language of Politics in the Age of Wilkes and Burke* (1963; Westport, Conn.: Greenwood P, 1975) 144.

3. Peter H. Melvin, "Burke on Theatricality and Revolution," *Journal of the History of Ideas* 36 (1975): 451.

4. Burke, *Letters on a Regicide Peace* 311.

5. Melvin 451.

6. Burke, *Letters on a Regicide Peace* 310.

7. E. P. Thompson, "Patrician Society, Plebeian Culture," *Journal of Social History* 7 (1974): 382–405. See also Ronald Paulson, *Popular and Polite Art in the Age of Hogarth and Fielding* (Notre Dame: U of Notre Dame P, 1979) 26–30.

8. Thomas Paine, *Rights of Man*, ed. Henry Collins (Harmondsworth: Penguin, 1969) 81–82, 72, 82.

9. Ronald Paulson, *Representations of Revolution (1789–1820)* (New Haven: Yale UP, 1983) 76.

10. Peter Stallybrass and Allon White, *The Politics and Poetics of Transgression* (London: Methuen, 1986) 108. On the carnivalesque and the interrelation of high and low culture, see also Mikhail Bakhtin, *Rabelais and His World*, trans. Helene Iswolsky (Cambridge, Mass.: MIT P, 1968), and Terry Castle, *Masquerade and Civilization: The Carnivalesque in Eighteenth-Century English Culture and Fiction* (London: Methuen, 1986).

11. Edmund Burke, *Reflections on the Revolution in France*, ed. Conor Cruise O'Brien (Harmondsworth: Penguin, 1968) 179 (hereafter cited as *Refl.*).

12. Burke, *Corr.* 2: 246.

13. Edmund Burke, *The Speeches of the Right Honourable Edmund Burke, in the House of Commons, and in Westminster Hall*, 4 vols. (London: Longman; J. Ridgway, 1816) 2: 178–79.

14. Cf. the account of the attack upon Versailles in *Memoirs of Madame de La Tour du Pin*, trans. Felice Harcourt (London: Harvill P, 1969) 131–37. For a discussion of the social composition of the crowds participating in the Gordon Riots, see George Rudé, *The Crowd in History, 1730–1848* (1964; London: Lawrence and Wishart, 1981) 60–61. See also, Dorothy Marshall, *Dr. Johnson's London* (New York: Wiley, 1968) 236–38.

15. Henry Fielding, *An Enquiry into the Causes of the Late Increase of Robbers* (London: A. Miller, 1751) 123. Douglas Hay's "Property, Authority, and the Criminal Law," in *Albion's Fatal Tree: Crime and Society in Eighteenth-Century England* (New York: Pantheon, 1975) 26–31, details the elaborate spectacle and ritual that surrounded the administration of justice in eighteenth-century England. Another essay in the same volume, Peter Linebaugh's "The Tyburn Riot against the Surgeons," 65–69, describes the theatrical and countertheatrical spectacle of public hangings in the period.

16. Fielding 123–24; Edmund Burke, "Some Thoughts on the Approaching Executions," in *Works* 6: 246.

17. John Brewer, *Party Ideology and Popular Politics at the Accession of George III* (Cambridge: Cambridge UP, 1976) 184. The incident was reported in *Gentleman's Magazine* (1771) 188, and in *Middlesex Journal* (2 Apr. 1771). George Rudé discusses this and similar incidents in *Wilkes and Liberty: A Social Study of 1763 to 1774* (1962; rpt. London: Lawrence and Wishart, 1983) 164 and passim. On crowd rituals, see also Paulson, *Popular and Polite Art* 24–30.

18. Adam Ferguson, *Essay on the History of Civil Society* (Edinburgh: A. Kincaid and J. Bell, 1767) 104. See also Brewer 183–84.

19. Thompson 400. See also Rudé, *The Crowd in History* 62.

20. John Brewer, "Commercialization and Politics," in Neil McKendrick, John Brewer, and J. H. Plumb, *The Birth of a Consumer Society: The Commercialization of Eighteenth-Century England* (London: Europa Publications, 1982) 247.

21. Nicholas Rogers, "Popular Protest in Early Hanoverian London," *Past and Present* 79 (May 1978): 77–79.

22. McKendrick, Brewer, and Plumb 248. See also Brewer 178–79; and Rudé, *Wilkes and Liberty*.

23. Alfred Cobban, *Edmund Burke and the Revolt against the Eighteenth Century*, 2d ed. (London: George Allen and Unwin, 1960) xii. Conor Cruise O'Brien, in the introduction to his edition of the *Reflections*, 56–67, offers a similar note of warning.

24. Michael McKeon, "Historicizing *Absalom and Achitophel*," in *The New Eighteenth Century: Theory, Politics, English Literature*, ed. Felicity Nussbaum and Laura Brown (New York: Methuen, 1987) 37.

25. Edmund Burke, *Thoughts on French Affairs*, in *Works* 4: 369.

26. Burke, *Speeches* 4: 64.

27. Ronald Paulson, *Representations of Revolution* 58.

28. James Mackintosh, *Vindiciae Gallicae*, in *The Miscellaneous Works of the Right Honourable Sir James Mackintosh* (Philadelphia: A. Hart, 1850) 448; Boulton 165.

29. Barbara A. Babcock, *The Reversible World: Symbolic Inversion in Art and Society* (Ithaca: Cornell UP, 1978) 17.

30. Ian Donaldson, *The World Upside-Down: Comedy from Johnson to Fielding* (Oxford: Clarendon P, 1970) 6.

31. Edmund Burke, *A Letter to a Member of the National Assembly*, in *Works* 4: 31, 33. See also Paulson, *Representations of Revolution* 62.

32. *A Complete Collection of State Trials, and Proceedings for High-Treason, and other Crimes and Misdemeanours*, 4th ed., 11 vols. (London: C. Bathurst, 1776–81) 2: 360 (hereafter cited as *State Trials*).

33. Quoted in Raymond Phineas Strearns, *The Strenuous Puritan* (Urbana: U of Illinois P, 1954) 330.

34. Richard Price, *The Evidence for a Future Improvement in the State of Mankind . . . Represented in a Discourse, Delivered . . . at the Meeting House in the Old Jewry, London* (London: H. Goldney, 1787) 51–52.

35. *England's Black Tribunall, Set Forth in the Triall of K. Charles, I* (London: J. Playford, 1660) 62. The author of *A Hand-kirchife for Loyal Mourners, or a Cordiall for Drooping Spirits* (London, 1649) develops the parallels with the Passion story in some detail. See also C. V. Wedgwood, *The Trial of Charles I* (London: Collins, 1964) 206–12.

36. Herbert Lindenberger, *Historical Drama: The Relation of Literature and Reality* (Chicago: U of Chicago P, 1975) 45.

37. *State Trials* 2: 359.

38. William Dugdale, *A Short View of the Late Troubles in England* (Oxford: M. Pitt, 1681) 370. Richard Perrinchiefe, *The Life of Charles I*, in *The Workes of King Charles the Martyr*, 2 vols. (London: R. Royston, 1662) 1: 9.

39. Perrinchiefe, *Life of Charles* 1: 92, 118.

40. O'Brien, Introduction to *Refl.* 43.

41. Burke, *Corr.* 6: 86; Paine 73.

42. Paulson, *Popular and Polite Art* 115.

43. Joseph Addison and Richard Steele, *The Spectator*, ed. Donald F. Bond, 5 vols. (Oxford: Clarendon P, 1965) 2: 353.

44. Paulson, *Popular and Polite Art* 116.

45. Anthony Ashley Cooper, third earl of Shaftesbury, *Characteristics of Men, Manners, Opinions, Times*, ed. John M. Robertson, 2 vols. (Indianapolis: Bobbs-Merrill, 1964) 1: 143.

46. Edmund Burke, *Speech in General Reply*, in *Works* 11: 308; Harvey C. Mansfield, Jr., *Statesmanship and Party Government: A Study of Burke and Bolingbroke* (Chicago: U of Chicago P, 1965) 218.

47. Burke, *Remarks on the Policy of the Allies*, in *Works* 4: 468; Bruce James Smith, *Politics and Remembrance: Republican Themes in Machiavelli, Burke, and Tocqueville* (Princeton: Princeton UP, 1985) 111.

48. Smith 116; Burke, *Remarks* 468.

49. Raymond Williams, *Keywords: A Vocabulary of Culture and Society* (London: Fontana, 1976) 206.

50. Paulson, *Representations of Revolution* 48.

51. Burke, *Letter to a Member* 28.

52. Burke, *Letter to a Member* 27.

53. Burke, *A Philosophical Enquiry into the Origin of Our Ideas of the Sublime and Beautiful*, ed. James T. Boulton (London: Routledge and Kegan Paul, 1958) 47.

54. Burke, *Philosophical Enquiry* 47.

55. Michael Freeman, *Edmund Burke and the Critique of Political Radicalism* (Chicago: U of Chicago P, 1980) 40.

56. Paine 80.

57. Paine 79.

58. E. P. Thompson, "Patrician Society, Plebeian Culture" 402; Paine 81.

59. Paine 81.

60. Paine 79.

61. Mary Wollstonecraft, *A Vindication of the Rights of Men* (London: J. Johnson, 1790) 26–27.

62. Wollstonecraft 32, 136–37.

63. Wollstonecraft 112–13.

64. Wollstonecraft 113–14.

65. Christopher Reid, *Edmund Burke and the Practice of Political Writing* (New York: St. Martin's P, 1985) 43. See also Frans De Bruyn, "Edmund Burke's Natural Aristocrat: The Man of Taste as a Political Ideal," *Eighteenth-Century Life* 11 (1987): 41–60; Neal Wood, "The Aesthetic Dimension of Burke's Political Thought," *Journal of British Studies* 4 (1964): 41–64; and R. T. Allen, "The State and Civil Society as Objects of Aesthetic Appreciation," *British Journal of Aesthetics* 16 (1976): 237–42.

THREE

---◄◉►---

Stripping the Queen: Edmund Burke's Magic Lantern Show

Tom Furniss

Although Edmund Burke's eulogy of Marie Antoinette in *Reflections on the Revolution in France* (1790) consists of only a single paragraph of about a page in length, its place and role in Burke's attack on the French Revolution is crucial. This is especially so in that it functions as the culmination of Burke's response to Richard Price's *Discourse on the Love of Our Country*, a radical sermon delivered to the Revolution Society on 4 November 1789, which presented the French Revolution as an example England might follow in order to protect and extend the "liberty" secured in 1688. By contrasting the "barbarity" of the desecration of Versailles on 5–6 October 1789—which Price had appeared to celebrate—with the civilized but vulnerable beauty of the ancien régime as embodied by Marie Antoinette, Burke's eulogy serves as an emotional touchstone for the various arguments Burke mounts in the more than 200 pages which follow.[1]

For James T. Boulton, the passage is crucially important: "The apostrophe is central to the work as a whole. At the risk of being censured by some for excessive emotionalism, Burke provides a memorable centrepiece which, in symbolic terms, focuses the philosophical significance of all that goes before it and acts as a seminal passage for what follows. . . . after the apostrophe [although] Burke is more and more concerned with the detail of governmental organisation . . . this passage remains in the mind by its imaginative force and persuasive suggestiveness."[2] Out of context, the apostrophe can appear as a quixotic vignette in praise of a figure regarded by most of "the world" as a "fallen woman"; indeed, the passage was one of those most frequently reprinted in contemporary newspapers and became the butt of many caricatures.[3] In its context, however, it can be seen as systematically juxtaposing aristocratic beauty with, or *exposing* it to, the democratic terror which Burke constructs in his account of the events at Versailles. In other words, these passages dramatically illustrate the paradoxical importance Burke ascribes to aristocratic beauty, since it is that aspect of the ancien régime most threatened by revolutionary terror and (in the form of the "pleasing illusions, which . . . incorporated into politics the sentiments which beautify and soften private society") constitutes a potential defense against such terror.[4]

Although some critics have argued that undue emphasis on Burke's treatment of the Versailles episode can lead to misreadings of the *Reflections*, and although it takes up only twenty pages in Conor Cruise O'Brien's edition (but it is curiously difficult to say where it begins and ends), I want to show that the account of 5–6 October foregrounds both the anxieties and the strategies which characterize and impel Burke's text.[5] This occurs partly because these passages constitute that moment when the interdependence between politics and aesthetics is most crucial in the *Reflections* because most threatened. In order to demonstrate why this interdependence becomes critically unstable at this juncture, I want to show how Price's sermon both appropriates Burke's aesthetics and reworks and exploits it in the promotion of a political project which seemed to endanger all that Burke had striven for in English public life. A close reading of the Versailles passage in the *Reflections* in conjunction with the texts it responds to and those which respond to it will reveal how Burke's political and rhetorical project is caught up in an irresolvable knot of mutually undermining positions. Like much contemporary conservative discourse, Burke strives to present what amounts to a partial understanding of political events and processes as natural and universal and thus attacks other viewpoints as rhetorical or ideological perversions. And yet, at the same time, Burke is driven to deploy the artifices of persuasion in an extraordinarily open way. This enables a "deconstruction" of Burke's position quite different from reductive criticism in that it shows how his text is wrestling with crucial ideological questions at a historical juncture in which a complex social formation faced an unprecedented crisis.

Setting the Scene:
Burke's "Triumph" over Richard Price

In order to understand why achieving a dominant representation of the Versailles affair was so important to Burke, we need to look more closely at the exchange between Burke and Price. Prior to reading Price's sermon (in January 1790), Burke typically represents the French Revolution as a dramatic spectacle characterized in terms drawn from his *Philosophical Enquiry into the Origin of Our Ideas of the Sublime and Beautiful* (1757–59). In private correspondence, for example, the Revolution is treated as sublime theater: "As to us here our thoughts of every thing at home are suspended, by our astonishment at the wonderful Spectacle which is exhibited in a Neighbouring and rival Country—what Spectators, and what actors! England gazing with astonishment at a French struggle for Liberty and not knowing whether to blame or applaud!"[6] Even in December 1789—well after the incident at Versailles—Burke seems able to think of the French Revolution as a distraction from the more painful situation within England: "perhaps the follies of France, by which we are not yet affected may employ ones curiosity more pleasantly, and as usefully, as the depravity of England which is more calculated to give us pain" (Burke to Francis, *Corr.* 6: 55). Thus Burke appears to regard the French Revolution as an aesthetic spectacle which might serve to divert attention from political unrest in England, rather than as posing any immediate danger.

Price also presents the Revolution as a sublime event, but in ways which have quite different political implications:

> What an eventful period is this! I am thankful that I have lived to it; and I could almost say, *Lord, now lettest thou thy servant depart in peace, for mine eyes have seen thy salvation.* . . . I have lived to see THIRTY MILLIONS of people, indignant and resolute, spurning at slavery, and demanding liberty with an irresistible voice; their king led in triumph, and an arbitrary monarch surrendering himself to his subjects. . . . And now, methinks, I see the ardour for liberty catching and spreading. . . .

Be encouraged, all ye friends of freedom, and writers in its defence!
The times are auspicious. . . . Behold, the light you have struck out, after
setting AMERICA free, reflected to FRANCE, and there kindled into a
blaze that lays despotism in ashes, and warms and illuminates EUROPE!

Tremble all ye oppressors of the world! . . . You cannot now hold the
world in darkness. . . . Restore to mankind their rights; and consent to
the correction of abuses, before they and you are destroyed together.[7]

The Enlightenment—which Burke calls "this new-conquering empire
of light and reason" (*Refl.* 171)—is figured here as fire and light, con-
suming the old order and illuminating the new with a momentum which
gathers exponentially. Light becomes a liberating sublime, driving out
the false, oppressive sublime of darkness and obscurity through which
kings terrorize the people. The people are figured as becoming *active*—
overthrowing their own slavery—through the strength of a collective
voice able to reverse the power relation between subjects and arbitrary
monarch.[8]

Thus it is the oppressors' turn to tremble at the rise of the people as
an irresistible political force. Price represents himself, and the peoples
of Europe, as fervently aroused by, and caught up in, a spirit of emu-
lation of what Wordsworth was to call the "verity" of "a whole nation
crying with one voice."[9] Burke's perception of the potential effects—
on Price's immediate congregation and on the English people—of this
"irresistible voice" of thirty million seems grounded in his early aesthetics, where "the shouting of multitudes[,] . . . by the sole strength of
the sound, so amazes and confounds the imagination, that in this stag-
gering, and hurry of the mind, the best established tempers can scarcely
forbear being borne down, and joining in the common cry, and common
resolution of the croud."[10] Price's sermon seems calculated, according
to Burke's own theory, likewise to stimulate his congregation and his
readers to participate in, or emulate, that revolutionary cry.

Price's sermon is therefore disturbing for Burke in a number of ways:
it replaces Burke's emphasis in his aesthetics on obscurity and irration-
ality by equating the sublime with light and reason; it reworks and
transvalues the sublime by exploiting its "democratic" potential (rather
than producing the hesitant spectators mentioned in Burke's letter, the
Revolution in Price promises to produce active participants). What's
more, this takes place in a text which criticizes the English constitu-

tion, stresses the servitude of the English people, and claims that the French Revolution indicates the "favourableness of the present times for all exertions in the cause of public liberty" (*Disc.* 49). Thus Price's sermon transforms the Revolution from a spectacle which might serve to distract attention from political problems in England to one which threatens either to exacerbate them (for Burke) or to strike at their very roots—for in Price's view, "the state [of England] is such as renders it an object of concern and anxiety [because it] wants . . . the grand security of public liberty" (*Disc.* 46), chiefly because of "the inadequateness of our representation" (*Disc.* 41).

Burke spends almost the first hundred pages of the *Reflections*—which culminate in his account of 5–6 October—wrangling, directly or indirectly, with Price's sermon. In contradistinction to Price and the Revolution Society, Burke would suspend his congratulations to the National Assembly (*Refl.* 90–91), claiming that he needs to consider France not in "the nakedness . . . of metaphysical abstraction" but in its actual circumstances (*Refl.* 89–90); this is because although liberty might be a good thing in the abstract, there are many instances (such as the liberation of madmen or murderers) where it might be an evil in actual affairs (*Refl.* 90). (Although they might appear to merely furnish an argument, Burke's examples and metaphors are never "innocent": he will go on to indict the Revolution as criminal madness and condemn it precisely for reducing both social institutions and the French queen to defenseless nakedness.)[11] He goes on to claim that events have enabled more circumspect observers "to discern, with tolerable exactness, the true nature of the object held up to our imitation" (*Refl.* 92). This is the cue for the well-known attack on the Revolution:

> It looks to me as if I were in a great crisis, not of the affairs of France alone, but of all Europe, perhaps of more than Europe. All circumstances taken together, the French revolution is the most astonishing that has hitherto happened in the world. The most wonderful things are brought about in many instances by means the most absurd and ridiculous; in the most ridiculous modes; and apparently, by the most contemptible instruments. Every thing seems out of nature in this strange chaos of levity and ferocity, and of all sorts of crimes jumbled together with all sorts of follies. In viewing this monstrous tragi-comic scene, the most opposite passions necessarily succeed, and sometimes mix with each other in the

mind; alternate contempt and indignation; alternate laughter and tears; alternate scorn and horror. (*Refl.* 92–93)

In the aforementioned letter to Lord Charlemont, "astonishment" is triggered by the "wonderful Spectacle" of "a French struggle for liberty"; in the *Reflections*, the Revolution is astonishing because it violates the principles of cause and effect: "wonderful things" are brought about—in a disruption of political and aesthetic order—by "means," "modes," and "instruments" that are "absurd," "ridiculous," and "contemptible." Such a disparity between cause and effect suggests that these relations, rather than being naturally motivated, are not only conventional but appallingly arbitrary. This is more than a philosophical crisis because it challenges and overturns the established social hierarchies by demonstrating that people from a class traditionally considered unfit to participate in political processes are capable of having significant effects on the state.

Burke would have his readers perceive the enormity and the absurdity of this and so presents the Revolution as a chaotic jumble of the terrible and the ridiculous—an event to recoil from or laugh at, but certainly not one to admire or imitate. Political events and affairs are presented in theatrical terms; the French Revolution is bad drama because it violates Aristotle's generic categories and emphasis on propriety and because its actors are not properly fit or fitted for their roles.[12] Producing a *succession* of "opposite" passions (contempt, laughter, and scorn *alternating* with indignation, tears, and horror) which "sometimes mix" but are not suspended in ambivalence and do not cohere, the Revolution fails to produce the "delightful horror" which characterizes Burke's formulation of the sublime and which is so indebted to Aristotle's theory of tragedy. And yet Thomas Weiskel's description of the sublime, via Kant, as "a rapidly alternating repulsion and attraction produced by one and the same Object," is remarkably akin to Burke's attempt here to identify the Revolution as a perversion of the sublime.[13] Given this—and given Burke's own argument that "if we attend coolly to the kind of sensible image" produced by the most sublime passages in literature, "the chimeras of madmen cannot appear more wild and absurd than such a picture" (*PE* 171)—it seems impossible, in the sublime's own terms, to distinguish the unimaginable from the nonsensical save by a recourse to questions of propriety which are themselves problematized by the aesthetic category they are brought in to constrain.

It has long been a critical donnée that the Revolution presented itself in theatrical terms;[14] Burke's strategy is to rewrite it as tragicomic farce in order to deflate any attempt to restage it in England. Burke therefore takes on the roles of scriptwriter, director, and principal protagonist against this infectious revolution. According to Peter Hughes, he thereby becomes "the embodiment of his own notion of the sublime, a dynamic performer we are meant to respond to with fear and wonder. He becomes the chief actor in a drama that he has also staged and written."[15] Burke's whole project depends, therefore, on the possibility of distinguishing between political forms in terms of good and bad drama.[16]

To this end, Burke employs all the rhetorical devices available to him to discredit and defame what he takes to be Price's triumphal representation of the march from Versailles with the royal family. He finds Price, "a preacher of the gospel," engaged in blasphemy, "prophaning the beautiful and prophetic ejaculation, commonly called '*nunc dimittis*,' made on the first presentation of our Saviour in the Temple, and applying it, with an inhuman and unnatural rapture, to the most horrid, atrocious, and afflicting spectacle, that perhaps ever was exhibited to the pity and indignation of mankind" (*Refl.* 159). Admonishing Price for the misuse of Simeon's pious prayer on seeing the child Jesus at the temple (Luke 2: 25–30) and for straying from his profession by introducing politics into the pulpit, Burke implies that the dissenting minister does not even know his own trade and sets out to correct him.

Yet although he criticizes Price's "profanation," Burke's presentation of it as exploiting the affective connotations of one context by applying them to another is curiously similar to his own account of how "compounded abstract" words may be used to powerful effect: "These words, by having no application, ought to be unoperative; but when words commonly sacred to great occasions are used, we are affected by them even without the occasions" (*PE* 166). Grounded in a Lockean theory of the arbitrary nature of linguistic signs, Burke's early aesthetics therefore makes the discrimination between appropriate and inappropriate uses of sacred texts awkwardly problematic. And yet the only recourse open to the *Reflections* is to invoke notions of propriety; Burke wants to show that Price errs in "applying" sacred words to the wrong place because in so doing he is revealed as unfit to be a preacher of the gospel—unfit because by "prophaning" the most sacred of texts he declares himself *outside* the temple, "not initiated into the religious rites or sacred mysteries."[17] Burke's recourse to notions of religious decorum reveals that he can differentiate his own textual processes from Price's only through an appeal to custom. And yet if custom itself is arbitrary, this distinction becomes not one of spiritual substance (if there could be such a thing) but a question of ideological hegemony. Burke is struggling for a particular set of customs as practiced in a particular socioreligious system.

Burke enters into a theological-cum-political contest with Price, striving to identify him as a false prophet. He "visibly triumphs" over the dissenting minister (as O'Brien puts it [*Refl.* 384 n. 50]) by exposing parallels between him and the Reverend Hugh Peters, who had ridden, Burke tells us, "*triumphing*" before Charles I in 1648, and had said "after the commencement of the king's trial . . . 'now I may say with old Simeon, *Lord, now lettest thou thy servant depart in peace, for mine eyes have seen thy salvation*'" (*Refl.* 158).[18] But in this struggle, Burke is not averse to employing the same tactics—the application of words commonly sacred to great occasions for ideological effect—for which he condemns Price. The latter's representation of the people's "triumph" at the leading of their monarch is replaced in the *Reflections* by what Hughes calls a "sacred parody" of the via dolorosa: "After they had been made to taste, drop by drop, more than the bitterness of death, in the slow torture of a journey of twelve miles, protracted to six hours, they were, under a guard, composed of those very soldiers who had thus conducted them through this famous triumph, lodged in one of the old palaces of Paris, now converted into a Bastile for kings" (*Refl.* 165).[19] Leading this procession, Burke has the heads of "two gentlemen . . . stuck upon spears" and the whole train "slowly [moving] along, amidst the horrid yells, and shrilling screams, and frantic dances, and infamous contumelies, and all the unutterable abominations of the furies of hell, in the abused shape of the vilest of women" (*Refl.* 164–65).[20]

Thus Price's Nunc Dimittis is shown to have been applied to a scene more appropriate to demonic or pagan rituals: "Is this a triumph to be consecrated at altars? to be commemorated with grateful thanksgiving? to be offered to the divine humanity with fervent prayer and enthusiastick ejaculation?—the Theban and Thracian Orgies, acted in France, and applauded only in the Old Jewry, I assure you, kindle prophetic enthusiasm in the minds but of very few people in this kingdom" (*Refl.* 165). In this way, Burke works to establish in his English readers' minds the proper response to this "triumph" by making it impossible to concur with Price's profane, inhuman, and unnatural enthusiasm for the Revolution. That his representation of Price's sacrilegious techniques is also an accurate description of his own rhetorical processes suggests how crucial yet precarious Burke's critique of Price is. The canonical and the evil, the pious and the sacrilegious, the constitutional and the revolutionary, exist not as opposites but as a peculiarly complicit and mutually dependent system. And yet the constitutional position needs aggressively to define itself by repudiating its "other"—and this is especially so in times of revolutionary crisis. Burke's text, then, seems both energized and compromised by the contradictions implicit in the terms it is compelled to wield in this battle of books.

The very energy with which Burke repeatedly returns to this scene, and the range of imagery employed, is striking. After condemning Price for profaning the Nunc Dimittis, he proceeds to intensify his indictment:

> This "*leading in triumph*," a thing in its best form unmanly and irreligious, which fills our Preacher with such unhallowed transports, must shock, I believe, the moral taste of every well-born mind. Several English were the stupified and indignant spectators of that triumph. It was (unless we have been strangely deceived) a spectacle more resembling a procession of American savages . . . after some of their murders called victories, and leading into hovels hung round with scalps, their captives, overpowered with the scoffs and buffets of women as ferocious as themselves, much more than it resembled the triumphal pomp of a civilized martial nation. (*Refl.* 159)

In this passage, the correct—the tasteful, or "English"—response to this "savage" spectacle is exemplified by the "stupified and indignant" response of the "several English" whom Burke scripts into the "audience." But apart from the problem of distinguishing this response from that produced by, or appropriate to, the "genuine" sublime, this passage raises the question of the distinction between "savage spectacle" and "the triumphal pomp of a civilized martial nation." Upon these distinctions rests Burke's attempt to delineate the "proper" response to the Revolution as that of a spectator who is civilized rather than savage,

Christian rather than profane, well-born rather than of the lower orders, English rather than French.

The National Assembly, impotent to control or even properly investigate such outrages as those of 5–6 October, emerges as the "captive" of a "monstrous" portion of the public rather than as a representative assembly of the French nation. Given such a situation, where a certain section of the populace has illegitimately usurped power, the National Assembly's role can only be a theatrical one (in the derogatory sense of the term):

> The Assembly, their organ, acts before [the people] the farce of deliberation with as little decency as liberty. They act like the comedians of a fair before a riotous audience; they act amidst the tumultuous cries of a mixed mob of ferocious men, and of women lost to shame, who, according to their insolent fancies, direct, control, applaud, explode them; and sometimes mix and take their seats amongst them; domineering over them with a strange mixture of servile petulance and proud presumptuous authority. As they have inverted order in all things, the gallery is in place of the house. (*Refl.* 161)

All the conventional codes of politics and theater are "inverted" here: the electorate direct the elective body, the audience take their seats upon the political stage and subvert the customary relation between gallery and house. His very need to present this as a farce, however, suggests how disturbing such disruptions of the "proper" relations between representative bodies and "the people" might be for Burke. Yet the only recourse open to him is the precarious one of attempting to establish an absolute distinction between proper and improper theater.

Mr. Burke's Magic Lantern Show

Although he represents himself as having been initially "at a loss to account for [Price's] fit of unguarded transport," Burke claims that by taking "one circumstance" into consideration:

> I was obliged to confess, that much allowance ought to be made for the Society, and that the temptation was too strong for common discretion; I mean, the circumstance of the Io Paean of the triumph, the animating cry which called "for all the BISHOPS to be hanged on the lampposts," might well have brought forth a burst of enthusiasm on the foreseen con-

sequences of this happy day. . . . I allow this prophet to break forth into
hymns of joy and thanksgiving on an event which appears like the precursor of the Millenium, and the projected fifth monarchy, in the destruction
of all church establishments. (*Refl.* 165–66)

Thus, for the second time in a few pages, Burke draws on English
memories of the fusion of political radicalism and unorthodox religious
sects (the Fifth Monarchists, by attempting to overturn Cromwell's Parliament and so reduce England to anarchy, had sought to induce the
long-awaited Second Coming).[21]

Exploiting the emotive power of yet more religious allusions, Burke
suggests that Price's congregation, "in the midst of this joy," have
something "to try the long-suffering of their faith" (i.e., in waiting for
Christ's second appearance): "The actual murder of the king and queen,
and their child, was wanting to the other auspicious circumstances of
this '*beautiful day.*' The actual murder of the bishops, though called for
by so many holy ejaculations, was also wanting. A groupe of regicide and sacriligious slaughter, was indeed boldly sketched, but it was
only sketched. It unhappily was left unfinished, in this great history-
piece of the massacre of innocents" (*Refl.* 166). In this passage, Burke
sarcastically reverses the story of Herod by suggesting that what was
lacking from the events at Versailles was the final sign of the Second
Coming—that is, the murder of the king by the populace. By exploiting the affective connotations of sacred texts in this way, Burke seems
therefore to participate in the rhetorical "perversions" and "profanities"
he condemns.

Burke supports his account of the "Io Paean" by referring to "a letter
written upon this subject by an eyewitness" (*Refl.* 166; see 166–68),
but for Paine this mention of the call to hang the bishops is the concluding evidence that Burke's account is spectacle rather than history:
"Mr. Burke brings forward his bishops and his lantern like figures in a
magic lantern, and raises his scenes by contrast instead of connexion."[22]
Burke's scene becomes further embroiled in controversy, however, in
that Price subsequently claimed, in prefatory remarks added to subsequent editions of the sermon, to have been referring not to the events
of 6 October but to the quite different "triumph" over the king in July.[23]
Burke never changed his attack on Price—perhaps because he did not
accept Price's disclaimer; but whatever the truth of the matter, Burke
saw that any celebration, after 5–6 October, of the French people's "tri-

umph" over their king could not help but refer to the terrifying scenes at Versailles. This was a weakness in Price's position, and Burke was not averse to exploiting it; he seems not to have been concerned with verisimilitude but with establishing a dominant representation of the Revolution, and such clarity and attention to detail find no place in his own aesthetic theory of how language works and of how, consequently, most effectively to influence opinion (see *PE* 173–76). The *Reflections*, then, emerges as a representation of the Revolution which abandons the "reflection" theory of representation, relinquishing any direct relation between representation and "object" or "event" represented. As Paine puts it, "It suits his purpose to exhibit the consequences without their causes. It is one of the arts of the drama to do so."[24]

That Burke never withdrew or qualified his attack on Price indicates how important it was for him to "triumph" over the dissenting minister. Burke is not concerned with veracity but with winning the struggle for English opinion. In the *Reflections*—which makes very little mention of the fall of the Bastille—the events of 5–6 October *are* the Revolution, and Burke's case succeeds or fails according to his success or otherwise in persuading the English public to accept his representation of them rather than Price's. To withdraw his attack on Price would have involved withdrawing the *Reflections* itself, because the whole text pivots around this central scene. This is the moment when Burke attempts to establish the horror of the Revolution and the unthinkability of countenancing its imitation in England; everything else in the *Reflections* depends upon the effective power of this attack on the Revolution and on the Revolution Society's enthusiasm for it.

Burke's representation of these events exploits the affective power not only of the sublime but of the beautiful as well, since it enables him to juxtapose the terror of revolution with the vulnerable beauty of the "natural order of things." Having established the barbarity of the triumphal procession to Paris, Burke switches attention to the preceding events at Versailles, where, according to his account, the king and queen had been "forced to abandon the sanctuary of the most splendid palace in the world, which they left swimming in blood, polluted by massacre, and strewed with scattered limbs and mutilated carcases" (*Refl.* 164).[25] Although "the king of France will probably endeavour to forget" these events, "history, who keeps a durable record of all our acts, . . . will not forget, either those events, or the aera of this liberal refinement in the intercourse of mankind" (*Refl.* 163–64). "History will record," and Burke is compelled to relate, that the queen of France was "startled" from her sleep on the morning of 6 October 1789:

> by the voice of the centinel at her door, who cried out to her, to save herself by flight—that this was the last proof of fidelity he could give— that they were upon him, and he was dead. Instantly he was cut down. A band of cruel ruffians and assassins, reeking with his blood, rushed into the chamber of the queen, and pierced with an hundred strokes of bayonets and poniards the bed, from whence this persecuted woman had but just time to fly almost naked, . . . to seek refuge at the feet of a king and husband, not secure of his own life for a moment. (*Refl.* 164)

In fact, "history" had not much more to go on than Burke or Paine when they produced their rival accounts. George Rudé suggests that the Châtelet inquiry, published March 1790, "far from throwing a bright light into dark corners, . . . served effectively to divert attention from the real authors of the October 'days.'" Although "fresh light" has been brought to the episode by recent historians, it remains "in some respects . . . more shrouded in mystery than any other similar event of the Revolution."[26]

Several of the key images of Burke's account remain controversial: Boulton claims that the murder of the "centinel" was a fiction and that Burke had this pointed out to him several times; Alfred Cobban's account of the incident implies that none of the demonstrators penetrated beyond the queen's antichamber; while Ronald Paulson says that there is "no evidence of Marie Antoinette's fleeing 'almost naked.'" Christopher Hibbert's more recent history of the French Revolution, however, more or less supports Burke's version of this episode, but does so in a melodramatic way which seems to repeat Burke's manner and to rely on the same sources. (Paine began a critical trend by saying that "Mr. Burke should recollect that he is writing History, and not *Plays*.") Hughes reveals how Burke's account of 5–6 October draws on and reverses the implications of the report in the *Gazette Nationale ou Le Moniteur Universel* of 12 October 1789, but argues that "his most brilliant and theatrical touches, the phallic thrusts into the queen's bed and her near naked and hair's breadth escape," are his own inventions.[27] This is not quite the case, however; like any dramatist of the period, Burke bases his "inventions" on prior "sources." *The Times* (London)

of 13 October 1789 presents Burke with an alternative contemporary
account of the incident at Versailles, reporting that "in the dead of the
night a party of the troops and mob forced their way into the Palace to
the Antichamber of the QUEEN's apartment: The noise was so sudden,
that her Majesty ran trembling to the KING's apartment with only her
shift on." In its report on 12 October, *The Times* informed its readers
that "at this moment, the fate of Europe depends on the actions—of
A BARBAROUS and UNRESTRAINED MOB!—a mob which has shown
itself so licentious, that the country which claims it, blushes at its cruel-
ties. The MURDER of the QUEEN has been attempted in the dead of
night."[28] In the *Reflections*, then, Burke simply exaggerates and drama-
tizes, for the most part, these already histrionic counterrevolutionary
reports: the queen "in her shift" becomes "almost naked," while the
assassins get beyond the antichamber and *penetrate* to the queen's bed
chamber—the structure of Burke's sentence giving the illusion that she
is still in her bed as they begin to pierce it with "an hundred strokes"
of their weapons. Burke's "historical record" of 5–6 October emerges,
then, as a theatrical production in which one set of discursive interpretations is put in contest with another; Burke's distinction between his
own historical veracity and the theatricality of revolutionary rhetoric—
a distinction vital to his ideological project—thus threatens to collapse
in its most critical moment.

The Rise and Fall of Marie Antoinette

Burke's dramatization of this day's events, and of his own reactions to
them, seems peculiarly compelled and unsettled by its own figurations.
He claims in one moment that "I knew, indeed, that the sufferings of
monarchs make a delicious repast to some sort of palates" but that there
"were reflexions which might serve to keep this appetite within some
bounds of temperance" (*Refl.* 165). And yet, far from desisting, Burke
represents himself to Jean-François Depont (the original addressee of
the *Reflections*) as driven to continue his narrative: "But I cannot stop
here. Influenced by the inborn feelings of my nature, and not being illuminated by a single ray of this new-sprung modern light, I confess to
you, Sir, that the exalted rank of the persons suffering, and particularly
the sex, the beauty, and the amiable qualities [of the French queen] . . .
instead of being a subject of exultation, adds not a little to my sensibility
on that most melancholy occasion" (*Refl.* 168).

Burke's comic irony here should not be allowed to mask the ways this response draws on his aesthetic treatise. In refusing to exult over the fall of the exalted—the slave's triumph over the master or mistress—Burke appears to refuse the sublimity of revolution and to take refuge in sensibility. In fact, his text "oversteps the bounds of temperance" in the very moment it sets those bounds; the impulses of "the inborn feelings of [his] nature" drive Burke to indulge or whet the "appetite" which he condemns as offensive to "good taste." Thus in the famous apostrophe which this "confession" announces, Burke rejoices to hear "that the great lady . . . has borne that day (one is interested that beings made for suffering should suffer well) . . . and the insulting adulation of addresses, and the whole weight of her accumulated wrongs, with a serene patience, in a manner suited to her rank and race, . . . that she feels with the dignity of a Roman matron; that in the last extremity she will save herself from the last disgrace, and that if she must fall, she will fall by no ignoble hand" (*Refl.* 169). If Burke's inborn feelings "naturally" present Marie Antoinette's situation in conventional stage images, he presumably relies on his readers' own "inborn feelings" to distinguish these images from the Revolution's perversion of the dramatic arts. Yet the language's very decorum ("the last disgrace" primarily evokes images of rape) plays upon the possibility of the queen's rape in the moment it pays her decorous homage (pays court to her). Burke's effect depends upon a shared set of social customs whose violation is calculated, here, to produce universal horror. Not only are these conventions "shared" in radically different ways (to the "lower orders" such an account of the queen's demise might well prove delightful), however, but Burke's exploitation of the emotive possibilities of rape is perhaps symptomatic of an implicit aggression toward (aristocratic) women operating within his "chivalric" text. After all, it is Burke's text, rather than the revolutionary "mob," which exposes the queen to "the last disgrace."

The apostrophe continues with Burke recalling his personal experience of meeting the French queen. In doing so, as Boulton notes, Burke exploits the same techniques he praises in Homer's presentation of Helen, which evokes her beauty not through minute description but through the *effect* it has on an observer, and which, according to his own aesthetic, is the best way to *affect* readers (*PE* lxxxi, 171–72): "It is now sixteen or seventeen years since I saw the queen of France, then the dauphiness, at Versailles; and surely never lighted on this orb, which she hardly seemed to touch, a more delightful vision. I saw her just above the horizon, decorating and cheering the elevated sphere she just began to move in,—glittering like the morning star, full of life, and splendour, and joy. Oh! What a revolution! and what an heart must I have, to contemplate without emotion that elevation and that fall!" (*Refl.* 169).

For Boulton, "the Queen . . . embodies some of the fundamentals of Burke's thought," and the apostrophe concenters them "in a memorable literary achievement."[29] It is curious, then, that this literary achievement is rife with puns that may intensify, but may equally puncture, the effect Burke is supposed to aim at, ridiculing the queen and all she stands for. When Burke, elevating his lady, writes that "surely never lighted on this orb, which she hardly seemed to touch, a more delightful vision," a series of puns compound, or perhaps refract, the effect: "lighted on" is at once "landed on" and "illuminated"; "this orb" is both "this earth" and "this eye"; "a more delightful vision" is at once an *object* of vision and vision as *perception*. Burke seems to opt for the first of each of these possibilities, producing a comically absurd image, when he continues: "I saw her just above the horizon, decorating and cheering the elevated sphere she just began to move in,—glittering like the morning star." That "elevated sphere" may be both the social or political sphere of the court and the "heavenly sphere"—the second option placing her just above the horizon, like a planet or "morning star," the first having her literally "floating" above the floor of the French court, once domain of the "sun king."

The then dauphine becomes an alternative source of illumination to the Enlightenment (on the previous page Burke refers disparagingly to "this new-sprung modern light"); but as a "morning star" she is also associated with Lucifer—the planet Venus (a suggestive allusion) in its matutinal guise, but also the revolutionary protagonist of Milton's *Paradise Lost* prior to his own disastrous fall.[30] This latter association, curiously enough, is reinforced in an unexpected way: if one of the clearest signs that there has been a revolution in manners in France is that previously "ten thousand swords must have leaped from their scabbards to avenge even a look that threatened [the queen] with insult" (*Refl.* 170), at the conclusion of Satan's revolutionary speech in hell,

> to confirm his words, out flew
> Millions of flaming swords, drawn from the thighs
> Of mighty cherubim.[31]

(These references to swords leaping from their scabbards and drawn from thighs also resurrect the phallic connotations of weapons evoked in the "rape" scene.)

"Oh! What a revolution!" Burke laments, referring to the political revolution embodied in the overthrow of the queen, but also allowing the planetary dauphine her own celestial change. Burke's pun therefore emphasizes how the revolutionaries' treatment of Marie Antoinette represents the subversion of natural, cyclical patterns of change by violent overthrow or fall—a revolution which the term "revolution" was itself undergoing at this historical moment.[32] Paulson suggests that Burke was the first writer in English to use "revolution" in its modern sense and that he "carried the day with his redefinition."[33] In his eulogy of Marie Antoinette, then, Burke seems intent on pointing up the contrast between the beauties of celestial cycles and the apocalyptic terrors of the French Revolution. Dramatizing his own response, Burke exclaims, "What an heart must I have, to contemplate without emotion that elevation and that fall"—having the queen literally "fall" from her "elevation" above the horizon/floor. Yet the reference to that "fall" leads back again to the ambiguous images of rape and suicide— "if she will fall, she will fall by no ignoble hand"—taken from the Roman, Shakespearean, and chivalric stage: "Little did I dream . . . that she should ever be obliged to carry the sharp antidote against disgrace concealed in that bosom; little did I dream that I should have lived to see such disasters fallen upon her in a nation of gallant men, in a nation of men of honour and of cavaliers" (*Refl.* 169–70). Burke fantasizes that the queen carries her own "sharp antidote" against the Revolution's threatened breach of decorum—a weapon concealed, suggestively, in "that bosom." The "disasters" that threaten her develop both the cosmological and the sexual imagery, yet such "disasters" were thought to have already "fallen" upon the queen at the hands of the French court— Marie Antoinette being rumored to have taken lovers from among those "gallant men" and "men of honour."[34]

Thus these textual tensions in the *Reflections* need to be seen in relation to those discourses of the period in which Marie Antoinette's sexuality was constructed. The *Reflections* decorously *excludes* these constructions, perhaps because they would complicate the clear-cut distinctions Burke seeks to delineate between revolutionary terror and aristocratic beauty. And yet that exclusion leaves its traces and produces its own tensions. Phillip Francis (who was allowed to see the *Reflections* as it progressed in manuscript and was, in Burke's opinion, "the only friend I have who will dare to give me advice" [*Corr.*, 6: 88]) reminds Burke that the "opinion of the world [about the French queen's virtue] is not lately but has been many years decided" (Francis to Burke, *Corr.* 6: 87). It is not, then, that the Revolution comes to despoil a chivalric reality but a "dream" of chivalry. Burke's text—like Don Quixote—seems able to maintain that dream only by excluding the sexual intrigue and the implicit fear of women which structures the chivalric code. And yet this intrigue and fear seem to return uncontrollably within the language of Burke's most chivalric moment, since the courtly apostrophe, couched in the language of decorum, is precisely that moment in the *Reflections* in which Burke's language—through uncontrolled puns, through the play of double entendre and innuendo—most explicitly exploits, and is exposed to, the radical disjunction between language and "event" or "object." This is necessarily to expose the duplicitous grounds of the "rococo" ideology and aesthetics being celebrated here.[35] Burke's language reveals itself as an inflated or bombastic prose whose index is precisely the fissure between the figure he celebrates and the earth she floats above.

In advising Burke, Francis's main apprehension was that the apostrophe to Marie Antoinette might endanger the principal object of the *Reflections*—which he saw as undertaking "to correct and instruct another Nation, and . . . appeal in effect . . . to all Europe" (*Corr.* 6: 86). (In this Francis failed to see that Burke's appeal was not to France or to Europe but to England, and that the apostrophe was central to that appeal; his apprehensions allow us to see, however, how Burke's text at once depends upon and is endangered by the eulogy to the French queen.) Because of the high seriousness of this end, Burke ought not to leave himself vulnerable to attacks from "Doctor Price":

> Let every thing you say be grave, direct and serious. . . . In my opinion all that you say of the Queen is pure foppery. If she be a perfect female character you ought to take your ground upon her virtues. If she be the reverse it is ridiculous in any but a Lover, to place her personal charms in opposition to her crimes. . . . On this subject, however, you cannot but know that the opinion of the world is not lately but has been many years decided. . . . are you such a determined Champion of Beauty as

to draw your Sword in defense of any jade upon Earth provided she be handsome? . . . The mischief you are going to do to yourself is, to my apprehension, palpable. (Francis to Burke, *Corr.* 6: 86–87)

Burke responds to Francis by saying that he is "astonish'd" that he could have thought that Marie Antoinette's beauty, by then "I suppose pretty much faded," was his only reason for condemning her treatment at Versailles: "What, are not high Rank, great Splendour of descent, great personal Elegance and outward accomplishments ingredients of moment in forming the interest we take in the Misfortunes of Men?" (Burke to Francis, *Corr.* 6: 89–90).

As to the queen's reputation, Burke chivalrously says that he cannot suspend his "Natural Sympathies . . . until the Tales and all the anecdotes of the Coffeehouses of Paris and of the dissenting meeting houses of London are scoured of all the slander" (*Corr.* 6: 89–90). His main object had been "to excite an horrour against midnight assassins at back stairs, and their more wicked abetters in Pulpits" (*Corr.* 6: 90), and to "expose them to the hatred, ridicule, and contempt of the whole world" (*Corr.* 6: 92). In order to achieve this, he had endeavored to interest others in the suffering of the king and queen in the same way that he had himself given way to the sentiments Euripides had wished to excite in the readers of the tragedy of Hecuba (*Corr.* 6: 90). In answer to Hamlet's question about why the Player can be so passionate over Hecuba's death (*Hamlet* 2.2.569–70), Burke responds rhetorically: "Why because she was Hecuba, the Queen of Troy, the Wife of Priam, and suffered in the close of Life a thousand Calamities. I felt too for Hecuba when I read the fine Tragedy of Euripides upon her Story: and I never enquired into the Anecdotes of the Court or City of Troy before I gave way to the Sentiments which the author wished to inspire; nor do I remember that he ever said one word of her Virtues" (*Corr.* 6: 90). In effect, Burke is suggesting that sympathy and compassion ought to be aroused not by a consideration of the person's character, nor by the fact that they share the human condition, but by their social and political position, by their "high Rank, great Splendour of descent, great personal Elegance and outward accomplishments." These considerations not only outweigh all others but preclude any inquiry into character or virtue. His unquestioning admiration of and sympathy for the queen of France is therefore emblematic of the attitude he is trying to foster toward political institutions—which should also be venerated and loved without the kind of inquiry which might strip them of their splendor and discover their "defects."

And yet Burke's rejoinder to Hamlet is particularly apposite and revealing. If Burke says that "the minds of those who do not feel" as he feels "are not even Dramatically right" (*Corr.* 6: 90), Shakespeare uses the tragedy of Hecuba in order to analyze the emotive power of drama. In Hamlet's assessment, Hecuba can mean "nothing" to the Player; that the Player can work himself up into a passion is a "monstrous" witness (*Hamlet* 2.2.561) of the power of dramatic language to affect human passions in an arbitrary fashion. Hamlet, on the other hand, who has a genuine "motive and . . . cue for passion" (line 571), can find no "authentic" means of expressing it because language is always already theatrically prostituted (lines 597–98). While Burke wants to suggest that there is a direct correspondence between our response to suffering in the theater and in reality, in the passage which he refers to in *Hamlet* there is an *inverse* relation. To ask that his readers respond to the suffering of Marie Antoinette as if she were a dramatic character is consistent with Burke's theory of the theatrical nature of political figures and institutions, but the particular example he chooses to justify this challenges his argument that there is a correspondence between ("proper") political theater and authentic emotions or the natural order of things. More serious still for Burke, however, is that Hamlet's insight into the arbitrary yet powerful effects of words is precisely Burke's own argument in the *Philosophical Enquiry*'s section on "Words" (*PE* 163–77). If Burke allowed himself to dwell upon the consequences of this for his own ideological position, he might become as perplexed as Hamlet himself in trying to untangle authentic from inauthentic theater, constitutional from revolutionary words. That is perhaps why, unlike Hamlet, Burke judiciously avoids and deflects attempts to inquire into "the natural order of things."

Since, according to the *Philosophical Enquiry*, the most effective way of evoking a woman's beauty and of moving a reader is to represent one's own emotions toward it (no matter that the emotion and the beauty were those of sixteen or seventeen years previously), Burke can answer Francis's criticism of the passage as follows:

> I tell you again that the recollection of the manner in which I saw the Queen of France in the year 1774 and the contrast between that brilliancy,

Splendour, and beauty, with the prostrate Homage of a Nation to her, compared with the abominable Scene of 1789 which I was describing did draw Tears from me and wetted my Paper. These Tears came again into my Eyes almost as often as I lookd at the description. They may again. You do not believe this fact, or that these are my real feelings, but that the whole is affected, or as you express it, "downright Foppery." (*Corr.* 6: 91)

If Burke claims that he is repeatedly affected to tears by his apostrophe to the queen, O'Brien informs us that "a correspondent of Burke's later reported to him that the passage had been brought to the attention of Marie Antoinette in her captivity: 'who before she had read half the Lines she Burst into a Flood of Tears and was a long Time before she was sufficiently composed to peruse the remainder.' "[36]

If we accept these statements—and Burke gains no public advantage by lying to Francis—then we are presented with the curious phenomenon that reading the apostrophe moved both its author and its central protagonist to tears. This says nothing, however, about Burke's feelings for Marie Antoinette outside the writing and reading of the apostrophe. In fact, it seems that in these passages Burke is moved by his own rhetoric (just as the Player is moved to tears by his own rendition of a speech about Hecuba) to sentiments quite at odds with those of other discursive moments. For instance, the editors of Burke's correspondence make this pertinent point:

One effect of Burke's contact with the *émigrés* [from France] was to intensify his private criticism, which did not appear in his published works, of the unhappy King and Queen of France. His correspondence shows that his public eulogies of Louis XVI and Marie Antoinette were far from representing his true opinion. . . .

Burke's distrust of Marie Antoinette, despite the rhapsody in the *Reflections*, was profound. He had been touched to know that when the famous passage about her was read to the Queen she burst into a flood of tears, but he shared the prejudices of Coblenz [where the *émigrés* had their headquarters] against her. (*Corr.* 6: xvi–xvii)

Both author and protagonist are therefore affected by the dramatic reproduction of these scenes—by identifying (like the Player) with the "part" rather than the "reality."

Whatever his "true opinion" or feelings were, Burke interestingly emerges here as a sentimental victim of his own dramatic spectacle; for, despite his attempt to answer Hamlet's question, we may still ask what *is* Marie Antoinette to Burke, or he to Marie Antoinette, that he should weep for her? Like Wordsworth attempting to feel and touch the dread of the September Massacres after the event, Burke seems to have "wrought upon" himself through the labor of a rhetoric "conjured up from tragic fictions."[37] This, indeed, is the opinion of Burke's first critics: for Paine (echoing Burke's criticism of Price) the *Reflections* is a series of "tragic paintings by which Mr. Burke has outraged his own imagination, and seeks to work upon that of his reader."[38]

In the *Reflections*, Burke rhetorically asks why he feels so differently from Dr. Price and his flock in order to claim that his own response is a *natural* one:

> For this plain reason—because it is *natural* I should; because we are so made as to be affected at such spectacles with melancholy sentiments upon the unstable condition of mortal prosperity, and the tremendous uncertainty of human greatness; . . . because in events like these our passions instruct our reason; because when kings are hurl'd from their thrones by the Supreme Director of this great drama, . . . we behold such disasters in the moral, as we should behold a miracle in the physical order of things. We are alarmed into reflexion; our minds (as it has long since been observed) are purified by terror and pity; our weak unthinking pride is humbled. (*Refl.* 175)

Burke invokes the authority of Aristotle's theory of tragic drama here, but he is equally drawing on his own theory of the sublime developed in the *Philosophical Enquiry*. Since the aesthetic experience of the sublime is based on a physiological theory, we necessarily respond to the king of France's deposition in the same way Burke does because *that is how we are made*. Such terror ought therefore to inspire us with fear for our own mortality and "purify" our minds; our passions instruct (or anticipate) our reason, and we are alarmed into reflection. It seems that the overpowering effect of the sublime moment is now indulged in its own right and gleaned for moral instruction (there is no proud flight here but rather a humbling of our pride).

But to point to Burke's dramatic metaphors in order to suggest that he is talking about art not nature is to be anticipated by Burke himself.

For Burke, there is, or ought to be, no difference between our response to theater and reality: "Some tears might be drawn from me, if such a spectacle were exhibited on the stage. I should be truly ashamed of finding in myself that superficial, theatric sense of painted distress, whilst I could exult over it in real life" (*Refl.* 175). The difference between theater and real life is collapsed in the text's very language:

> Indeed the theatre is a better school of moral sentiments than churches, where the feelings of humanity are thus outraged. Poets, who have to deal with an audience not yet graduated in the school of the rights of men, and who must apply themselves to the moral constitution of the heart, would not dare to produce such a triumph as a matter of exultation. There, where men follow their natural impulses, they would not bear the odious maxims of a Machiavelian policy, whether applied to the attainment of monarchical or democratic tyranny. They would reject them on the modern, as they once did on the antient stage. . . . No theatric audience in Athens would bear what has been borne, in the midst of the real tragedy of this triumphal day; a principle actor weighing, as it were, in scales hung in a shop of horrors. (*Refl.* 176)

Burke, then, attempts to ground the proper response to theater in nature—in "the moral constitution of the heart" and in our "natural impulses."

In a suggestive way, however, the theater becomes one of the best *schools* of "moral sentiments"; the moral constitution of the heart knows how to respond to the theater because it has been schooled there, rather than in the "school of the rights of men." If this is so, the human constitution which causes us to respond with melancholy sentiments to the "real tragedy" of political events turns out to be made in the theater rather than by nature. The difference between good and bad drama, then, can be decided only in theatrical terms rather than by appealing to nature. The distinction between nature and artifice (which is meant to correspond to a fundamental difference between Burke's politics and French radicalism) therefore reveals itself as an unstable distinction between proper theater and superficial theatricality. In the *Philosophical Enquiry*, the sublime—however much Burke tries to ground it in the physical properties of the object and the physiological makeup of the nervous system—always reads like a moment of theater; indeed, it is a drama that needs to suspend disbelief or it may collapse into comedy or madness. And since the natural object in Burke's aesthetic treatise is at its most sublime when presented through particular kinds of verbal description, the criteria of sublimity are not physiological but rhetorical.[39]

In the *Philosophical Enquiry*, the sublime resources of language derive from its *arbitrary* relation to ideas and/or reality; thus the only way of discriminating between genuine and false sublimity is through convention, propriety, decorum. But since these are themselves arbitrary—the constructions of particular classes used to promote a historically specific hegemony as "natural"—then Burke's attempt to distinguish between his own and Price's dramatization of the events of 5–6 October reduces to the question of who controls the criteria.

The ironic aspect of this, however, is that Burke cannot control the effects of his own theatrical account of 5–6 October. Variously producing admiration, irritation, laughter (or ridicule), and tears, the effects of Burke's apostrophe—supposedly the centerpiece of his *Reflections* and of his political philosophy and aesthetic theory—thus come to resemble his own representation of the French Revolution's contradictory and incongruous effects. Attempting to deflect the revolutionary urge by contrasting the queen's beauty with the unlicensed terror of the revolutionary mob, Burke's text turns out to be unexpectedly complicit with the exposure of that beauty to that terror. At the same time, Burke exposes himself, or is exposed, as a ridiculous lover of a queen and ideology that are themselves exposed to ridicule through his equivocal overtures. Indeed, this might offer one way of understanding the contradictory effects the *Reflections* produced—energizing both counterrevolutionary terror and, as James K. Chandler puts it, becoming the occasion of the English Jacobin movement's "greatest flowering."[40]

Notes

1. There are numerous modern accounts of the events at Versailles on 5–6 October 1789; see, for example, Alfred Cobban, *A History of Modern France, 1715–1799* (Harmondsworth: Penguin, 1957) 161–62.

2. James T. Boulton, *The Language of Politics in the Age of Wilkes and Burke* (London: Routledge and Kegan Paul, 1963) 132–33.

3. For an account of such responses, see F. P. Lock, *Burke's Reflections on the Revolution in France* (London: Allen and Unwin, 1985) 138–43.

4. Edmund Burke, *Reflections on the Revolution in France*, ed. Conor Cruise O'Brien (Harmondsworth: Penguin, 1968) 171 (hereafter cited as *Refl.*).

5. O'Brien argues in his Introduction that the "Gothic and pathetic" manner of these passages, "which many have been taught to think of as typical Burke," is only one of three fundamentally different styles employed in the *Reflections* (43). Gerald Chapman even argues that a too exclusive concentration on the Versailles passage has caused critics to misread Burke's overall position (*Edmund Burke: The Practical Imagination* [Cambridge: Harvard UP, 1967] 194–96). But I am interested in these passages partly because they *have* so obsessively preoccupied Burke's readers and partly because, as I will show, they are both central to the rest of the *Reflections* and constitute some of its most vulnerable moments.

6. Burke to Charlemont, 9 Aug. 1789, *The Correspondence of Edmund Burke*, ed. Thomas W. Copeland et al. 10 vols. (Cambridge: Cambridge UP; Chicago: U of Chicago P, 1958–78), 6: 10 (hereafter cited as *Corr.*).

7. Richard Price, *Discourse on the Love of Our Country* (London: Cadell, 1789) 49–51 (hereafter cited as *Disc.*).

8. The University of East Anglia English Studies Group, on the other hand, argues that the "underlying passivity of the 'People' is evident [in this passage]; they are joined to no concrete verbs of action" ("Strategies for Representing Revolution," in *1789: Reading, Writing, Revolution*, ed. Francis Barker et al. [Chelmsford: U of Essex, 1982] 81–100 [95]). But not to see linguistic acts as themselves concretely political is to overlook the politicization of language which is especially characteristic of this period (see Olivia Smith, *The Politics of Language 1791–1819* [Oxford: Clarendon, 1984]).

9. William Wordsworth, *Prelude* (1805) 10.211–12.

10. Edmund Burke, *A Philosophical Enquiry into the Origin of Our Ideas of the Sublime and Beautiful*, ed. James T. Boulton (London: Routledge and Kegan Paul, 1958) 82 (hereafter cited as *PE*).

11. In an important and provocative article, Gary Kelly suggests that "figures of crime and madness are the presiding ones in all of Burke's 'reasonings' on the revolutionaries and their British sympathizers" ("Revolution, Crime, and Madness: Edmund Burke and the Defense of the Gentry," *Eighteenth Century Life* 9.1 [1984]: 16–32 [17]). According to Kelly, one of the Revolution's principal dangers was that it "makes its admirers resemble itself" (24); Burke's figuration of the Revolution as criminal insanity can be seen primarily as an ideological ploy for "putting it in a kind of intellectual quarantine" (27).

12. Burke's concept of the sublime clearly draws on Aristotle's descriptions of tragedy (the *Philosophical Enquiry* makes few overt references to Aristotle, yet the idea that an event or drama can be both painful and pleasurable seems to derive from *The Poetics* [see *Philosophical Enquiry* 44]). Burke's response to the

Revolution in the *Reflections* seems to make specific use of Aristotle's discussion of "Fear and Pity." Aristotle argues that although fear and pity "may be excited by means of spectacle," it is more "artistic" to achieve these effects through the plot alone; he goes on to assert that "those who employ spectacle to produce an effect, not of fear, but of something merely monstrous, have nothing to do with tragedy, for not every kind of pleasure should be demanded of tragedy, but only that which is proper to it" (*On the Art of Poetry*, in *Classical Literary Criticism*, trans. and with an intro. by T. S. Dorsch [Harmondsworth: Penguin, 1965] 49). In presenting the Revolution as "monstrous," then, Burke seeks to score an aesthetic point; but it could be argued that it is Burke himself who breaches propriety here by constructing a spectacle of something merely monstrous and deploying it to achieve certain effects. But, as in Burke, Aristotle's attempt to differentiate between the tragic and the monstrous relies, in the end, on a notion of "propriety" which resists formulation.

13. Thomas Weiskel, *The Romantic Sublime: Studies in the Structure and Psychology of Transcendence* (Baltimore: Johns Hopkins UP, 1976) 105.

14. For a thorough account of this aspect of the Revolution, see Lynn Hunt, *Politics, Culture, and Class in the French Revolution* (Berkeley: U of California P, 1984) 19–119. Marx's description of the Revolution's adoption of theatrical costume in *The Eighteenth Brumaire of Louis Bonaparte* is well known (see *Surveys from Exile*, ed. David Fernbach [Harmondsworth: Penguin, 1973] 146–49).

15. Peter Hughes, "Originality and Allusion in the Writings of Edmund Burke," *Centrum* 4.1 (1976): 32–43 (41).

16. For the fullest discussion of Burke's dramatic conception of politics, see Paul Hindson and Tim Gray, *Burke's Dramatic Theory of Politics* (Aldershot: Avebury, 1988).

17. *Oxford English Dictionary*, S.V. "profane," def. 1b.

18. "Hugh Peters (1598–1660), independent minister, and chaplain in the Parliamentary army; at the restoration executed on a charge of concerting the king's death" (O'Brien, in *Refl.* 379 n. 8).

19. For Hughes, this passage represents "an attempt to transform the incidents at Versailles and during the return to Paris into a parodied allusion, but a sacred parody, of Christ's via dolorosa, of the Way of the Cross" (39).

20. For Thomas Paine, Burke's "account of the expedition to Versailles" employs all the devices of the theater to produce "a stage effect" (*Rights of Man* [1791/92], ed. Henry Collins [Harmondsworth: Penguin, 1969] 81); in place of "Mr. Burke's drama" (86), Paine offers "the sober style of history" (83).

21. For a brief discussion of the Fifth Monarchists, see Christopher Hill, *The Century of Revolution, 1603–1714* (London: Nelson, 1961) 168–69.

22. Paine 86.

23. See Boulton, *Language of Politics* 128 n. 2. For Burke's use of the letters in support of his attack on Price, see *Refl.* 157n. and 182n. The king made two "escorted" journeys from Versailles to Paris in 1789, the first on 17 July "escorted by fifty deputies" when, on being "received by the victors at the City Hall and, in token of acquiescence in the turn of events, [he] donned the red, white and blue cockade of the Revolution" (George Rudé, *Revolutionary Europe, 1783–1815* [Glasgow: Fontana/Collins, 1964] 98).

24. Paine 82.

25. For a textual source of these images and incidents, see the *Times* (London), 13 and 14 Oct. 1789.

26. George Rudé, *The Crowd in the French Revolution* (Oxford: Oxford UP, 1959) 61–63. For Paine's version of these events, see *The Rights of Man* 81–86.

27. Boulton, *Language of Politics* 129; for Cobban's account of the events at Versailles, see *A History of Modern France* 161–62; Ronald Paulson, *Representations of Revolution (1789–1820)* (New Haven: Yale UP, 1983) 60; Christopher Hibbert, *The Days of the French Revolution* (New York: Morrow Quill, 1981) 100–105; Paine 72; Hughes 39.

28. For a useful though selective collection of the *Times'* reports of the Revolution, see *The Times Reports the French Revolution*, ed. Neal Ascherson (London: Times Books, 1975).

29. Boulton, *Language of Politics* 130.

30. See John Milton, *Paradise Lost* 5.706–707 and 7.131–35.

31. Milton 1.663–65.

32. See Paulson 49–59 and Raymond Williams, *Key Words: A Vocabulary of Culture and Society* (London: Fontana, 1976) 271–72.

33. Paulson 51.

34. Desmond Seward, in *Marie Antoinette* (London: Constable, 1981), shows that the French queen's reputation for sexual license was constructed by political intrigue in the French court (see Seward's account of the affair of the Diamond Necklace, 87–107). Far from epitomizing the corruption of the ancien régime, Seward argues, Marie Antoinette actually introduced a vogue for "naturalness" and simplicity in the French court.

35. A recent art historian's celebration of rococo paintings of women reveals how Burke's aesthetics is implicated within its historical context (and, incidentally, how that aesthetic may still affect the [male] gaze). Women are central to rococo art, and are represented in ways which recall Burke's "memory" of Marie Antoinette; whereas in Watteau, women "were natural beings, they have become goddesses to the high rococo" (Michael Levey, *Rococo to Revolution: Major Trends in Eighteenth-Century Painting* [London: Thames and Hudson, 1966] 90). In Giovanni Battiste Tiepolo's *Madonna del Carmelo*, the Virgin is "borne

aloft, tall and calm in the heart of the agitation, . . . effortlessly [holding] . . . the Child—weightless, equally aerial. . . . This concept of woman, which can be disconcerting in religious work, found perfect expression in Tiepolo's profane decorations, where every woman becomes a queen, and queens themselves acquire a new aura" (Levey 95). But it is in Levey's descriptions of François Boucher's work that the parallels with Burke emerge most suggestively: "His mythological world was more frankly feminine . . . than Tiepolo's; it hardly tries to astonish the spectator, and its magic is no exciting spell but a slow beguilement of the senses, a lulling tempo" (Levey 103). Just as Burke strips Marie Antoinette, so Boucher strips Tiepolo's women "to complete nudity, warmed by love or lust"; in *The Birth of Venus* he blends "the natural and the artificial to make a completely enchanted scene, exuberant yet relaxed, an aquatic frolic and yet also an air-born, sea-born vision . . . [in which] the goddess remains a ravishingly pretty, demure girl, half-shy of the commotion of which she is the centre . . . divinely blond and slender, touched with a voluptuous vacancy, a lack of animation, which perhaps only increase her charm" (Levey 104–105). The high rococo was to be replaced, by the end of the century, by an art form which emphasized "education" and "the dignity of labour" (Levey 140)—a shift which seems to find its ideological pivot in the exchange between Burke and Wollstonecraft over the events of 5–6 October 1789.

36. O'Brien, in *Refl.* 385 n. 63; see Edward Jerningham to Burke, before 18 Jan. 1791, *Corr.* 6: 203–204 (O'Brien refers to the correspondent as "Jeringham").

37. Wordsworth 10.38–82.

38. Paine 71.

39. This point is derived from Frances Ferguson's insightful reading of the *Philosophical Enquiry* in "The Sublime of Edmund Burke, Or the Bathos of Experience," in *Glyph: Johns Hopkins Textual Studies* 8 (1981): 62–78 (66–68).

40. James K. Chandler, *Wordsworth's Second Nature: A Study of the Poetry and Politics* (Chicago: U of Chicago P, 1984) 17.

FOUR

———◄◦►———

Burke, Rousseau,
and the French Revolution

Peter J. Stanlis

C'est la faute a Rousseau; c'est la faute a Voltaire is a
claim few now would wish to make: the French
Revolution cannot *simply* be ascribed to the work of
Rousseau or Voltaire, of philosophes or Jansenists, of
reforming administrators or reactionary parlements,
or of any other writers, traditions or practices to
which its putative origins have been traced by one or
another historiographical school. On the contrary, it
was a radical political invention, the elements of
which were derived from many sources, and the
consequences of which were anticipated by none of
the political actors involved.

Keith Michael Baker, *The French Revolution and the Creation of
Modern Political Culture*

Undoubtedly, the multiple and complex etiology of the French Revolution can never be wholly identified, nor can the scale in importance of
the diverse determinants ever be accurately ascertained, which is why
Keith Baker's statement probably expresses the strong consensus that
exists among current scholars. If, however, a complete knowledge of
the role of Jean-Jacques Rousseau in the Revolution, as understood by
Edmund Burke, has yet to be fully explicated through new empirical

evidence and scholarship, then the Revolution as a "radical political invention" (to use Baker's phrase) may be still better understood by a consideration of Rousseau's thought, without ascribing to him any causal "putative origins." In this context, I propose to provide a general frame of reference for precisely such an understanding.

It is an unfortunate fact that most readers of Burke's *Reflections*, including those who agree with his political philosophy, perceive it as primarily an attack on the French Revolution, and not as a defense of a two-thousand-year-old European civilization. It is much easier to perceive what Burke was attacking than what he was defending, particularly if a reader lacks knowledge of the specific political and social philosophy which grounds his assault on the Revolution. Perhaps the most common fallacy, particularly among Marxist scholars, is the conviction that Burke was defending the status quo in France; that he doggedly opposed change; that he championed the absolute monarchy, with all its abuses of power, real or imaginary; that he defended the nobility and clergy against the confiscations of their estates and the destruction of their corporate orders; in short, that he was an obfuscationist, whose arguments opposed the creation of liberty, equality, and fraternity, which the Revolution was attempting to establish.

Critics who approach Burke and the Revolution through their own restricted ideologies often perceive him solely in terms of class conflicts between the rich and the poor. Consequently, Burke is portrayed as a defender of privilege, as a man who supported the dominant class and hence advanced his own career. From this peculiar reading, it follows that what drove Burke to rage and despair was not his conviction that the rationalistic madness of an abstract revolutionary ideology was destroying the twenty-centuries-old civilization of Europe, but that the privileges of the Old Regime were being destroyed. Indeed, it is ironic that even the monarchs and aristocrats of Europe did not understand that they were being assailed by an unprecedented hostile power until Burke repeatedly stressed the point. Even then, some, like the king of Prussia, hastened to placate the revolutionaries, while Burke was advocating war on the Revolution. If the interpretations of Marxist critics about Burke and the Revolution were valid, Burke's sustained critique would long ago have been discarded. Marxist interpretations of Burke either omit or misrepresent his conception of history and his vision of the crucial role of religion in civil society. Hence they dismiss his appeals to moral natural law as meaningless rhetoric or as shrewd, calculating expediency in defense of capitalism. But this line of argument is essentially reductionist; it distorts Burke within the confining perimeters of an imposed ideology that presupposes his defense of the ancien régime.

To understand the norms that Burke was defending and the theories he was attacking, it is necessary to examine Burke's conception of history, which underscores his lifelong reverence for the inherited continuum of civil society in Europe. In the same year that he wrote his satirical *A Vindication of Natural Society* (1757), attacking those social-contract theorists who thought it possible or desirable to establish a "natural society" such as they imagined to have existed before historical society was organized, he also wrote *An Essay towards an Abridgment of English History* (1757). In this work, Burke set forth his considered notion on the origin and nature of European civil society and man's past, as well as his conception of the moral nature of humanity. The importance of this work for a valid comprehension of his early intellectual development in political and social theory can hardly be overestimated. It is also crucial for an understanding of his relentless attacks on the French Revolution.

Burke's English history reveals an extensive knowledge of both English and European society from the ancient Romans to the reign of King John. It also supplies the first explicit evidence of his profound respect for the historical modus operandi of Montesquieu, as applied to civil society—an empirical method wholly at variance with Cartesian rationalism and the abstract speculative theorizing of Hobbes, Locke, and Rousseau. It was a method he employed in almost every page he ever wrote on politics and society. To Burke, the only reliable evidence on man as a civil-social animal was to be found within recorded history, never in any imaginary or hypothetical pre-civil "state of nature," out of which a fictional social contract evolved before society existed. In the *Reflections*, he is very clear about this: "I have in my contemplation the civil social man, and no other. . . . Men cannot enjoy the rights of an uncivil and of a civil state together."[1] It was totally unacceptable to him to omit history—the actual empirical record of what humanity had achieved in its enduring struggle to create a better society—and to substitute instead the idyllic fictions of a hypothetical, prehistorical "state of nature," such as was posited by Locke and Rousseau. Therefore, he attacked the speculative notion of a pre-civil "social contract" as the norm by which historical civil society should be judged. In the preface to his satire on "natural society," Burke had called such ideological speculations "the fairy land of philosophy." Even within empirical history, the fictional speculations of rationalist theories posed a grave danger to the very existence of organized civil society. Burke asked a fundamental question in the preface to his satire, a question which has great importance for an understanding of his attack on the French Revolution thirty-three years later: "Even in matters which are, as it were, just within our reach, what would become of the world, if the practice of all moral duties, and the foundations of society, rested upon having their reasons made clear and demonstrative to every individual?"[2] No society could withstand the impossible criterion of having to justify the historical, civil, and social inheritance of Europe to the satisfaction of every individual's reason.

In his *Abridgment of English History*, Burke clearly identified the chief elements that, in various combinations in different areas of Europe, comprised the real foundations of European civilization—Graeco-Roman culture and especially Roman civil law, Christian religion and morality, and the Teutonic customs and manners of the tribes which had overrun the Roman Empire. These basic elements of Western civilization always commanded his veneration and respect. They were embodied in church and state; they infused family and provincial loyalties; and they extended to all the subordinate institutions of society. They provided the moral clothing for mankind, without which man would be naked and exposed to the power of barbarian forces. They provided the moral, intellectual, aesthetic, and social norms for the value system of European civilization.

Burke had no philosophy of history, nor did he hold a "historicist" theory such as Leo Strauss and his students have attributed to him: that he accepted whatever the historical process threw up for man's acceptance, including political tyranny. Nothing in Burke's view of history was inconsistent with his belief that freedom, good order, and justice were the great ends of man in civil society. His view of European history reveals a conception of man's important place in temporal events, under the mysterious dispensations of God, that dovetails with his view of history, religion, and political philosophy. In varying degrees and at different times, Burke contended, the nations of Europe

evolved from similar social forms: they "grew imperceptibly into freedom, and passed through the medium of faction and anarchy into regular commonwealths. Thus arose the republics of Venice, of Genoa, of
Florence, Sienna, and Pisa, and several others. . . . All the kingdoms
on the continent of Europe were governed nearly in the same form;
from whence arose a great similitude in the manners of their inhabi-
tants."[3] Burke argued that all the nations of Europe had evolved from
some fusion of Roman law, Christian morality, and Teutonic customs
and manners, and that this complex of nations constituted a "commonwealth of Europe," the product of slow historical development over
many centuries.

Burke did not believe that history, as "the known march of the ordinary providence of God," contained any law of necessary progress, but
he did believe that improvements in the civil-social life of Europeans
could and did continue to occur. He regarded all the basic institutions
of society—family, church, state, schools, guilds, commercial organiza-
tions—all corporate bodies, as the necessary instrumental means for the
full development of human nature in its spiritual and temporal dimensions. All such institutions were "natural"; that is, normal for man, the
product of his will and reason, created artfully for his improvement.
Burke summarized his defense of the institutions of civilization in an
epigram: "Art is man's nature." Because civil society was the normal
condition for human nature, the legal and moral systems of social institutions, and not a fictional pre-civil state of nature, nor the private
reason of isolated men, provided the norms by which individuals and a
society should be judged.

Therefore, Burke saw the French Revolution as an attack upon the
whole conception of European civilization as a Christian commonwealth
of nations. Forty years after his English history, in his *Letters on a Regicide Peace* (1796–97), he repeated with variations the very language and
thesis of his early history. He noted that the unity found among the
"many nations of Europe" was derived from their common Christian
culture and heritage:

> The cause must be sought in the similitude throughout Europe of reli-
> gion, laws, and manners. At bottom, these are all the same. The writers
> on public law have often called this aggregate of nations a common-
> wealth. They had reason. It is virtually one great state, having the same

basis of general law, with some diversity of provincial customs and local
establishments. The nations of Europe have had the very same Christian
religion, agreeing in the fundamental parts, varying a little in the ceremonies and in the subordinate doctrines. The whole of the polity and
economy of every country in Europe has been derived from the same
sources. It was drawn from the old Germanic or Gothic Customary,—
from the feudal institutions, which must be considered as an emanation
from that Customary; and the whole has been improved and digested
into system and discipline by the Roman law. From hence arose the several orders, with or without a monarch (which are called States), in every
European country; the strong traces of which, where monarchy predomi-
nated, were never wholly extinguished or merged in despotism. In the
few places where monarchy was cast off, the spirit of European monarchy was still left. Those countries still continued—countries of states,—
that is, of classes, orders, and distinctions, such as had before subsisted,
or nearly so. Indeed, the force and form of the institution called States
continued in greater perfection in those republican communities than
under monarchies. From all those sources arose a system of manners and
of education which was nearly similar in all this quarter of the globe,—
and which softened, blended, and harmonized the colors of the whole.
There was little difference in the form of the universities for the education of their youth, whether with regard to faculties, to sciences, or to
the more liberal and elegant kinds of erudition. From this resemblance
in the modes of intercourse, and in the whole form and fashion of life,
no citizen of Europe could be altogether an exile in any part of it. There
was nothing more than a pleasing variety to recreate and instruct the
mind, to enrich the imagination, and to meliorate the heart. When a man
travelled or resided, for health, pleasure, business, or necessity, from his
own country, he never felt himself quite abroad.[4]

The similarity throughout Europe of its culture was also reflected in
its various governments:

The states of the Christian world have grown up to their present magni-
tude in a great length of time and by a great variety of accidents. They
have been improved to what we see them with greater or less degrees of
felicity and skill. Not one of them has been formed upon a regular plan
or with any unity of design. As their constitutions are not systematical,

they have not been directed to any *peculiar* end, eminently distinguished, and superseding every other. The objects which they embrace are of the greatest possible variety, and have become in a manner infinite. In all these old countries, the state has been made to the people, and not the people conformed to the state. Every state has pursued not only every sort of social advantage, but it has cultivated the welfare of every individual. His wants, his wishes, even his tastes, have been consulted. This comprehensive scheme virtually produced a degree of personal liberty in forms the most adverse to it. That liberty was found, under monarchies styled absolute, in a degree unknown to the ancient commonwealths. (*Reg.* 5: 373)

This Classical-Christian-Germanic system of civil society and its governments shaped and suffused the corporate nature of Europeans and was transmitted through tradition and history to each new generation. Moral prudence, which Burke called the first of political virtues, together with the norms built into the institutions and traditions of European society, provided the basis for how important changes should be made in society and government.

Since the Christian commonwealth of Europe was for Burke the norm for civilized society, the French Revolution was "a total departure of the Jacobin republic from every one of the ideas and usages, religious, legal, moral, or social, of this civilized world." Therefore, he condemned the Revolution "for tearing herself from this communion with such studied violence" (*Reg.* 5: 320). It had rejected the basic elements which had formed European society for centuries, and substituted for them entirely different elements: "Instead of the religion and the law by which they were in a great politic communion with the Christian world, they have constructed their republic on three bases, all fundamentally opposite to those on which the communities of Europe are built. Its foundation is laid in regicide, in Jacobinism, and in atheism; and it has joined to those principles a body of systematic manners which secures their operation" (*Reg.* 5: 308). As a "violent breach of the community of Europe" (*Reg.* 5: 320), the Revolution was much more than a change in government: "It has not been, as has been falsely and insidiously represented, that these miscreants had only broke with their old government. They made a schism with the whole universe" (*Reg.* 5: 320). Politically, the revolutionists held "that all government, not being a democracy, is an usurpation,—that all kings, as such, are usurpers, and, for being kings, may and ought to be put to death, with their wives, families, and adherents" (*Reg.* 5: 308). Burke insisted that the Revolution, while including government, was far more than political: "It is not a revolution in government. It is not the victory of party over party. It is the destruction and decomposition of the whole society" (*Reg.* 5: 325), because "this pretended republic is founded in crimes, and . . . is at war with mankind" (*Reg.* 5: 325–26).[5] Therefore, he refused to recognize the revolutionaries as anything but usurpers: "The Regicides in France are not France. France is out of her bounds" (*Reg.* 5: 326). To the end of his life, he adhered to the concept of the Christian commonwealth of Europe as the norm by which to judge the Revolution.

Great Britain was to be the most persistent and constant enemy of the French Revolution until the final defeat of Napoleon in 1815, and it is significant that Burke refers to "Englishmen . . . as citizens of the great commonwealth of Christendom" (*Reg.* 5: 304), asserting that they are allied to "the body of Christendom," which includes all the nations at war with revolutionary France (*Reg.* 5: 245). In fighting the Revolution, Europe is at war with "atheism by establishment," and the revolutionary government is "the synagogue of antichrist" (*Reg.* 5: 245, 309–12). In the second of his *Letters on a Regicide Peace*, Burke took issue with Englishmen who thought the war with revolutionary France was like their old nationalistic wars: "It is a war between the partisans of the ancient civil, moral, and political order of Europe against a sect of fanatical and ambitious atheists which means to change them all. It is not France extending a foreign empire over other nations; it is a sect aiming at universal empire, and beginning with the conquest of France" (*Reg.* 5: 345–46). To perceive that "France [is] subversive of the whole ancient order of the world" (*Reg.* 5: 359), Englishmen needed to perceive "our country . . . as a part of the commonwealth of Europe" (*Reg.* 5: 345). France was once a part of that commonwealth, as was evident in its old system of laws: "The methodized reasonings of the great publicists and jurists form the digest and jurisprudence of the Christian world. . . . There the relations of ancient France were to be found amongst the rest" (*Reg.* 5: 360).

But the revolutionaries subverted the jurisprudence of Europe, including prescriptive law, so that "the present system in France" cannot be admitted "into the brotherhood of Christendom" (*Reg.* 5: 360).

Revolutionary France had to be defeated, Burke argued, in order "to preserve Europe from the return of barbarism" (*Reg.* 5: 344) and to restore "the balance of power throughout the Christian world" (*Reg.* 5: 452). Throughout his *Letters on a Regicide Peace*, he makes it clear that the great issue is between the militant atheism and dogmatic political ideology of the Revolution and "the Christian world," or "the great commonwealth of Europe" (*Reg.* 5: 344, 469). Burke believed that the Revolution signified a great spiritual crisis in the life of Europe, that "a silent revolution in the moral world preceded the political, and prepared it" (*Reg.* 5: 379). Nothing less than the survival of "the nations which compose the old Christian world" (*Reg.* 5: 415) was at stake in the war with the French Revolution.[6]

With this background and in light of his criticism of Rousseau's real or supposed role in the French Revolution, including assessments by recent scholarship, a thorough review of Burke's critique would be fruitful. Burke was, of course, aware that there were multiple causes behind the Revolution, but he laid great stress on its speculative rationalist ideology, derived largely from the abstract theories of man and society emanating from Enlightenment philosophes and the "sensibility" of Rousseau. Yet he also wrote: "I have reason to be persuaded that it was in this country, and from English writers and English caballers, that France herself was instituted in this revolutionary fury" (*Reg.* 6: 62). Unfortunately, Burke does not identify these English writers, but it is well established that many revolutionary leaders were tinctured with the philosophy of Voltaire, Diderot, Helvétius, and the other philosophes. Burke was also aware that their writings had contributed to the great discontent with traditional French society, even in the midst of increasing prosperity. He also knew of the growing cult of Rousseau and of the widespread belief in an idyllic "state of nature" and a fictional social contract.

He knew of the new faith in the natural moral goodness of man, as distinct from the acquired goodness taught by orthodox Christianity and organized civil society. Burke believed that when all the basic institutions of society were stripped away, and men were thrown upon nothing but the resources of their private passions and reason, the result would be precisely the social anarchy, violence, terror, and wars that France experienced under the Revolution. In contrast to his view that man is by nature insufficient and hence subject to sinful temptations, the French revolutionaries believed that the "artificial" institutions of society, such as church and state, were the causes of man's corruption and misery. If men were by nature morally good, social institutions were impediments to liberty, and to establish liberty required the destruction of church and state as they had functioned throughout history. Burke became convinced that no one was more responsible for advocating the removal of the moral restraints upon men in France than Rousseau.

In his sustained attack on Rousseau in *A Letter to a Member of the National Assembly* (1791), he is aware of the widespread cult of the Genevan among the revolutionaries, and he states that "Rousseau is a moralist or he is nothing." After describing the "unfashioned, indelicate, sour, gloomy, ferocious medley of pedantry and lewdness—of metaphysical speculations blended with the coarsest sensuality," which are "the general morality of the passions to be found in their famous philosopher, in his famous work of philosophic gallantry, the *Nouvelle Eloise*," Burke concludes: "I am certain that the writings of Rousseau lead directly to this kind of shameful evil."[7] He was criticizing Rousseau's "morality of the passions"—passions based on eighteenth-century "sensibility"—a theory of ethics concerning the moral nature of man which reversed the normative morality of orthodox Christianity in relation to feelings. Whereas Christianity taught that man felt deeply about a moral action or a violation of moral law, "sensibility" taught that an action was moral or immoral depending upon how deeply man felt about it. If man was "by nature" morally good, then his passions were also good and trustworthy, requiring no controls by the church or any other external social agency. In contrast to this doctrine of sensibility, Burke held that restraints upon human passions were to be reckoned among the true rights of man in society. To him, the duties of man merely required conformity to the imperative norms of the Decalogue. Undoubtedly, Burke's strong criticism of Rousseau's moral theory had much to do with his charge that the latter constituted one of the founding principles of the French Revolution.[8]

But beyond Rousseau's theory of ethics and his conception of man as naturally "good," other theories in his writings contributed to render his philosophy revolutionary. For instance, his *Discourse on the Arts and Sciences* (1750) attacked the historically developed social institutions of Europe as the source of moral corruption in human nature, and not, as Burke believed, the necessary instrumental means of redeeming man out of his natural limitations. In regard to his disciples during the Revolution, Norman Hampson notes that "Rousseau had taught them to be suspicious of corporate bodies."⁹

In his *Discourse on the Origin of Inequality* (1755), the same antithesis between "art" and "nature" is assumed, with "art" identified with man's depravity and "nature" with his innate goodness. In this work he argues that men were originally "equal" in a state of nature, and that private property is the source of inequality among men in society. The opening sentences of the second part reverberate with revolutionary implications: "The first man who, having enclosed a piece of ground, bethought himself of saying, 'This is mine,' and found people simple enough to believe him, was the real founder of civil society. From how many crimes, wars, and murders, from how many horrors and misfortunes might not any one have saved mankind, by pulling up the stakes, or filling up the ditch, and crying to his fellows: 'Beware of listening to this imposter; you are undone if you once forget that the fruits of the earth belong to us all, and the earth itself to nobody.'" Rousseau also argues that "one man could aggrandize himself only at the expense of another," thus making the wealth of the rich the cause of the poverty of the poor, and implicitly suggesting a concept of class warfare for revolutionary theorists. His statement that "the man who meditates is a depraved animal" is an indictment of civilization as a corrupting force and constitutes a prelude to his appeal for the total moral regeneration of mankind.¹⁰ The fact that he also defends the right of private property, and seems to contradict his case against civilization, does not nullify the revolutionary nature of his theory.

In his *Discourse on Political Economy* (1755), which initially appeared in Diderot's *Encyclopaedia*, Rousseau first mentions "the general will," making it the basis of all laws within society, setting it against the original "social contract" out of a state of nature. He contends that "the general will" is infallible: "legitimate or popular government, . . . whose object is the good of the people, is . . . to follow in everything the general will. But to follow this will it is necessary to know it, and above all to distinguish it from the particular will, beginning with one's self: this distinction is always very difficult to make, and only the most sublime virtue can afford sufficient illumination for it."¹¹ In this work, and even more thoroughly and explicitly in *The Social Contract* (1762), Rousseau identifies the general will with "the people," an abstraction centered in numbers, never, as with Montesquieu and Burke, in the corporate "people," embodied in their civil and social institutions. Such corporate entities were regarded by Rousseau as particular wills, in conflict with the general will. Thus, the corporate community life of man in society was ignored by Rousseau in favor of social and political collectivism.

Perhaps nowhere did Rousseau reveal more clearly the consequences of his theory of popular sovereignty derived from the general will than in book 4, chapter 8, entitled "Civil Religion," in *The Social Contract*. Like Hobbes, Rousseau reduced the church to a department of the state, whose main function was to inculcate patriotism rather than to maintain religion:

> There is therefore a purely civil profession of faith of which the Sovereign should fix the articles, not exactly as religious dogmas, but as social sentiments without which a man cannot be a good citizen or a faithful subject. While it can compel no one to believe them, it can banish from the State whoever does not believe them—it can banish him, not for impiety, but as an anti-social being, incapable of truly loving the laws and justice, and of sacrificing, at need, his life to his duty. If any one, after publicly recognizing these dogmas, behaves as if he does not believe them, let him be punished by death: he has committed the worst of all crimes, that of lying before the law.[12]

On Rousseau's principle, politicians who controlled the National Assembly could execute or exile anyone who was insufficiently patriotic, and such an act could be legally justified by an appeal to the general will.

In Rousseau's other writings, *La Nouvelle Héloïse* (1762), *Emile* (1762), and his *Confessions* (1783 and 1790), his revolutionary disciples—Mercier, Brissot, Marat, Robespierre, and Saint-Just—found much to admire, and his *Lettres de la Montagne* (1762), together with the penultimate chapter of *The Social Contract*, inspired Robespierre (in his speech on 7 May 1794) to commit the country to worship the Supreme Being in the fete on 8 June.[13]

Critics have, of course, argued that there is another Rousseau. The Genevan's constitutions for Corsica and Poland are generally cited by his defenders as evidence of the "conservative" dimensions of his social and political philosophy. His statement to the Corsicans, maintaining that the state has no right to confiscate private property, is seemingly "conservative," yet he ends by stressing the social right to property over private rights. He also urged the Poles to exercise caution when considering changes in their feudal society, but that in itself is not necessarily conservative. Although he recommended that the Corsicans look to the Middle Ages, and the Poles to classical antiquity, for their social and political models, his prescriptions for Corsica and Poland were irrelevant to the French Revolution. As Norman Hampson has noted: "Rousseau's contemporaries could not read his advice to the Corsicans, which was not published until much later, and they do not seem to have paid much attention to what he told the Poles, which was perhaps just as well for his reputation during the Revolution." But even these so-called "conservative" constitutions contained principles which were inimical to individual freedom: "Rousseau's proposals for Corsica and Poland show how far he was prepared to go in practice to force recalcitrant human nature on to the Procrustean bed of republican principle."[14]

But the central question still remains: to what extent can the social and political ideas expressed in Rousseau's major works be said to have been embodied in the French Revolution? Burke, contrary to many modern historians, certainly believed that Rousseau was a chief source, among many, for the practical programs of the revolutionaries. Among the revolutionaries who expressed admiration for Rousseau were Mirabeau, Mme Roland, Bertrand Barère, Sylvain Maréchal, Jean-Paul Marat, Sebastian Mercier, Jean-Pierre Brissot, Maximilien Robespierre, Louis-Antoine de Saint-Just, Gracchus Babeuf, Anarcharsis Cloots, and Abbé Sieyès. Would this array of admirers and disciples be sufficient to prove that Rousseau was one of the chief progenitors of the Revolution? In itself, it proves no cause-and-effect connections between his ideas expressed in the 1760s and the revolutionary programs initiated and carried forward from 1789 until the end of the Terror.

One of many difficulties in any discussion of Rousseau and the French Revolution is that he died in 1778, more than a decade before the king convened the States General; and hence there is no way of knowing with absolute certainty what he would have thought about the events of 1789 and afterward. Since his social and political philosophy is fraught with ambiguities and paradoxes, and, as some scholars would insist, with irreconcilable contradictions, it becomes a matter of weighing one set of speculations and ideas against another to contend that he would have approved or disapproved of the Revolution, or approved some of its aspects but not others. For example, on 13 November 1792,

Saint-Just responded to the arguments about the legality of putting the king on trial by asserting that Louis XVI was already condemned, since monarchy was an illegitimate form of government and was contrary to nature. He appealed to Rousseau's theory that the populations of European society had been corrupted by centuries of unnatural government and concluded that the king inevitably had to be executed.[15]

In opposition to Saint-Just's claim, Romain de Sèze, one of the lawyers who volunteered to defend Louis XVI after Guy-Jean-Battiste Target had abandoned the king, appealed to Rousseau against the claim that the trial was legal and that popular will superseded the law: "It has been further said, that there existed no law which could be applied to Louis, therefore the *will* of the *people* should pronounce *without one*—here is my answer, Citizens—I read these words in Rousseau's *Social Compact*, article IV. 'In the case where I see neither the law, which it is necessary to follow, nor the judge who should pronounce, I cannot *rely* on the *general* will. The general will, being general, cannot pronounce on a man or on a fact.'"[16] Clearly both revolutionists and antirevolutionaries found it possible to appeal to Rousseau to justify their views.

Perhaps the strongest point against the claim that Rousseau would have approved of the Revolution was his statement that monarchy was appropriate for large countries and that democratic forms of popular sovereignty and government were applicable only in a small society, such as the city-state of Sparta, which he so admired, or modern Geneva, which he portrayed in such idealistic terms in *The Social Contract*. Rousseau made it quite clear that he never intended his idea of democracy should be applied to a large country such as France. Moreover, although Rousseau denies any right of legitimate political sovereignty to monarchs, he has some good points to make in favor of aristocracy. It is a matter of record that, at the beginning of the Revolution, conservatives appealed to Rousseau against the Revolution.[17]

Gordon H. McNeil has noted that Edme Champion, in *J. J. Rousseau et la Révolution française* (1909), presents a wealth of documentation suggesting that Rousseau cannot validly be considered even a precursor of the Revolution, because his basic political principles were antirevolutionary. In addition, conservative critics of the Revolution argued that Rousseau would have opposed the merging of the three orders into one, the illegal assumption of permanent power by the National Assembly, the limits placed upon the king's veto, and the confiscation of church property.[18] The Comte Ferrand, who first advocated calling the States General, but soon became one of its most fierce opponents, quoted passages from Rousseau's *Social Contract* to demonstrate that his political philosophy was strongly opposed to the specific acts passed by the National Assembly. When Barere de Vieuzac, a radical delegate, presented a bust of Rousseau to his colleagues in June 1790, the antirevolutionaries attacked this as an outrage against his memory.[19] Later that year, the radical revolutionaries voted to erect a statue of Rousseau, with the inscription: "La Nation française libre a J.-J. Rousseau." This provoked cries of outrage by antirevolutionary writers.[20] But in the end, by 1792, the radical majority seemed to have won the argument by drafting a constitution which they claimed was consistent with Rousseau's politics.

The strongest case against Rousseau's real or supposed influence on the French Revolution is Joan McDonald's *Rousseau and the French Revolution: 1762–1791*. The author states that there is "great imprecision and error in previous estimates of Rousseau's influence upon the political theory of the Revolution and the revolutionary generation." She grants that the prerevolutionary literary cult of Rousseau, centered in his concept of the moral regeneration of human nature, was transformed through politics into a revolutionary cult by his self-proclaimed "disciples" but discounts his influence on them because they were more enthusiastic than knowledgeable about his writings and philosophy. In addition, because Rousseau's name was evoked for a variety of causes, "when it was convenient" to use his literary popularity, the specific practical politics of the Revolution cannot be said to have been greatly influenced by such appeals.[21]

But this thesis is based on the period 1788–91, during which time Rousseau's influence upon practical revolutionary politics was indeed slight. McDonald made no attempt to trace the development of political ideology as the Revolution unfolded after 1791. Moreover, she limits herself to published pamphlets and National Assembly debates during 1789–91 and makes much of the few references to Rousseau's *Social Contract* within this restricted area of political debates. The antirevolutionaries were quick to point out the discrepancies between the revolutionaries' appeals to Rousseau and their actual political behavior. McDonald seems quite unaware of any relation between the qualitative cultural influence of Rousseau upon society and politics through *La*

Nouvelle Héloïse, Emile, and the *Confessions,* in manners, morals, and "sensibility," as these bear upon the revolutionaries' ideology and action. Consequently, the real significance of the cult of Rousseau in shaping the totalitarian democratic politics of the Jacobins is largely ignored. In this regard, John W. Chapman's *Rousseau—Totalitarian or Liberal* is a far more accurate work of scholarship.[22]

In addition, Norman Hampson's *Will and Circumstance: Montesquieu, Rousseau, and the French Revolution* provides substantial evidence that such revolutionary figures as Mercier, Brissot, Marat, Robespierre, and Saint-Just were deeply indebted to either Montesquieu or Rousseau (and in Brissot's case to Voltaire) for their essential political ideas. In light of Hampson's study, Burke's comment on these writers takes on considerable significance. In January 1790 he wrote the following to an unknown correspondent:

> You say, my dear sir, that they read Montesquieu—I believe not. If they do, they do not understand him. He is often obscure; sometimes misled by system; but, on the whole, a learned, and ingenious writer, and sometimes a most profound thinker. Sure it is, that they have not followed him in any one thing they have done. Had he lived at this time, he would certainly be among the fugitives from France. With regard to the other writers you speak of, I do believe the directors of the present system to be influenced by them. Such masters, such scholars. Who ever dreamt of Voltaire and Rousseau as legislators? The first has the merit of writing agreeably; and nobody has ever united blasphemy and obscenity so happily together. The other was not a little deranged in his intellects, to my almost certain knowledge. But he saw things in bold and uncommon lights, and he was very eloquent—But as to the rest!—I have read long since the *Contract Social.* It has left very few traces upon my mind. I thought it a performance of little or no merit; and little did I conceive, that it could ever make revolutions, and give law to nations. But so it is.[23]

Hampson noted repeatedly that revolutionary writers—particularly Marat, Robespierre, and Saint-Just—turned increasingly to Rousseau between 1789 and 1791, during the time when almost all French institutions were being transformed by the Revolution. They took to heart Rousseau's "The Legislator," in book 2, chapter 7 of *The Social Contract,* and each of them by turn presumed that he was the destined lawgiver who would transform the moral nature of man and perfect a new society for France and all Europe.

Rousseau had defined the nature, function, and objective of his lawgiver as follows:

> He who dares to undertake the making of a people's institutions ought to feel himself capable, so to speak, of changing human nature, of transforming each individual, who is by himself a complete and solitary whole, into part of a greater whole from which he in a manner receives his life and being; of altering man's constitution for the purpose of strengthening it; and of substituting a partial and moral existence for the physical and independent existence nature has conferred on us all. He must, in a word, take away from man his own resources and give him instead new ones alien to him, and incapable of being made use of without the help of other men. The more completely these natural resources are annihilated, the greater and the more lasting are those which he acquires, and the more stable and perfect the new institutions; so that if each citizen is nothing and can do nothing without the rest, and the resources acquired by the whole are equal or superior to the aggregate of the resources of all the individuals, it may be said that legislation is at the highest possible point of perfection.[24]

As Hampson notes, Rousseau's lawgiver was hence an active political prophet, "a kind of political Moses who could guide—and when necessary bully—his recalcitrant charges toward a Promised Land of whose precise location only he was aware. It was a position for which there were to be quite a few candidates during the French Revolution."[25]

Similarly, Brissot, Marat, Robespierre, and Saint-Just believed that *vertu* was the ultimate objective of a morally transformed society: "For contemporaries, the republic was a regime whose principle was *vertu*. . . . Henceforth the state was dedicated . . . to . . . the eradication of every form of moral and political vice. . . . For some Frenchmen at least, the objective was now the full Rousseauist Utopia in all its glory."[26] In practice, this policy included all who did not measure up to the standard of *vertu* of the ruling political faction—whether Girondins or Montagnards; they determined who was not considered a legitimate member of society, and could be proscribed or, if necessary, executed. As Burke said of this psychology, which became the moral basis of the Terror, by hating vices too much the revolutionaries came to love men too little. Indeed, as Hampson notes, "the range of the guilty grew all the time," and his paraphrase from Marat provides a revealing illustration of the Revolution's transformation into the republic of virtue: "In July 1789 it would have been sufficient to murder only 500 people. False humanity then meant 10,000 would have to die now. For a year or so this figure remained constant but inflation set in and by the autumn of 1791 it had risen to 2–300,000." Marat even suggested that the Committee of Public Safety appoint him as director, so that he might restore order through mass executions. Hampson comments that this development "raises the disquieting question of whether *Maratisme* should be considered, not as the aberration of an individual, but as the natural destination of any-one who tried to adopt Rousseauist principles to the circumstances of revolution."[27]

Marat, Robespierre, and Saint-Just adopted other Rousseauist principles in their practical politics. All of them agreed that the law must be the expression of the general will, which they located either within their own persons or in the Paris Commune.[28] "Like Rousseau, Robespierre opposed the survival of any corporate bodies that could interpose their sectional interests between the citizen and the state."[29] As Burke noted, the revolutionary state was all in all. Robespierre's version of the social contract was a paraphrase of Rousseau's *Social Contract*. Hampson has summarized the extent to which that radical dictator had absorbed his thought: "Throughout the whole course of the revolution his thinking was dominated by the influence of Rousseau. . . . Rousseau was invoked all the time, occasionally by name but more often by some such epithet as 'the virtuous philosopher of Geneva,' 'the sublime and true friend of humanity,' as though his very name were too sacred to be pronounced lightly. Robespierre quoted him, paraphrased him and saw politics in Rousseauist terms." The September massacres, the lynching of prisoners at Orléans on 10 April 1793, and the executions during the Terror were all justified by Robespierre as "revolutionary justice," because he believed "the greatest service that the legislator can render men is to force them to be honest." Hampson concluded that "Rousseau might not have been happy about all this, but it was a logical consequence of seeing politics in terms of moral regeneration by a collective will."[30] The revolutionary republic of virtue rested upon the dialectic of *vertu* and terror: *vertu* in directing the "people," *terror* for enemies of the revolution.

Saint-Just, Robespierre's chief supporter, published *De la Nature* in 1792, a social theory based upon Rousseau's principle that man is by nature good and becomes corrupted by his civil institutions. He believed in "natural society," that is, a social order without political power or institutions, which he thought was a harmonious and self-regulating system requiring no external restraints on anyone. Thus, as Hampson notes, "crime was a consequence, rather than a cause of repressive laws. 'Crime is born of force; it is not in men's hearts.' The way to suppress crime was therefore to abolish punishment. 'No one on earth should command; all power is illegitimate.'"[31] Like Rousseau, Saint-Just assumed that all men were equal in "natural society" and that civil institutions warped men's true nature by restraining their desires. Ironically, Saint-Just believed literally in the theory of man and society that Burke had satirized in *A Vindication of Natural Society* in 1756. Like his colleagues, Saint-Just wished to consolidate the central power of his revolutionary faction; he therefore favored abolishing the newly created departments of France. He too justified the Terror as necessary for the moral regeneration of man, as well as for the preservation of the Revolution.

Several important recent works of scholarship on Rousseau have confirmed and greatly extended the theme of Hampson's book—that the prerevolutionary literary and cultural cult of Rousseau, centered on manners and morals, carried over into the practical politics of the Revolution and thereby greatly influenced its spirit, course, and direction. James Miller's *Rousseau: Dreamer of Democracy* (1984) refutes Joan McDonald's claim that Rousseau had little political influence on the Revolution because, among other facts, between 1775 and 1790 not one new edition of Rousseau's *Social Contract* was published in France. He notes that between 1789 and 1799 at least thirty-two editions appeared. His book stresses how thoroughly Rousseau's ideas and symbolic image had percolated down to the lower classes, and how far his moralistic rhetoric and language appeared as revolutionary slogans on the rights of man, popular sovereignty, *vertu,* and in the "general will" as embodied in the single, unicameral National Assembly.

Carol Blum's *Rousseau and the Republic of Virtue* (1986) substantiates and adds to the work of McDonald, McNeil, Henri Peyre, L. Sozzi, and J. L. Talmon and most especially to the extensive scholarship of Lester G. Crocker, among many others, to demonstrate in great detail

Rousseau's vital role in providing a language of ideas that inspired the creation of the Republic of Virtue. The subtitle of Blum's book is significant: "The Language of Politics in the French Revolution." Robespierre, Saint-Just, and others used Rousseau's ideas and language in their political discourses, but even more important was the image of Rousseau, partly historical and partly mythical, which formed the cult of his followers. Rousseau's discourses, novels, and *Confessions* are more important than *The Social Contract* in creating the archetypal myth of the good man persecuted by a corrupt, unfeeling, and tyrannical society. Rousseau as the virtuous and innocent martyr became the model for his revolutionary disciples, and they viewed the antagonist world of evil "counterrevolution" through his virtuous, threatening language. Because Rousseau had been persecuted during the Enlightenment by "evil" men, his revolutionary disciples, also untouched by corruption, were prepared to destroy all nefarious people—products of the morally bankrupt ancien régime—who opposed the politics of their revolutionary Republic of Virtue. The Terror that followed was based upon the highest moral ideals of Robespierre, Saint-Just, and others who believed that the only function of the state was to compel men to be virtuous. For almost two years, from the imprisonment of the king on 11 August 1792 to the Comité de Salut Public (9 Thermidor), Robespierre and the Mountain shaped the revolutionary government through Rousseau's language.

The law of 22 Prairial eliminated the cumbersome operations of the courts—which required evidence, witnesses, due process, and the right of self-defense—so that enemies of the people could be punished directly by revolutionary tribunals which supposedly embodied revolutionary conscience. Louis XVI was the first victim of a terrorist method of prosecution by revolutionary intuition; the Terror began with the king's trial. Blum's work is an incisive analysis of the paradoxical connection between Rousseau's violent and destructive statements against others and his self-image as a morally uncorrupted man, as they relate to the apparently same antithetical values reproduced by the Revolution.

The most direct political influence of Rousseau on the Revolution is in the constitutions of Abbé Sieyès, who modified Rousseau's principles to fit the circumstances created early in the Revolution. His vital role as a constitution maker is described by Bronislaw Baczko, in "Le contrat social des Francais: Sieyès et Rousseau."[32] Sieyès was one of the chief political theorists of the Revolution; he was nominally a Christian cleric, but more a man of the Enlightenment, devoted to Anne-Robert-Jacques Turgot, Etienne Bonnot de Condillac, and Rousseau. His pamphlet "What Is the Third Estate?" excluded the nobility and clergy from a legitimate role in reforming France and precipitated the merging of the three orders into a one-chambered Constituent Assembly. Like many revolutionaries, Sieyès identified the general will with popular sovereignty, and denied the king's right of absolute veto as contrary to that will. More than anyone, he was responsible for the new division of France into eighty-three departments.

Sieyès was a member of the first committee to frame a revolutionary constitution, and later, in May 1799, he was elected to the Directory, as a member of which he helped frame the subsequent constitution that facilitated Napoleon's rise to power. Rousseau's theory of government expounded in *The Social Contract* had a deep influence on the early constitution framed by Sieyès, which was modified to fit the practical politics of the Revolution. He tried to reconcile such diverse and paradoxical notions as individual rights and the general will, but without much success. He argued for a complete break with tradition and the legacy of the past in considering political validation, maintaining that modern government finds its legitimacy "in the authentic archives of the people" and in "reason." Burke satirized him as an ideologically insane constitution-monger in his *Letter to a Noble Lord* (1795).

Thus we return full circle to Burke's criticism of the Revolution in general and of Rousseau in particular. The major need of scholarship on Burke and the French Revolution is a correlation of the manifold empirical details that he possessed of the French scene prior to the Revolution, and his comments on particular persons and events from 1789 to 1797, with an especially strong focus on his criticism of Rousseau. In light of recent scholarship on Rousseau and the Revolution, which has established the close connection between the literary and cultural aspects of the cult of Rousseau and the practical politics of the Revolution, such a study of Burke and the French Revolution would contribute to a better understanding of both.

Notes

1. Edmund Burke, *Reflections on the Revolution in France*, in *The Works of the Right Honourable Edmund Burke*, 12 vols. (Boston: Little, Brown 1904), 3: 309 (hereafter cited as *Works*).

2. Edmund Burke, Preface to *A Vindication of Natural Society* (1757), in *Works* 1: 6–7.

3. Edmund Burke, *An Essay towards an Abridgment of English History*, in *Works* 7: 731.

4. Edmund Burke, *Letters on a Regicide Peace*, in *Works* 5: 318–20 (hereafter cited as *Reg.*).

5. See also *Reg.* 5: 335.

6. As "the common enemy of all nations" (*Reg.* 5: 415–16), the Revolution was to Burke "the most unchristian republic" (*Reg.* 5: 104), that is, the antithesis of the Christian commonwealth of Europe. The fourth of his *Letters on a Regicide Peace* is peppered with such phrases as "the commonwealth of Christian Europe" (*Reg.* 6: 17); "the lawful sovereigns of the Christian world" (*Reg.* 6: 28); "the general liberty and independence of the great Christian commonwealth" (*Reg.* 6: 30); "the ancient system of Europe" (*Reg.* 6: 61); "the Christian world" (*Reg.* 6: 76); "the poor relics of Christian Europe" (*Reg.* 6: 77); and "the remnant of Christianity" (*Reg.* 6: 81).

7. Edmund Burke, *A Letter to a Member of the National Assembly*, in *Works* 4: 31.

8. For a full account of Burke's attack on Rousseau's ethical theory, see Peter J. Stanlis, "Burke and the Sensibility of Rousseau," *Thought* 36 (1961): 246–76.

9. Norman Hampson, *Will and Circumstance: Montesquieu, Rousseau, and the French Revolution* (London: Gerald Duckworth, 1983) 154.

10. Jean-Jacques Rousseau, *The Social Contract and Discourses*, trans. G. D. H. Cole (London: Dent, 1973) 76, 87, 51.

11. Rousseau 120–21, 123.

12. Rousseau 276.

13. See Hampson 240.

14. Hampson 41–42, 46. Hampson adds: "One wonders if those who have contrasted the abstractions of *Du contrat social* with the sense of reality he is supposed to have shown when advising the Corsicans and the Poles, have actually read what he wrote" (46).

15. See Hampson 252–53.

16. See David Jordan, *The King's Trial: Louis XVI vs. the French Revolution* (Berkeley: U of California P, 1979) 131. Cf. *The Trial at Large of Louis XVI. Late King of France. containing a most complete and authentic narrative of every interesting and impartial Circumstance attending the Accusation—Trial, Defence, Sentence—*

Execution, etc. of this unfortunate monarch. communicated in a series of letters by a Member of the late National Assembly, to a Member of the British Parliament. To which is subjoined a copy of His Majesty's will (London: H. Macleish, 1794) 58; emphasis in the original.

17. See Gordon H. McNeil, "The Anti-Revolutionary Rousseau," *American Historical Review* 58 (July 1953): 808–23. McNeil argues that Rousseau did not create or help to create the Revolution, but that the reverse occurred—the Revolution created the myth of Rousseau as a revolutionist.

18. See McNeil, "The Anti-Revolutionary Rousseau" 809–10.

19. See *Mercure de Paris*, no. 27 (3 July 1790): 32–33.

20. See McNeil, "The Anti-Revolutionary Rousseau" 812–13.

21. Joan McDonald, *Rousseau and the French Revolution: 1762–1791* (London: Athlone P, 1965) 155–73.

22. For a more detailed account of the relation between the prerevolutionary literary cult of Rousseau and revolutionary politics after 1789, see Gordon H. McNeil, "The Cult of Rousseau and the French Revolution," *Journal of the History of Ideas* 6 (1945): 197–212.

23. *The Correspondence of Edmund Burke*, ed. Thomas W. Copeland et al., 10 vols. (Cambridge: Cambridge UP; Chicago: U of Chicago P, 1958–1978) 6: 80–81.

24. Rousseau 194–95.

25. Hampson 31.

26. Hampson 158–59.

27. Hampson 205. The sense of Marat's thought is that because of previous revolutionary weakness ("false humanity"), more "enemies" of the Revolution will now have to die.

28. Hampson 224.

29. Hampson 219.

30. Hampson 218, 230, 233.

31. Hampson 250.

32. See *The French Revolution and the Creation of Modern Political Culture*, ed. Keith Michael Baker (Oxford: Pergamon P, 1987) 1: 493–513.

FIVE

---<◉>---

Desire and Sympathy, Passion and Providence: The Moral Imaginations of Burke and Rousseau

Daniel E. Ritchie

Among the most furious passages in the writings of Edmund Burke is his denunciation of Jean-Jacques Rousseau in *A Letter to a Member of the National Assembly*:

> Everybody knows that there is a great dispute amongst their leaders, which of them is the best resemblance of Rousseau. In truth, they all resemble him. His blood they transfuse into their minds and into their manners. Him they study; him they meditate; . . . he is their standard figure of perfection. . . . We have had the great professor and founder of *the philosophy of vanity* in England. As I had good opportunities of know-ing his proceedings almost from day to day, he left no doubt on my mind that he entertained no principle either to influence his heart, or to guide his understanding, but *vanity*. . . . He melts with tenderness for those who only touch him by the remotest relation, and then, without one natural pang, casts away as a sort of offal and excrement, the spawn of his dis-gustful amours, and sends his children to the hospital of foundlings. The bear loves, licks, and forms her young; but bears are not philosophers. Vanity, however, finds its account in reversing the train of our natural feelings.[1]

While this is Burke's longest reference to Rousseau in his counter-revolutionary writings, his acquaintance with Rousseau's writings dates from at least 1759, when he reviewed Rousseau's *Lettre à d'Alembert sur les spectacles* for the *Annual Register*. And in that review, Burke alludes to two of the earlier *Discourses*. In 1762, he reviewed Rousseau's *Emile*, Rousseau's book on education, for the *Annual Register*. Elsewhere in the passage quoted above, Burke refers to the *Confessions* and *La Nouvelle Héloïse*. Burke also read *The Social Contract*, although he "thought it a performance of little or no merit" and admitted in 1790 that it "left very few traces upon my mind."[2]

Burke's greater familiarity with *Emile* and *La Nouvelle Héloïse* reflects the general reception of Rousseau up to 1791. Those two books inspired a vast literature in the decades between their publication and the French Revolution, while *The Social Contract* inspired relatively little. Moreover, the cult of Rousseau, against which Burke reacted so strongly in the selection from *A Letter to a Member of the National Assembly*, antedated the Revolution and was largely inspired by *Emile* and *La Nouvelle Héloïse*.[3]

Joan McDonald describes the prerevolutionary cult of Rousseau thus:

> In this legend [Rousseau] featured as a captivating genius, a man of charm and gentleness, whose sufferings had not prevented him from laying down those sublime truths which he had learned in solitary communion with Nature, nor from being hounded by a perverse authority and betrayed by false friends. Seen through the eyes of that *sensibilité* of which he was the greatest eighteenth-century exponent, Rousseau's own person appeared larger than life; he became for his admirers the prototype of the natural and virtuous man whose education he had planned in *Emile*, and a living exemplar of the complex humanity which he had described in the *Nouvelle Héloïse*, and later in his own *Confessions*.[4]

Clearly, Burke considered Rousseau the educator of the French revolutionaries, both by word and example. "I am certain that the writings of Rousseau lead directly to this kind of shameful evil," said Burke of the revolution in sexual morality, which he considered a completion of the revolutionary "plan of leveling" (*LM* 540). To admire the French Revolution, wrote Burke, was instantly to resemble the Revolution in its "elements and principles, . . . members and its organs."[5]

Burke was not alone in considering Rousseau as an educator whose theories had revolutionary significance. Madame de Staël considered *Emile* his best work, and it marked a turning point in the life of the Girondist leader Jean-Pierre Brissot.[6] Kant considered the publication of *Emile* comparable in importance to the French Revolution itself, and Rousseau himself ranked it first among all his writings.[7]

I will argue that the revolutionary significance of *Emile* comes from Rousseau's account of the origin of social bonds and language. Both social bonds and language—and hence, imaginative language and the imagination itself—come from desire, or "love of self." For Burke, by contrast, social bonds and imagination depend upon "sympathy." This sympathy reaches out to persons living and dead, and, by extension, to the habits and culture (including literary culture) they have passed on.

These two different approaches to imagination and society have great consequences for the views of Rousseau and Burke regarding morals, imaginative literature, and the relation of nature and art. The moral bond for society, as Rousseau envisions it, is compassion ("pity"). Burke's sympathy for a wide range of cultural predecessors, by contrast, accepts an entire "wardrobe" of moral bonds—"the wardrobe of a moral imagination"—chief among which are veneration and natural law. Because Rousseau locates the origin of imagination in desire, he is naturally suspicious of the *false* desires that imagination can create. He is thus suspicious of older literature. Burke, however, welcomes older authors as essential to the identity of the individual and the citizen. Some of his characteristic imagery, that of "inheritance," suggests a sympathetic attachment to gifts from the past. Not surprisingly, Rousseau often opposes nature to art and casts his book on education, *Emile*, as a guide to natural, as opposed to artificial, education. Burke, by contrast, sees art as completing or perfecting nature, as much of his medical imagery suggests.

Finally, by locating the origins of society and imagination in desire, Rousseau ultimately needs to sublimate desire—especially sexual desire—into some other channel, such as love for God, to prevent desire from tearing society apart. Burke, in contrast, did not associate sexual passion with "the sublime," and therefore he does not need or want to sublimate it in some other direction. Rather he associates it with "the beautiful." He considered beauty a "social quality" that led to the creation of society and the propagation of the species.[8] The sublime, a far more powerful force than the beautiful, is aroused by religious terror and ecstasy, tragic loss, danger, and fear of pain. By keeping the sublime and beautiful separate, Burke can separate the most powerful ("sublime") imaginative responses from politics. By mixing the sublime and beautiful, Rousseau provides a theoretical basis for introducing the most powerful human passions *into* politics and the subsequent need to sublimate the fearful and dangerous aspects of those same passions *out* of politics.

The revolutionary consequences that Burke sees in Rousseau's persona and in his more popular writings come ultimately from the large place Rousseau gives to desire. Burke believed the French revolutionaries were enacting this side of Rousseau, occasionally to the neglect of other, more salutary aspects of the citizen of Geneva.

Rousseau's Project and Burke's Response

In comparing the two men, some have said that Rousseau seems to have had the more rigorous, ambitious, and philosophical mind.[9] In a way, this could hardly help but be true, for in *Emile* and elsewhere, Rousseau is self-consciously doing a new thing, making a new system. Burke, by contrast, does not claim to be doing anything new. Rousseau gives us a rereading of Plato's philosophy of love in *La Nouvelle Héloïse* and a rereading of Plato's *Republic* in *Emile*.[10]

Burke correctly perceives Rousseau's ambitions and throws his own imaginative energies entirely against them. In doing so, Burke has sometimes been accused of misreading Rousseau, or of unfairly attributing to him the worst evils of the French Revolution.[11] While Burke was never shy of overstatements or attracted by disinterested interpretations of philosophy, he would question whether philosophers could be so easily exonerated from events produced by men who claimed to be their disciples. Indeed, he would note that three of the major founders of modern philosophy—Rousseau, Marx, and Nietzsche—all inspired cults and, later, revolutions by men and women claiming to be their followers, and yet many modern intellectuals have tried to exonerate the philosophers themselves of the sufferings caused by those revolutions. Burke, however, responds to the persona of Rousseau as well as to his words. His approach is rooted in his sympathetic response to all the factions of society affected by Rousseau and his cult. He does not feel free to divorce ideas from unforeseen consequences.

Burke and his intellectual forebears are responsible for the historical and imaginative worlds that they create. The sympathetic imagination is also, for Burke, a morally responsible one. This responsibility, which is partly inherited by Burke and partly created by him, helps to explain his extraordinarily allusive style. By alluding to an older author, whose work had created in Burke a sympathetic response, Burke is incorporating the older author into his present moral and political life.

Burke's sympathetic imagination worked in this way. It reached true understanding, as William Hazlitt implies, when his mental impressions were heightened by powerful and passionate sympathies.[12] These impressions ranged from Burke's encounter with historical writing and classical works to English literature, contemporary politics, and persons. Burke quotes older authors not because his subject and theirs are identical in every dry, empirical circumstance. Rather, he receives a similar, often quite powerful, impression through his sympathetic identification with his subject and theirs. Books are almost human things to Burke, not merely papers or collections of maxims. To say that books "contain" sympathies is too mechanical; they convey the impressions of former times, into which Burke enters with deep sympathy. "Men are not tied to one another by papers and seals," he remarks about treaties.[13] "They are led to associate by resemblances, by conformities, by sympathies." A line remembered from older literature unites Burke and his audience, sympathetically, with Terence or Vergil, the Hebrew prophets or Shakespeare. Burke's allusiveness is essential to the larger, inherited community, which he must appropriate and add to, in order to find his identity. His actions and the actions of others are intelligible, as Alasdair MacIntyre has said in a more general context, because he is living out a narrative—a story—and he understands his own life in terms of the narratives of others.[14]

At times it seems quite unnecessary for Burke to go to Rome or Athens for a sentiment or aphorism, but he goes there anyway. For instance, when Richard Price, Burke's "revolutionary" antagonist, compliments George III on being "more properly the servant than the sovereign of his people," Burke quotes Terence: "Haec commemoratio est quasi exprobatio."[15] Why does he need to quote Terence? He doesn't need to, of course, but (having sympathized with Terence at some time in the past) he wants the company of Terence in his present struggle. Burke requires more of Terence than his aphorism: he requires the entire "narrative" surrounding the aphorism.

The authors he quotes help Burke to "cover the defects of [his] naked shivering nature" and furnish him with "the wardrobe of a moral imagination" (*Refl.* 171). These authors modestly cover his nakedness, providing the clothes—"the decent drapery of life"—without which he is unfit to enter society. Burke's perception of shared sympathies between himself and them, sympathies whose perception is the function of the imagination, equip him for the discovery and exercise of morality in society.

Irving Babbitt explained Burke's "moral imagination" in this way:

> He saw how much of the wisdom of life consists in an imaginative assumption of the experience of the past in such fashion as to bring it to bear as a living force upon the present. The very model that one looks up to and imitates is an imaginative creation. A man's imagination may realize in his ancestors a standard of virtue and wisdom beyond the vulgar practice of the hour; so that he may be enabled to rise with the example to whose imitation he has aspired. The forms of the past and the persons who administer them count in Burke's eyes chiefly as imaginative symbols.[16]

By sympathizing with authors and historical characters from the past, Burke's imagination finds its morality—not so much in a set of aphorisms but in many sets of narratives.

Rousseau's Aesthetic of Desire

Rousseau's approach is entirely different. He knows classical authors as well as Burke, but he remarks, "I hate books. They only teach one to talk about what one does not know" (*E* 184). Up through the pre-adolescent years of Emile (ages twelve to fourteen), Rousseau prohibits all books except *Robinson Crusoe*. The reason for this stricture, which most notably implicitly prohibits Emile from reading the Bible, is not due to Rousseau's critique of organized religion or to obscurantism. Instead, it is due to his view of the imagination, which engages Emile's desires but cannot ultimately resist desire: "for as I have said countless times, the senses are awakened by the imagination alone. Their need is not properly a physical need. It is not true that it is a true need" (*E* 333).[17] The imagination, then, is likely to produce false "needs," hopes, and fears. Initially, man is constituted by nature with only the proper desires, but "imagination, the most active of all [faculties], is awakened and outstrips them" (*E* 80–81). Rousseau rejects fables—which again would include implicitly the tales of the Bible—because they go beyond the truth and cover it with a veil (*E* 113).[18]

For Rousseau, the imagination produces supplements to truth, rather than truth itself. But what is the relation between "imagination as supplement" and "desire"? And did Burke have any inkling of the importance of desire in Rousseau's thought?

Burke was very much aware of Rousseau's skepticism of imaginative literature, for he chose to quote—although he does not comment on—some of Rousseau's most skeptical passages about books in his 1762 review of *Emile*.[19] The context for Burke's quotation is Rousseau's recommendation of geometry as propaedeutic to moral education, a notion which Burke utterly rejects in his later political writings. Among the reasons for his rejection is Burke's belief, clearly implied in his practice, that education in universal moral truths comes only through the narratives and intellectual traditions of one's particular culture. Rousseau, by contrast, begins his discussion of moral philosophy by asking us to "suppose a philosopher cast a-shore on a desert island. . . . It is probable he would never after look in a book, during his whole life: but he certainly would not fail to explore the island, however extensive, even to its remotest corner."[20] Instead of using maps and globes, Rousseau will actually point out geographical phenomena to Emile. Instead of making speeches to the child—"no flowers of speech, no tropes and figures, no poetry"—the tutor will use language which is "clear, simple, and cold."[21]

In this entire passage, which Burke quotes, Rousseau views the instruments of education, from maps to books, as "supplements," to use the language of Derrida.[22] They are supplements for actual observation and "natural" learning. That is why the learning of the castaway Robinson Crusoe is later recommended, in all seriousness, as "the most felicitous treatise on natural education" (*E* 184).[23] The implication of Rousseau's teaching, as Derrida has explained, is the removal or self-destruction of all such supplements, including language itself.

Desire, especially in the various forms of self-love, is the most basic characteristic of human life, according to Rousseau. Language originates as a substitution for tears when the baby finds he can satisfy his desires by speaking (*E* 77, 80). Rousseau cautions against substituting signs (or any other supplements) for things—implying a deep, mutual suspicion between language and its referents—if one can possibly avoid it (*E* 170). The most natural education, therefore, is that of Robinson Crusoe, which apparently makes no use of imaginative supplements at all, for language itself is unnecessary on the island.

Moral Consequences of Rousseau's Aesthetic

Although language arises from desire, originally as a supplement to tears, its illusions can be put to positive use. The first, clearly beneficial use of the imagination in *Emile* is Jean-Jacques's attempt in book 4 to dissuade his sexually maturing student from indulging his newly awakened desires. At this point (the beginning of adolescence), Rousseau introduces the first moral maxims in Emile's education. Justice is to be based on pity (or "compassion"), which comes from the common weaknesses and sufferings of humanity. By having compassion (or pity) on those worse off than himself—which includes even the wealthy and famous men of the past as well as the bourgeois men of the present, for their education, unlike his, was "unnatural"—Emile's compassion extends to all humanity (*E* 221–53). Rousseau thus accepts Hobbes's notion that human society is grounded in self-love and self-interest, but (unlike Hobbes) he grounds our duties to others in our pleasure in acting compassionately.[24] Compassionate action, one should note, is not virtuous. Rather, the pleasure one derives from acting compassionately gratifies the passion of self-love: "When the strength of an expansive soul makes me identify myself with my fellow, and I feel that I am, so to speak, in him, it is in order not to suffer that I do not want him to suffer. I am interested in him *for love of myself*."[25]

Rousseau's "compassion" is quite different from Burke's "sympathy." While Burke is aware that "we have a degree of delight . . . in the real misfortunes and pains of others" (because we ourselves are unaffected), "our Creator has designed we should be united by the bond of sympathy."[26] What Rousseau bases on self-love and desire, Burke bases on the Creator. And clearly (for Burke) the Creator "willed . . . the state" (*Refl.* 196). For Burke, sympathy is a means of binding together a social unit under God's authority, with the benefit of past generations. For Rousseau, compassion is a means of turning self-love to good use, especially at the moment when Jean-Jacques's pupil is feeling the oncoming of adolescent sexual desire.

When Emile reaches adolescence, Jean-Jacques requires a great deal of help from the imagination, despite its untrustworthy character, for the moment of sexual maturity has come before the completion of Emile's political education. He must make his student disgusted with what Boswell would call "low gallantry" and yet somehow take advantage of the moment, which he designates the "true moment of nature" (*E* 316). Emile has not yet gone out into society, and will not until he is twenty (*E* 317, 331, 332). Emile's self-love (*amour-de-soi,* which, unlike *amour-propre,* is a good passion) should attach him securely to his tutor, more as a friend now than as a pupil, and enable him to fight successfully, passion against passion (*E* 316–17, 327). Nevertheless, Jean-Jacques is apparently anxious lest the libertine passions should win, destroying Emile's education at the very moment when he is nearly ready for the final educational step—political education. Rousseau seizes this moment, turning the greatest threat to Emile's education into his greatest resource, by means of the imagination.

Instead of fighting adolescent passions, or ignoring them, Rousseau bravely promises that the student's "adolescent fire, far from being an obstacle to education, is the means of consummating and completing it. . . . As soon as he loves, he depends on his attachments. Thus are formed the first bonds linking him to his species" (*E* 233). Rousseau appeals to Emile's imagination by presenting it an image that will satisfy its desires, while sublimating them from the most dangerous passions and instincts. Now that the proper time has come, he presents Emile with the image of a woman, Sophie.[27]

"Sophie" and her Consequences
for the Imagination

The image of Sophie has important consequences for Rousseau's view of wisdom, desire, local attachments, and the imagination. The name implies wisdom, the female counterpart and complement to Emile. The image in its sexual aspect suggests the extraordinarily large place that sexual desire has in completing the political education of a Rousseauvian. The image appeals to basic human nature, not to any national, local, or customary connections. By means of sexual passion, properly sublimated in "the beautiful [objects] of all sorts" until his marriage to Sophie, Emile has deferred the enjoyment of his lower passions and developed acceptable attachments to persons other than his tutor (*E* 344).[28]

Emile is thus ready to become a citizen, attached to his species. It follows that his attachments to his particular country or traditions are arbitrary.

Perhaps more fundamentally, however, the image of Sophie defines Rousseau's beliefs regarding the imagination. Sophie is introduced, with all the power of the imagination, to supplement the tutor's power. Notice how Rousseau attempts to substitute the pleasurable image of Sophie for the actual pleasures of "low gallantry": "It is unimportant whether the object I depict for him is imaginary; it suffices that it make him disgusted with those that could tempt him. . . . And what is true love itself if it is not a chimera, lie, and illusion?" (*E* 329). This is the first time Rousseau has preferred the imagination to "truth" and the products of the imagination to the actual objects for which they are (in his view) supplements.[29] Rousseau has not explained why one ought suddenly to prefer, for the first time, an image rather than the promptings of "the master," nature. Indeed, his entire treatment of the imagination has previously made the imagination appear as an agent of deception.

Sophie appears very soon after the end of the confession of the Savoyard Vicar, in which the old priest tells Rousseau (but not Emile) of his loss of faith in revealed religion and his conversion to an entirely "natural" religion. I do not believe the arrangement is accidental, for "revelation" is similar to "imagination": both are necessary in order to prevent chaos, but for Rousseau they are mere supplements to truth. Often they obscure truth. Allan Bloom relates the confession of the Savoyard Vicar to the introduction of Sophie in this way:

> The Vicar teaches the dualism of body and soul, which is alien and contradictory to the unity which Emile incarnates. In keeping with this, the Vicar is otherworldly and guilt-ridden about his sexual desires, which he deprecates, whereas Emile is very much of this world and exalts his sexual desires, which are blessed by God and lead to blessing God. . . .
>
> Thus at the dawn of a new day, Emile learns that the peak of sexual longing is the love of God mediated by the love of a woman. Sublimation finally operates a transition from the physical to the metaphysical. But before speaking to Emile, Rousseau explains to his readers how difficult it is to be a good rhetorician in modern times. . . . Now the world has been deprived of its meaning by Enlightenment. The land is no longer peopled by spirits, and nothing supports human aspiration anymore. . . . He wants to use imagination to read meaning back into nature. The old meanings were also the results of imaginings the reality of which men

believed. . . . Rousseau suggests a new poetic imagination motivated by love rather than the harsher passions, and here one sees with clarity Rousseau's link with romanticism.

With this preface, he proceeds to inform Emile what the greatest pleasure in life is. He explains to him that what he desires is sexual intercourse with a woman, but he makes him believe that his object contains ideas of virtue and beauty without which she would not be attractive. . . . If Emile and Sophie can be constituted as a unit and individualism thereby surmounted, then Rousseau will have shown how the building blocks of a society are formed.[30]

By the time Emile and Sophie turn their sexual longing into love of God, desire is no longer a threat, having been redirected already into love of one's fellow man ("compassion") and love of virtue. In *La Nouvelle Héloïse*, the love of Saint-Preux for Julie is also sublimated—in this case into love of nature (*NH* 1. xxiii, 64–66). The point is that in both of Rousseau's works, crucial to the cult that grew up after him and flourished in the Revolution, desire is seen as the most basic aspect of our humanity. In both works, Rousseau describes desire with the most intense imaginative powers at his disposal—powers that Burke would reserve to "the sublime." In both cases, Rousseau calls for aid from the very products of imagination he had elsewhere banished for their illusion-creating effects on the senses.

On what basis can Rousseau now know that imagination, which was formerly regarded as a faculty to be avoided, is now to be regarded as a potential ally? How does he decide that now is the time to fight against nature (in its sexual aspect), which was formerly the "master" to be obeyed? There is indeed an arbitrariness to Rousseau's invocation of the powers of the imagination, as Derrida has implied, against those of nature. The arbitrariness, I believe, comes from Rousseau's foundation of imagination and social bonds in desire. But as Burke discerned in the life of Rousseau and his followers, the virtues derived from this theory have a way of turning into vices. The sublime, when used to build society out of the redirected passions of desire, turns into the truly horrible. Let us now turn to Burke's alternative vision of society and to his critique of Rousseau.

The Basis of Society in Burke's Thought

Burke sees the building blocks of society in domestic life, not in sexual desire: "No man will glory in belonging to the Checquer, No 71, or to any other badge-ticket. We begin our public affections in our families. No cold relation is a zealous citizen. We pass on to our neighbourhoods, and our habitual provincial connections. . . . Such divisions of our country as have been formed by habit, and not by a sudden jerk of authority, were so many little images of the great country in which the heart found something which it could fill" (*Refl.* 315). Burke too wishes to incorporate "into politics the sentiments [of] private society." But he has something entirely different in mind from either Rousseau's compassion (as Rousseau defines it) or sexual desire.

For Burke, the social passions, including sexual ones, are associated with the beautiful, not with the more powerful, even terrifying, category of the sublime. The sublime pleasures of the imagination derive ultimately from our passion for self-preservation. The sublime is aroused by experiences of the divine, or of danger, terror, or fear, especially fear of pain and death. The sublime is appropriate to prophetic, epic, and tragic themes and modes. These themes could presumably be political if a writer were to treat the deaths of kings and empires. In general, however, works that treat social themes and their sexual basis do not (in Burke's view) naturally incline toward the titanic, powerful imagery of the sublime. They incline toward the beautiful. He considers "beauty a social quality."[31] Since response to the sublime comes ultimately from the passion for self-preservation, so the response to the beautiful comes from the "passions of society," especially the passions between the sexes. The beautiful is aroused by delicacy, grace, "gradual variation," and even smoothness and smallness.[32]

Burke's aesthetic theory does imply a relation between sexuality and politics, but it is very different from Rousseau's. For Rousseau, desire is the most important aspect of our humanity, and it requires the most powerful efforts of the imagination—efforts that Burke would associate with the "sublime"—to sublimate it into socially acceptable channels. Burke associates politics with the beautiful, not with the sublime. To mix the two is a confusion of categories, in his aesthetic. The practical consequences of mixing the sublime with sexuality and politics are, implicitly, what Burke reacts against so strongly in the "Rousseau cult," represented by the persona of Rousseau and his self-described followers in the Revolution.

Burke's writing in the American speeches lacks the prophetic, epic, or "sublime" strain that is so evident in his counterrevolutionary writings. The sublime strain enters Burke's rhetorical arsenal, in part, from the revolutionaries' incorporation of this aspect of Rousseau into their imaginations. Burke responds in kind, hurling against his opponents the plots and characters of the most sublime literature produced by the Western imagination, from Homer and Vergil to Shakespeare and Milton.

By contrast, when Burke prepares his call for incorporating private sentiments into politics, he alludes to an institution that he would associate with "the beautiful"—chivalry (*Refl.* 170–71). Chivalry for Burke reverses the all-too-human tendency to believe that "might makes right."[33] Chivalry requires the powerful—those capable of inspiring others with the fear of death, terror, and the other aspects of the sublime—to subordinate their power to the interests and needs of the weak. The origin of this idea is not in Rousseauvian compassion but in the historical traditions of European Christendom, with which Burke so vividly sympathized.[34] The images associated with this idea are images of the beautiful queen of France rather than the awesome sublime. When Burke is speaking of the social relations he admires instead of those he abhors, he generally chooses images that are more beautiful than sublime—images of houses, cultivated landscape, and even graceful clothing.

Burke's "Moral Imagination" and his Imagery

Paul Fussell's book *The Rhetorical World of Augustan Humanism* has explicated Burke's use of the imagery of architecture and clothing, noting especially the dependence of such imagery on shared human conventions.[35] Burke's most important metaphor for politics, however, is that of "inheritance":

> You will observe that from Magna Charta to the Declaration of Right, it has been the uniform policy of our constitution to claim and assert our liberties as an *entailed inheritance* derived to us from our forefathers, and to be transmitted to our posterity. . . . By this means our constitution preserves an unity in so great a diversity of its parts. . . .

This policy appears to me to be the result of profound reflection; or rather the happy effect of following nature, which is wisdom without reflection, and above it. . . . Whatever advantages are obtained by a state proceeding on these maxims, are locked fast as in a sort of family settlement; grasped as in a kind of mortmain for ever. By a constitutional policy, working after the pattern of nature, we receive, we hold, we transmit our government and our privileges. . . . The institutions of policy, the goods of fortune, the gifts of Providence, are handed down, to us and from us, in the same course and order. Our political system is placed in a just correspondence and symmetry with the order of the world. . . . By adhering in this manner and on those principles to our forefathers, we are guided not by the superstition of antiquarians, but by the spirit of philosophic analogy. In this choice of inheritance we have given to our frame of polity the image of a relation in blood; binding up the constitution of our country with our dearest domestic ties. . . .

Through the same plan of a conformity to nature in our artificial institutions, and by calling in the aid of her unerring and powerful instincts, to fortify the fallible and feeble contrivances of our reason, we have derived several other, and those no small benefits, from considering our liberties in the light of an inheritance. Always acting as if in the presence of canonized forefathers, the spirit of freedom, leading in itself to misrule and excess, is tempered with an awful gravity. This idea of a liberal descent inspires us with a sense of native dignity. . . . [Our liberty] has a pedigree and illustrating ancestors. It has its bearings and ensigns armorial. It has its gallery of portraits. (*Refl.* 119–21; Burke's emphasis)

Burke's imagery has profound implications for his view of nature and art and of social relations, especially family relations.

The metaphor, or "philosophic analogy," of inheritance depends upon human traditions, just as advances in architecture and clothing do. Nature is completed, or perfected, by the human contribution to the inheritance one receives, whether in architecture, politics, or moral philosophy. "Art is man's nature," Burke notes in *An Appeal from the New to the Old Whigs*.[36] No phrase more succinctly separates his imagination from Rousseau's. For Rousseau, the primary purpose of education is to enable man's nature to exfoliate, like a plant, according to its natural desires. Insofar as possible, man should get along without the ruinous effects of human art—literature, medicine, globes, and the range of artificial supplements attacked in *Emile* and *La Nouvelle Héloïse*. For Burke, the educated imagination enables man to reform what he receives from nature, thus acting, *imago dei,* as a created and creative being.

Inheritance, in Burke's imagery, blends the natural inclination to propagate with the artificial, presecriptive manners and laws that govern families. In *Present Discontents*, he notes that "Commonwealths are made of families."[37] One is obligated to use one's reason and imagination in defending or reforming those manners and laws, yet reason often produces but "feeble contrivances," which must in turn be fortified by powerful, natural instincts. These instincts do not produce illusory, chimerical images, intended to deceive true natural passions, as the image of Sophie is meant to do. Rather, they complete human nature and teach it true liberty.

Burke thought that the basis for society was not ultimately in the human passions, as Rousseau believed, but in Providence, especially in God's provision of families. Hence he believes that an orderly society is bounded by obligations that have little to do with human choice and only secondarily to do with passion: "They arise from the relation of man to man, and the relation of man to God, which relations are not matters of choice."[38] He believes that because the revolutionaries do not fear God, they become scourges to each other and to all mankind.[39] Burke would have had no confidence in Rousseau's proposal to sublimate the antisocial passion of *amour-propre* in any other object, or to oppose it with any other passion.

Burke believed that Providence had placed men in families so that their social attachments could begin in infancy and childhood. Rousseau, by contrast, takes Emile out of a family and makes him into an orphan before his education begins. In *La Nouvelle Héloïse*, Julie's sexual passions effectively separate her from her family. Rousseau does not see the need to sublimate the sexual passions of Julie or Saint-Preux, one should note, until after she is removed from her family and her habitual, received social relations. Virtually every paragraph on "natural" education in both *Emile* and *La Nouvelle Héloïse* is a polemic against the bad social relations Rousseau finds before his own education cultivates the natural desires of his characters.

The Burkean imagination, by contrast, is equally the product of nature and art. The "monumental inscriptions" and "gallery of portraits" point to real ancestors, but they are clearly arranged in an artful way so as to strike the imagination and inspire love and "natural" affection in it. The "relation in blood" requires one to imagine an actual family member, but it points to an "artificially arranged" constitution. The arrangement of the portraits and the constitution do not oppose nature by creating inhuman social relations; instead they complete nature and bestow upon the present generation an inheritance. One can enter into this inheritance, through one's sympathetic identification with the images and narratives of the past, or refuse to do so. It follows, however, that if one does not contribute to one's inheritance, one is guilty of ingratitude, which Burke considers the chief vice of the revolutionaries.[40]

The Natural and Artificial
in Burke's Medical Imagery

Apart from "inheritance," Burke's imagery of agriculture and husbandry likewise combine the natural and artificial. Plants and animals reach their perfection under human art.[41] But medical imagery offers perhaps the best means of comparing Burke and Rousseau. Rousseau was one of the early exponents of what we would now call "natural medicine," trusting in a benevolent nature to heal the body and distrusting the knowledge and technology of doctors. The contemporary, imperfect technology of smallpox inoculation, for instance, provokes some of Rousseau's most revealing comments: "Shall we have [Emile] inoculated with it at an early age, or wait for him to get it naturally? . . . The second choice is more in accord with our general principles of letting nature alone in everything, in the care it is wont to take by itself and which it abandons as soon as man wants to interfere. The man of nature is always prepared; let him be inoculated by the master; it will choose the moment better than we would" (*E* 131).[42] Earlier in *Emile*, Rousseau has rejected most of medicine, except hygiene, because it teaches us to be afraid of death and to resist nature. Conquering the fear of death is among Rousseau's chief objectives in the book.

Burke is, of course, perfectly aware of the dangers of false diagnoses and of the willingness of quack doctors to treat hypochondriacs. One of his favorite French authors, Molière, had a great deal to say on this subject, and Burke alludes to the *Malade imaginaire* both in the *Reflections* and in the *Regicide Peace*.[43] In the latter of these two references, Burke compares his opponents to the quack doctor for whom each worsening of the "public malady" is a "happy prognostic of recovery." Elsewhere in the *Reflections* he imagines his antagonists prescribing two inappropriate drugs, an aphrodisiac to stimulate the British love of liberty, and mercury sublimate, the dangerous cure for syphilis: "I confess to you, Sir, I never liked this continual talk of resistance and revolution, or the practice of making the extreme medicine of the constitution its daily bread" (*Refl.* 154).

It is worth noting that these two images take seriously the Rousseauvian association of politics, sexual desire, and the sublime. (Here, the sublime is aroused by the powerful fears of self-preservation produced by the Revolution.) But far from having sublimated the passions of the sublime in acts of compassion, as Rousseau wished Emile and Sophie to do, politics serves Burke's antagonists as an aphrodisiac and source of venereal disease.

These images also show that Burke is aware of the possible abuses of the medical arts. He is nonetheless capable of using medical imagery in a positive vein as well. To Burke, the proper use of medical arts can represent the natural and reasonable application of artifice to human affairs. "Cast your eyes on the journals of parliament," he urges in his *Speech on Parliamentary Reform* [1782]: "It is for fear of losing the inestimable treasure we have, that I do not venture to game it out my hands for the vain hope of improving it. I look with filial reverence on the constitution of my country, and never will cut it in pieces, and put it into the kettle of any magician, in order to boil it, with the puddle of their compounds, into youth and vigour. On the contrary, I will drive away all such pretenders; I will nurse its venerable age, and with lenient arts extend a parent's breath."[44] In this excerpt, Burke not only gives himself the role of physician to the British body politic, he associates himself with both Alexander Pope and Dr. Arbuthnot (in Arbuthnot's capacity as the queen's physician) by paraphrasing line 410 from Pope's "Epistle to Dr. Arbuthnot": "With lenient Arts extend a Mother's breath."[45]

Even though the image above has to do with medicine, it also includes the constitution and the family. The patient is a parent. The medical arts are "lenient" ones, which is to say palliative or mitigating, to use Johnson's synonyms for "lenient" and related words in his 1755 *Dictionary*. Burke fears death in this passage not because of pain or even personal loss but because (in his "philosophic analogy") it threatens the "inestimable treasure" represented by the inherited constitution, here imagined as a parent. Burke alludes to the same myth of Medea in the *Reflections*: "[Man] should approach to the faults of the state as to the wounds of a father . . . [rather than] rashly to hack that aged parent in pieces" (*Refl.* 194).

Deconstructing the Revolution

In summary, Burke's implicit critique is that everything favored by Rousseau and his revolutionary cult turns rapidly into its opposite.[46] I do not believe Burke would have been surprised that deconstruction has found in Rousseau so fertile a ground for its initial experiments. As Steven Blakemore has shown, Burke himself was aware of the infinite flexibility of language, once the "cosmic ordering of the Logos" is assaulted.[47]

By beginning with desire as the fundamental characteristic of man, language emerges (for Rousseau) as a substitution for tears, and writing (as Derrida says of Rousseau's theory) as "destruction of presence and as disease of speech."[48] The deconstructionists' belief in the arbitrariness of language, as evidenced in Rousseau, would have been perfectly understandable to Burke. Nor would Burke be surprised at the other, antithetical tendencies in Rousseau. Both gratitude and compassion, in *Emile*, are founded on self-interest. Sexual passion is now an instrument for dividing families, now a means to complete one's political education. Burke himself sees that, among the cult followers of Rousseau, compassion for the historical figures of the past or the bourgeois turns rapidly into contempt. Gratitude, valued so highly in *Emile*, turns rapidly into ingratitude. Burke went so far as to call ingratitude the revolutionaries' "four cardinal virtues compacted and amalgamated into one" (*LNL* 138). Rousseau's most hated vice—vanity, or deformed *amour-propre*—turns into his very guide, in the judgment of Burke: "With this vice he was possessed to a degree little short of madness" (*LM* 536). According to Burke, the *douce humanité*, which Emile's compassion should produce, turns into the savage massacres and confiscations of the Revolution.[49] *Lèse majesté* turns into *lèse humanité*. The revolutionaries' emphasis on following nature ends up requiring the most artificial laws, religious rites, and even geographical divisions.

Burke seems to imply that if the world really is founded on desire, as Rousseau believed, the deconstructionists are right—both about Rousseau and about literature in general. Burke did indeed write "a revolutionary book against the Revolution."[50]

All understanding involves a faith commitment—a commitment to some experience, usually to a "revelation" that explains all other experiences. For Rousseau, the experience of nature above all other social relations and culture has this function. *Emile* ambitiously works out Rousseau's innovative faith. By contrast, Burke's mind works by synthesizing and balancing opposites, sympathizing with past narratives and characters, and finding their relevance for contemporary life. Rousseau's project entails rethinking the very foundations of philosophy. It is both more exciting and original, in the most obvious respects, than Burke's. Burke's political thought was intensely practical and occasional, requiring the practical intelligence to approach actual circumstances in principled yet prudent ways.[51]

Rousseau's thought releases the most powerful of human desires by incorporating the sublime into politics. Burke engages the deep sympathies, incorporating the beautiful. For Rousseau, sexual maturity marks the end of Emile's education and his arrival on the scene as a citizen. For Burke, political education is a continual process, through the seasons of growth, decay, and renovation. Rousseau attempts to draw out the potential of the young soul, away from the prejudices and customs of society. Burke believes that individuals achieve their humanity only within their particular, inherited traditions, including social customs, manners, narratives, and even prejudices, which on balance are useful in shaping and extending human sympathies. Their different views point to two different possibilities for instructing the imagination in morality. The revolutionary men and women who were inspired by the persona of Rousseau and by *La Nouvelle Héloïse* and *Emile* may not have cared about *The Social Contract*. But perhaps they, and Burke, were closer to understanding the true spirit of Rousseau.

Notes

1. Edmund Burke, *A Letter to a Member of the National Assembly* [1791] (hereafter cited as *LM*), in *The Works of the Right Honourable Edmund Burke*, 9 vols. (London: Henry G. Bohn, 1854–62) 2: 535–37 (hereafter cited as *Works*). Since he was prohibited from living in France or Geneva, Rousseau left Paris with David Hume, at Hume's invitation, and sailed for England on 4 Jan. 1766. Frank Brady and Frederick A. Pottle suggest that opposition rose against Rousseau

throughout the preceding year, in part because of growing rumors (to which Burke alludes) of his having fathered five illegitimate children whom he deposited in a foundling hospital. Rousseau's highly publicized stay in England (until May 1767), especially his quarrel with Hume, left an impression of madness, vanity, and ungratefulness among many English people. Burke's *Correspondence*, however, does not record any contemporary impressions of Rousseau. Rousseau's mistress, Thérèse, followed him to England in Feb. 1766, escorted by James Boswell, who seduced her during what the editors of his journal call "their leisurely crossing from Paris to London." See Brady and Pottle, *Boswell on the Grand Tour* (New York: McGraw-Hill, 1955) 259, 277. See also Edward Duffy, *Rousseau in England* (Berkeley: U of California P, 1979) 23–31.

2. Edmund Burke, *The Correspondence of Edmund Burke*, ed. Thomas W. Copeland et al., 10 vols. (Cambridge: Cambridge UP; Chicago: U of Chicago P, 1958–78) 6: 81.

3. Joan McDonald, *Rousseau and the French Revolution, 1762–1791* (London: Athlone P, 1965) 44–46, 161–62.

4. McDonald 161–62.

5. Edmund Burke, *Letter to a Noble Lord* (hereafter cited as *LNL*), in *Works* 5: 111.

6. McDonald 49, 52. McDonald also notes (52) that the numerous *éloges* to the memory of Rousseau, written between 1788 and 1791, refer mostly to *Emile*, *La Nouvelle Héloïse*, and the first and second *Discourses*—not to *The Social Contract* or other political writings. Many of the comparisons of Burke and Rousseau have excellent discussions of their political ideas (notably Cameron), but few mention the issues of imagination and education that appear in *Emile* and *La Nouvelle Héloïse*, as I propose to do.

7. Allan Bloom, Introduction to *Emile, or On Education*, by Jean-Jacques Rousseau (New York: Basic, 1979) 4 (hereafter cited as *E*).

8. The political implications of Burke's association of the beautiful with politics have been explored by Frans De Bruyn, "Edmund Burke's Aesthetic Politics: The Relation Between His Aesthetic Theory and His Political Writings" (Ph.D. diss., U of Virginia, 1982).

9. Werner Dannhauser, "Religion and the Conservatives," *Commentary*, Dec. 1985: 51–5.

10. For the reference to Plato's philosophy of love, see Rousseau's second note to Letter II in part 2 of *La Nouvelle Héloïse* in the translation and abridgment by Judith H. McDowell (University Park: Pennsylvania State UP, 1968), 191 (hereafter cited as *NH*, where Roman numerals refer to part, and letter divisions and Arabic numerals refer to pages in the McDowell translation). For the argument that *Emile* is a rereading of Plato's *Republic*, see *E* 40, and Bloom, Introduction, 4, 12.

11. Duffy writes of Burke's "rather far-fetched congruity between [Rous-

seau] and the Revolution" (*Rousseau in England* 30). Raymond Williams says that the confutation of Burke on the French Revolution is a mere "one-finger exercise" (*Culture and Society* [New York: Columbia UP, 1958] 4).

12. Hazlitt's references to Burke are many and various. I have collected them in "Edmund Burke's Nineteenth-Century Literary Significance in England" (Ph.D. diss., Rutgers U, 1985), chap. 3. Interestingly, Hazlitt remarks Rousseau's resistance to the "moral uses of the imagination" in order to contrast him, in that respect, to Burke. See "On Reason and Imagination" in Hazlitt's *Plain Speaker,* in *The Complete Works of William Hazlitt,* 21 vols. (London: Dent, 1930–34) 12: 52–53. Burke writes often about the imaginative function of sympathy in his *Philosophical Enquiry into the Origin of Our Ideas of the Sublime and Beautiful* (2d ed., 1759), ed. James T. Boulton (London: Routledge and Kegan Paul, 1958); see esp. V.vii, "How Words Influence the Passions."

13. Edmund Burke, *Letters on a Regicide Peace* (hereafter cited as *Regicide Peace*), in *Works* 5: 213, Letter 1.

14. Alasdair MacIntyre, *After Virtue,* 2d ed. (Notre Dame: U of Notre Dame P, 1984) 211–12.

15. "Such a reminder is almost a rebuke" (Edmund Burke, *Reflections on the Revolution in France* [1790], ed. Conor Cruise O'Brien [Harmondsworth: Penguin, 1968] 114, 381 n. 23 [hereafter cited as *Refl.*]).

16. Irving Babbitt, "Burke and the Moral Imagination," *Democracy and Leadership* (Boston: Houghton Mifflin, 1924) 103–104.

17. The context for this quotation is Emile's awakening sexual desire. Jean-Jacques warns against the images that become "more seductive than the objects themselves," culminating in his famous admonition against "this dangerous supplement" of masturbation. Cf. Bloom, Introduction, 7.

18. See also Bloom's notes to this passage on 484–85 n. 34–37.

19. Burke's review quotes three passages from *Emile.* The corresponding quotations may be found in Bloom's translation: the first, on 92–96 (beginning with "All the instruments" and ending with" should feel himself subjected"); the second, which includes the critique of literature, on 167–69 (beginning with "To the activity" and ending with the final word, "cosmography"); the third, on 386–89 (beginning with "I have already said" and ending with "of our institutions"). The substance of this review (minus the quotations) is reprinted in Peter J. Stanlis, *Edmund Burke: Selected Writings and Speeches* (Chicago: Regnery-Gateway, 1963), along with the 1759 review of the *Lettre à d'Alembert sur les spectacles* (see Stanlis 89, 94–95). Burke's review of the earlier work censures Rousseau for unsettling "our notions of right and wrong, [which will] lead by degrees to universal scepticism." While he commends certain parts of *Emile,* he sees very clearly that it proposes a revolutionary new system of education. "To know what the received notions are upon any subject, is to know

with certainty what those of Rousseau are not. . . . In this system of education there are some very considerable parts that are impracticable, others that are chimerical; and not a few highly blameable, and dangerous both to piety and morals." Four years after the review of *Emile*, Rousseau came to England, when (as noted above) Burke says he knew "his proceedings almost from day to day" (*LM* 536).

20. When quoting from a selection that appears in Burke's review, I have quoted the translation used by Burke. This one corresponds to *E* 167.

21. Quoted by Burke; corresponds to *E* 169.

22. Jacques Derrida, *Of Grammatology*, trans. Gayatri Chakravorty Spivak (Baltimore: Johns Hopkins UP, 1976) 2.2.

23. Similarly, in *NH* (I.xii, 49), it is noteworthy that in his role as Julie's tutor, Saint-Preux consults, rather than shapes, the taste of his student and beloved. It is she—or rather, it is her love—that is the true teacher. Cf. *NH* I.xxi.

24. Bloom, Introduction, 18–19.

25. Rousseau's note to *E* 235 (my emphasis).

26. Burke, *Philosophical Enquiry* I.xiv, 45–46.

27. She is first named on 329. Rousseau waits until the last possible moment to introduce a sexually appealing image. On 320, he had temporarily succeeded in sublimating Emile's desires in the sport of hunting.

28. It is significant that at this moment Rousseau leaves off speaking of Emile altogether and (through the end of book 4) describes his personal utopia. He is a citizen of the world, attached to no particular city, fully prepared (in his own estimation) to live in society, as promised on 327.

29. Cf. *E* 323, where figurative language is also seen as a supplement to truth.

30. Bloom, Introduction, 20–22. The confession of the Savoyard Vicar ends on *E* 313, sixteen pages before Sophie is introduced. Bloom points to *E* 426 (book 5) for the sublimation of sexual longing in love for God.

31. Burke, *Philosophical Enquiry* I.x, 42.

32. Burke derives beauty from the social passions at *Philosophical Enquiry* I.x, 40. He describes beauty at length in part III of the *Philosophical Enquiry*, recapitulating his remarks at III.xviii, 117.

33. Peter J. Stanlis gave this interpretation to Burke's words on chivalry at the conference entitled "Edmund Burke's Significance in the Twentieth Century," Liberty Fund, Chicago, 21 May 1988.

34. Of course chivalry itself may be looked upon as a way of sublimating the powerful sexual passions into courtly love and knightly service. There is the chivalry of Gottfried's Tristan, which is emphatically sexual in origin. By contrast, however, there is the chivalry of Gottfried's contemporary and rival, the author of the *Queste del Saint Graal*, in which courtly love is rejected for the quest of the Holy Grail. Burke is clearly aware of the sexual element in chivalry,

as his reference here to Marie Antoinette suggests. But I doubt he would have considered chivalry explainable, ultimately and essentially, in sexual terms.

35. Paul Fussell, *The Rhetorical World of Augustan Humanism* (Oxford: Clarendon, 1965) 204–32.

36. Edmund Burke, *An Appeal from the New to the Old Whigs*, in *Works* 3: 86.

37. Edmund Burke, *Present Discontents* (1770), in *Works* 1: 373.

38. Burke, *An Appeal* 79.

39. *LNL* 141. It is strange that Burke does not refer (so far as I am aware) to the removal of the Jesuits from French colleges, beginning in 1762, and their expulsion from the country in 1764. One would think that Burke would emphasize the fact that education in French colleges was performed by the clergy until the Revolution. See R. R. Palmer, *The School of the French Revolution* (Princeton: Princeton UP, 1975) 14, 22.

40. *LNL* 138.

41. "We wished at the period of the Revolution [of 1688], and do now wish, to derive all we possess as *an inheritance from our forefathers*. Upon that body and stock of inheritance we have taken care not to inoculate any [scion] alien to the nature of the original plant" (*Refl.* 117; Burke's emphasis).

42. Nature is also called "the master," with regard to the visual arts, on 144 and 341. Rousseau's earlier rejection of medicine occurs on 54–56.

43. *Refl.* 360; *Regicide Peace* 370, Letter 4.

44. Edmund Burke, *Speech on Parliamentary Reform*, in *Works* 6: 153. This mythological image is also used in *Refl.* 194. E. J. Payne notes that the image had been used previously in at least two other political contexts, Thomas Hobbes's *De corpore politico* 2.8 and (applied to Cromwell) in Abraham Cowley's "Essay on the Government of Oliver Cromwell." See E. J. Payne, *Burke: Select Works*, 3 vols. (Oxford: Clarendon, 1874–78) 2:350.

45. I owe this suggestion to David Venturo of the University of Cincinnati. Pope mentions Arbuthnot's attendance on Queen Anne in line 417 of the poem.

46. In *Rousseau and the Republic of Virtue* (Ithaca: Cornell UP, 1986), Carol Blum makes related points throughout her book. For instance, on p. 87 she notes that "pity" for Rousseau is a "blending of sensual pleasure and enhanced self esteem." On p. 94, quoting Jean Starobinski, she remarks that for Rousseau, "'the certitude of personal innocence is inseparable from a no less unshakable faith in the guilt of others.'"

47. Steven Blakemore, "Burke and the Fall of Language: The French Revolution as Linguistic Event," *Eighteenth-Century Studies* 17 (Spring 1984): 306.

48. Derrida, *Of Grammatology* 142.

49. *E* 252; *LNL* 140. To these inversions, I would add that the purely "natural" education of Emile turns into a utilitarian one, taking Robinson Crusoe for its guide. (Rousseau reads Defoe's novel without regard to its fictional struc-

tures.) Emile must continually be motivated by his interest in a subject, which becomes a more and more utilitarian one as the book progresses.

50. Novalis, quoted in Gerald Chapman, *Edmund Burke: The Practical Imagination* (Cambridge: Harvard UP, 1967) 3.

51. One can imagine Burke's reaction to the education of Maria Edgeworth's brother, Richard, which was modeled on *Emile*. According to Marilyn Gaull, Edgeworth never acquired enough basic information about history, languages, aesthetics, and Western civilization to function in his world. Thomas Malthus was also educated on this pattern. One can judge for oneself whether Malthus became a model lover of humanity. On the other hand, Thomas Day tried to educate two female foundlings, whom he named Lucretia and Sabrina, after the model of Sophie. "They quarreled constantly and contracted smallpox. After the first year, Lucretia was sent to London, . . . and Sabrina became the sole object of his attention. Failing to develop her tolerance for pain and discomfort by dropping hot sealing wax on her arm or firing off pistols by her ear, he turned her over to Anna Seward" (*English Romanticism: The Human Context* [New York: Norton, 1988] 54–55). R. R. Palmer states that *Emile* had little direct influence on organized education in France (*The School of the French Revolution* [Princeton: Princeton UP, 1975] 22).

SIX

Burke and the Revolution: Bicentennial Reflections

Steven Blakemore

When Edmund Burke responded to the French Revolution two hundred years ago, he initiated an intellectual counterrevolution; the subsequent attacks on and reaffirmations of his position now constitute a fundamental part of the continuous debate about the Revolution's significance. Because the French Revolution was a supreme political event, how one views Burke often corresponds to how one views the Revolution. Many opposed to Burke have seen him as the stereotypical reactionary—the apologist for Europe's privileged elite and its oppressive orders: Burke feared the French Revolution because he was inbred within the old order's political culture and was opposed to the necessary transformations of eighteenth-century society.

This characterization poses some problems, however. To begin with, Burke was not an antirevolutionary per se: he defended a people's right to revolution, albeit as a last resort, when possibilities were exhausted and reformation circumvented. Because he believed reformation was essential to a resilient political order, he also believed that oppressive tyrannies were unreformable.

In addition, Burke was, throughout his life, a consistent opponent of oppression in its multitudinous forms, and he was a consistent defender of the oppressed. An Irishman of modest means and background, he suffered ridicule and discrimination in England—a biographical detail some have connected to his passionate defense of powerless people.[1] His generosity toward the poor is still proverbial in Beaconsfield, where an anecdote still circulates about his cook's complaint that Burke had given the evening meal (a side of beef) to a hungry man.[2] In England, he defended the right of religious dissenters to practice their own religion privately (not, however, those he believed were trying to subvert the English constitution), and he defended homosexuals from social persecution (they could be prosecuted and pilloried). In addition, he espoused the mitigation of the laws sanctioning life imprisonment for debt, and he drew up a plan for the eventual abolishment of the slave trade (which he envisioned taking place in 1800). In the House of Commons, he worked to limit royal patronage and court influence.

He also supported the Americans in their remonstrations against exorbitant British interference (in an effort to keep America in the British colonial orbit), and he opposed Protestant oppression of Catholics in Ireland and the exploitation of the people of India by the East India Company. None of these was a popular position identified with the status quo; in fact, if Burke had not opposed the French Revolution, he would likely be remembered as "progressive" by many who have subsequently discovered a Tory Burke disguised in Whig clothing.

On the other hand, Burke has been canonized by many of his hagiographers, who envision him as the reproachless knight of the Western world engaged in apocalyptic battle against the forces of darkness and evil. Both caricatures, however—of a reactionary Burke and of Burke as Saint Edmund—contain an ironic half-truth. Burke was generous, brilliant, and brave; and he was also an elitist who believed in a political order based on a limited constitutional monarchy, primogeniture, and a restrictive class suffrage. Even in the eighteenth century, this political order appeared to many to be both antiquated and reactionary. That Burke seems to mean so many different things to so many people is problematically complex. Today Burkean criticism is exploring this complexity by deconstructing the apparent contradictions of his thought, for, in many ways, Burke's contradictions have always been a central focus for those interested in his critique of the French Revolution.

In his own time, for instance, Burke was accused of contradicting his own principles: how could the defender of the oppressed in India and Ireland—the supporter of the Americans—how could this "progressive" Burke not also defend the French in their struggle against ancient, oppressive forces? Burke insisted, of course, that his opposition to the French Revolution was consistent with everything he had thought or done in the past, and thus to understand his resistance to the Revolution, we need to reconstruct how Burke envisioned and experienced the eighteenth-century European world that the Revolution was transforming.

I

To Burke, this prerevolutionary world was a prescriptive, traditional world of European Christian commonwealths connected by a common system of manners, sentiments, and beliefs—all reinforced by a shared language of ideas. In *Reflections on the Revolution in France*, he refers to "the patrimony of knowledge" bequeathed "by our forefathers,"[3] and in the first of the letters in *Letters on a Regicide Peace*, he notes that the Christian nations and their peoples are tied together by correspondences in "law, customs, manners, and habits of life."[4] These prescriptive powers transcend the "force of treaties," for "men are not tied to one another by papers and seals" but rather by "obligations written in the heart" (*Reg.* 5: 317). In this context, Burke traces the links of a collective and coherent European order to "the similitude throughout Europe of religion, laws, and manners" (*Reg.* 5: 318)—"the whole of the polity and economy of every country in Europe has been derived from the same sources": Roman civil law, the Christian religion, and Teutonic customs and manners (*Reg.* 5: 319).[5] From all these sources "arose a system of manners and education which was nearly similar in all this quarter of the globe," where "no citizen of Europe could be altogether an exile in any part of it" (*Reg.* 5: 319). Burke believed this prerevolutionary world still existed where the Revolution was contained, and it was precisely this "order of things long established in Europe" that he intended to die in.[6]

Europe hence consisted of a series of social, political, and moral "links," and it was this collective inherited order, an order Burke believed was constituted by God, that the Revolution threatened to destroy (*Reg.* 5: 320). Since France was a constituted "part" of Europe— a fundamental link in the Christian commonwealth—the Revolution threatened the entire communal, collective order of Europe as Burke envisioned it. Burke's defense of this traditional order is therefore not tied to a specific country or regime but to the entire inherited social, political, and moral order of Christian Europe. He contended in Letter 2 that the counterrevolutionary war was not really against France; it was against a fanatical faction within France: "It is a war between the partisans of the ancient civil, moral, and political order of Europe" and a fanatical sect "aiming at universal empire . . . beginning with the conquest of France" (*Reg.* 5: 345–46). He argues that the Revolution is not a revolution of an entire people but one controlled by a militant minority intending to overthrow the entire European order.[7] Burke was the first to argue that the Revolution was not an isolated or limited phenomenon—it was a "schism" within "the whole universe"—a schism that "extended to almost everything, great and small" (*Reg.* 5: 320). As J. M. Roberts notes, "Burke, before anyone else, gave the Revolution its full weight as an event in the history of civilization."[8]

Burke's defense of Europe's orthodox order also corresponded with his defense of Europe's traditional constitutions. Because he saw the established European state as an "archetype" consecrated by God (*Refl.* 361), any revolutionary attacks on the constituted order of Europe entailed, for him, a cosmic assault on God's ontological order. The ancient constitutions were part of this order, consisting of the specific "parts" that made each country what it is. In France, for instance, the ancient constitution consisted of the traditional orders that comprised the States General: the monarchy, church, nobles, and the Third Estate. In England, this generally corresponded to the monarchy and the British Parliament. Complementing his vision of a united European order, Burke contended that Europe's ancient constitutional orders comprised an essential part of the coherent European commonwealth. Indeed, each constitution was part of the entailed inheritance bequeathed by previous generations to the collective, communal order. A country's constitution had its roots in a prewritten past—the subsequent documents, charters, and "written" constitutions merely reaffirmed the traditional inherited order—the past out of which the present and future flowed.

But as the Revolution threatened Europe's traditional orders, Burke's vision of the ancient constitution expanded to include all the "parts" that constitute a country. He envisioned the ancient constitution as an analogue of Christ's *corpus mysticum*: just as the church is the mystical body of Christ, uniting all the church's transitory parts into one eternal whole, so each European state consists of its perishable members temporally united through the inherited constitutional order that perpetuates each member's legacy to the country and hence to the European commonwealth.[9] This explains why Burke, as early as 1790, was proclaiming that the French Revolution constituted a radical, antihistorical threat to European civilization. He saw the Revolution as attacking European heritage rather than a particular regime. Thus while Burke was not uncritical of France's Old Regime and while he recognized that the monarchy had to be reformed—the state finances had to be reordered, and "feudal" vestiges had to be abolished—he saw the changes instituted by the Revolution not as a reformation but as a radical transformation of France's historical reality.[10] Given his vision of an inherited, interconnected European order, Burke reacted consistently with alarm when any "reformable" part of the European body politic was radically transformed, since he felt the entire European order imperiled when any of its parts was changed. Burke's vision of a "prelapsarian" Europe was not, of course, historically "true," although (and this was probably more important to his European audience) it was mythically "true." He did, however, understand that the revolutionaries intended something more than a mere numerical change in the Third Estate.[11]

On another level, Burke envisioned the prerevolutionary world in terms of the Chain of Being—an image that permeates his writings. He had, of course, a hierarchic understanding of the world in which "parts" are again linked to each other in an ascending chain of subordination and meaning. Each person, for instance, had a place—an ontological link that established his historical being, providing him his social and political identity—his cumulative moral meaning in the chain of existence.[12] Thus, to pursue the metaphor, while the lower links were subordinate to higher links of being—including social and political being—each link complemented the rest: each simultaneously supported and depended on the others. To the rejoinder that this hierarchic vision of the world enabled the powerful to rationalize the *theodicy*, by which the "haves" could keep the "have nots" in their assigned place—Burke believed, first, that the European order was not inherently oppressive—it was a resilient, reformable order, as witness the very reforms Louis XVI was instituting; second, he believed that it was precisely European man's link to his entailed history that crystallized his social, political, and moral identity, liberating him to be who he really was within a cumulative chain of meaning. Without a historical identity within a legitimate ontological order, "man" was an empty abstraction—an abstraction stripped of *history,* of any meaningful relation to reality. In Burke's thinking, the hierarchic links lead man from his "littlest platoon"—his family and place in his community—to his larger place in his country, uniting him with the connecting links of European civilization and ultimately with the Logos. He believed that attachment to our littlest platoon connects us to larger battalions of existence, uniting us with all that makes us fully human.

It follows, then, that an attack on any "link" threatened the entire chain of meaning—an attack that Burke sees the Revolution initiating. In his *Speech on Army Estimates* (1790), he contends that the Revolution transforms everything to "one incongruous, ill connected mass," breaking "all those connections, natural and civil, that regulate and hold together the community by a chain of subordination."[13] The Revolution's endeavor to abolish the past, extirpating the links uniting the generations, creates a radically antihistorical hatred of historical existence. It denies civilization its cumulative essence, destroying the historical process by which a civilization is perpetuated and passed down to future generations. Thus the revolutionaries' delight in "changing the state," according to innumerable "floating fancies or fashions," ensures that "the whole chain and continuity of the commonwealth" is broken and that "no one generation" is linked "with the other" (*Refl.* 357).

Likewise, since the nobility "forms the chain that connects the ages of a nation," oedipal sons who betray their family heritage break "to pieces a great link of society."[14] Thus to Burke, English supporters of the French Revolution attempt to sever the connecting parts of the British constitution by attacking the House of Commons—"that link which connects both the other parts of the Constitution (the Crown and the Lords) *with the mass of the people,* it is to that link . . . that their attacks are directed."[15] In France the revolutionaries "destroyed the principle of obedience in the great essential critical link between the officer and soldier, just where the chain of military subordination commences, and on which the whole of that system depends" (*Refl.* 525). In short, Burke contends that the Revolution destroyed a chain of historical being that had sustained a coherent world order.

Burke undoubtedly romanticized the idea of a communal European commonwealth united through its common links, and while he begs the question by assuming that the poor, for instance, are "naturally" consoled by their "place" in a hierarchic European world, it is the vision of this world and its inclusive, supportive links that he posits against a divisive revolutionary power threatening to sunder Europe.

II

Having posited the prerevolutionary world, Burke is essentially interested in how the antagonistic revolutionary world came into being, and he provides a series of interconnected explanations. First, there was the fallen nature of man, and Burke's depiction of the Revolution is a voluminous catalog of arrogance, vanity, cruelty, and greed.[16] These vices had always existed of course, but Burke contends that the civilized restraints of Christianity and chivalry had held them in check, containing them with the "decent drapery" that clothed man's naked, fallen nature. But by the eighteenth century, the comprehensive political and moral order of Europe was being challenged and rejected, and the result was, for Burke, a second Fall, by which man lost his protective innocence (the sustaining belief in this entailed order). Consequently, European man, like Adam, was suddenly conscious of his existential nakedness and exposed to the Revolution's pernicious disorders. To Burke, the Revolution is a new force empowered by old ideas, and he documents the triumphant emergence of ancient, erroneous ideas (formerly rejected or contained), and hence he traces the Revolution's pedigree to the "illegitimate" origins and sources of a discredited past.

In this context, Burke explored the intellectual origins of the French Revolution and advanced the thesis that many ideas of the Enlightenment (various of which predated it) had a contributory connection to the Revolution's success. By this he did not mean that these erroneous ideas about the nature of man and society solely caused the Revolution but that they had made the Revolution possible. Specifically, to Burke, this meant the debilitating attack on Christianity, the pernicious questioning of established principles and legitimate authority, and the subversive corruption of the traditional manners and sentiments of Europe. Burke believed that these ideas were intentionally aimed at the inherited structures of Europe; he believed that the Enlightenment had infected the European mind. Thus while he was aware of the many contradictory differences between, for instance, the philosophes, he also argued that they had engaged in a concerted attack against their common enemy:

the traditional institutions and values of filiopietistic Europe. As early as *A Vindication of Natural Society* (1756), Burke had satirized certain Enlightenment ideas by parodying its vocabulary. By the time of the Revolution, he refers to the adulatory use of *enlightened* in new revolutionary dictionaries, and he sarcastically refers to "the solid darkness of this enlightened age" (*Refl.* 487, 554).[17] Although Burke shared some ideas of the Enlightenment, he believed its aggressive assault on Christianity and tradition reified itself in the Revolution.

Referring to the "October Days" (October 5 and 6) of 1789, he laments the "revolution in sentiments, manners, and moral opinions," and he continues to argue that the Revolution is primarily an ideological assault on Christian Europe (*Refl.* 337). In *Letters on a Regicide Peace*, he refers to a "silent revolution in the moral world that preceded the political, and prepared it" (*Reg.* 5: 379, Letter 1). Hence, like John Adams and Thomas Paine, Burke argued that a revolution is generally preceded by a revolution in thinking which makes the physical revolution possible. In contrast to Marx, Burke believed that ideas initially transform the "material base."[18]

Once the revolution in ideas began changing the way people thought about themselves and society, the new monied bourgeois, according to Burke, began to expand ambitiously. No longer content with their place in society and enviously coveting the honors and distinctions of the Second Estate, they began collaborating with political men of letters and the popular press to undermine further the traditional order.[19] It is this crucial nexus between the new monied class, men of letters, and "above all, the press, of which they had in a manner entire possession" that created a "kind of electric communication everywhere," resulting in a subversive monopoly of public discourse (*Reg.* 5: 380).[20]

In his *Letter to William Elliot* (1795), Burke reviewed the origins of the French Revolution, which he cast in a series of chronological stages. First, a general state of prosperity caused "laxity and debility" in the aristocracy and court, while it created ambition and conspiracy in the Third Estate. Second, Enlightenment ideas, "a false philosophy," passed from the academies into the courts and salons, infecting "the great themselves" with theories that contained the seeds of the nobility's destruction.[21] Third, there was a consequential epistemological revolution as knowledge was "diffused, weakened, and perverted." Burke then summarizes this chronological process with generic details: general wealth "loosened morals, relaxed vigilance, and increased presumption." Ambitious "men of talent" decided that they deserved more power and prosperity, and once the revolutionaries discovered that a "struggle between establishment and rapacity" could be maintained—"a practicable breach was made in the whole order of things, and in every country."[22] The result was the subversion of France's traditional value system: religion, ideas, and prescriptive prejudices. Property and patrimony were left undefended, and traditional authority had neither the will nor the force to defend itself.[23] Burke reviews the origins of the Revolution, passing from its precursors to its effects—all generated, according to him, from an astonishing revolution in ideas and sentiments.

In his *Letters on a Regicide Peace*, Burke again turned from origins to the essential components of the Revolution. In Letter 1 he contends that the Revolution has three fundamental bases: *Regicide*—the revolutionary axiom that all nondemocratic governments are ipso facto despotic and that consequently kings and their families should be murdered; *Jacobinism*—"the revolt of the enterprising talents of a country against its property," by which individuals form associations and conspire to destroy the country's prescriptive laws and institutions, securing "themselves an army" by dividing expropriated estates "amongst the people of no property," and creating the conditions of class war by legalizing class robbery;[24] *Atheism*—the denial of God, the abolishment of the Christian religion, and the persecution of its ministers, replacing both with a state religion of Reason and a state education system that indoctrinates the young with the false knowledge the Revolution promotes (*Reg.* 5: 308–10).[25] Burke's analysis of the Revolution's bases corresponds to its attack on the monarchy and the first and second estates of the ancient constitution. It is, at the same time, a reductive caricature of the Revolution's complexity.

Finally, Burke contends that the revolutionaries corrupt "the *correspondent system of manners*," which, according to him, "vex or sooth, corrupt or purify, exalt or debase, barbarize or refine us" (*Reg.* 5: 310). The traditional modes of behavior are denigrated and replaced with "a system of manners, the most licentious, prostitute, and abandoned that ever has been known, and at the same time the most coarse, rude, savage, and ferocious" (*Reg.* 5: 310–11).[26] Moreover, the revolutionaries have systematically institutionalized this corruption: "Nothing in the

Revolution, no, not to a phrase or a gesture, not to the fashion of a hat or shoe, was left to accident. All has been the result of design; all has been matter of institution" (*Reg.* 5: 310–11). Patriotism, for instance, is debased into hysterical exhibitions of state loyalty, as family members denounce each other for betraying the *patrie* (*Reg.* 5: 311). Burke, in effect, comes full circle in his analysis of the Revolution, for the traditional manners are based on prescriptive ways of thinking and feeling, and their subversion is a continuation of the Revolution's systematic assault on the French mind. In the end, Burke's conspiratorial theory of the Revolution is, at points, perceptive, yet ultimately unhistorical, for like many of the revolutionaries, he often turns revisionist history into political demonology.

III

Because Burke did not oppose revolution per se, his opposition to the French Revolution emanated from two premises: first, the French constitution was reformable and hence the Revolution unjustifiable; second, the Revolution was an unprecedented event in the history of Western civilization—a "complete revolution" extending to the mind of man.[27] Burke's analyses hence comprise a series of interlocking moral, social, political, epistemological, and linguistic critiques. First, and this is a continuation of his critique of the Enlightenment, he sees the Revolution as a hostile ideological invasion incarnated in sinister books and pamphlets deluging Europe. He contends that in France the Revolution reinforced ideological conformity by monopolizing the media and by indoctrinating the French people with incessant repetitions of revolutionary ideology—a contention ironically reminiscent (for the modern reader) of Marx's *The German Ideology*. Burke opposed this by waging a new Battle of Books, opposing the "wisdom" of the ancients to the "folly" of the revolutionaries. In both the revolutionary and counter-revolutionary writing of the time, there is a resonant intertextual context: both respond frequently to a correspondent antitext.

Burke, for instance, responds critically to a series of dissident anti-texts, starting with Richard Price's *Discourse on the Love of Our Country* (1789)—which initially provoked his response in the *Reflections*.[28] Like-wise, he attacks the subversive books circulated by the Constitutional Society as well as a cluster of erroneous books from the past, read only

by English radicals engaged in intellectual incest and mutual quotation
(*Refl.* 236–37, 344, 349).[29] In France, the National Assembly turns out
adulterated decrees like *assignats,* and the country is consequently del-
uged with devalued words: "They renew decrees and proclamations as
they experience their insufficiency, and they multiply oaths in propor-
tion as they weaken in the minds of men the sanctions of religion." Burke
sees a nexus between pernicious ideas and physical consequences, since
he has "no doubt" the French army is supplied the "sermons of Voltaire, d'Alembert, Diderot, and Helvétius" and hence it is well supplied
with the "ammunition of pamphlets as of cartridges" (*Refl.* 516–17). In
A Letter to a Member of the National Assembly (1791), he argues that the
"writings of Rousseau lead directly" to much of the "shameful evil" the
Revolution is producing.[30] In *Thoughts on French Affairs* (1791), he denounces defeatist literature and "mutinous manifestoes" circulated by
"emissaries of sedition."[31] In *Observations on the Conduct of the Minority*
(1793), he contends that English supporters of the Revolution "cooper-
ate with the Jacobin army in politics" by circulating "mischievous [see
Dr. Johnson, *Dictionary,* "mischievous," defs. s.v. 1 and 2] writings" at a
time "in which the press has been the grand instrument of the subversion of order, of morals, of religion, and . . . of human society itself."[32]
Burke thus responds to the Revolution as a malignant consequence of
the Enlightenment, and he responds to proliferating revolutionary anti-
texts by highlighting the dominant biblical and classical sources which
eventually establish a semantic space where his world and vision are
brought into presence. But there is only a brief respite in Burke's antirevolutionary oeuvres, for the Revolution impinges continually on his
conscience.

   One of the critical metaphors Burke uses to explain the Revolution's
metaphysical madness is that of the Fall. Thus the infectious spread of
erroneous knowledge constitutes for Burke a new fall into the knowledge of evil, in which revolutionary man becomes obsessed with society's "evil" origins and hence questions all oppositional "tradition."
Burke responds with a critique of the revolutionaries' nihilistic episte-
mology, since, to him, the obsession with discovering evil results in a
pathological paralysis: the revolutionary is constitutionally incapable of
reformation, constitutionally incapable of responding to reality. Hence
he reacts, according to Burke, by destroying everything that does not
correspond to his own fantasies—promoting a self-fulfilling episte-
mology that postulates evil in all that is "other" and posits good in a

world that is imaginary. Thus the revolutionary rationalizes all present revolutionary violence by appeals to a fantasied future that will mysteriously justify it.[33]

This new fall in knowledge corresponds to a new fall in language—a second Babel that transforms the traditional meaning of the European world through a revolution in language. Burke sees the Revolution as, inter alia, an astonishing linguistic event by which the traditional meaning of the European world is "rewritten," affecting man's understanding of himself and society. He contends that as man conceives and experiences the "world" through language, the new linguistic revolution infects both his thinking and perception of reality. Thus the revolutionaries attempt to reduce their country to a metaphoric text that can be scribbled on (*Refl.* 440). Although Burke distrusted the abuses of human language and the confusion of word with thing, he also believed that the "real" meaning of words is an expression of the Logos and that there is a linguistic link between both. He hence stressed the semantic inheritance conserved and transmitted to a posterity engaged in a dialogue with its own past and future. He felt that the Revolution threatened this dialogue by sundering the linguistic links between man and Logos, whether it was through the new revolutionary semantics expressed in Enlightenment and revolutionary ideology or in the new dictionaries produced in France and England in the 1790s.

Burke understood that by changing the traditional meaning of words, the correspondent meaning of the "inherited" world was also changed, and hence he produced a linguistic critique of the Revolution that complemented his epistemological critique. But he was also blinded by his insightful language from seeing that the revolutionary revolt against the traditional patriarchal language was precisely in terms through which the Revolution was being presented: as a liberation from the old oppressive order—the semantic Bastille which psychologically conditioned and imprisoned its victims.[34] He failed to understand the revolutionary critique of the language he defended; he was also, in this sense, a prisoner of his language. But by focusing on distortions and deviations from the traditional meaning of words and ideas and, by extension, the traditional meaning of a coherent European world, he did attempt to reestablish the semantic links between the Old World and its language, for as Burke focused on the meaning of words and world, he attempted to recover that world through the language that made it flesh.

In this context, Burke envisioned "traditional" language as an "en-

tailed inheritance" passed down to posterity, ensuring semantic continuity, conserving the prescriptive meaning that constituted European
patrimony—a patrimony that included the patriarchal structures em-
bodying prescription and primogeniture. Thus when he documents the
Revolution's assault on traditional patriarchal institutions, his defense
of these institutions coincides with his defense of "entailed inheritance"
as a principle of world order. Moreover, both the apologies for and the
attacks on patriarchy were an extension of both Burke and the revolutionaries' war over sources and origins: the revolutionaries attacking
the ancien régime's foundations—its oppressive origins of illegitimate
kings and bastard governments—while Burke and his supporters attack
the illegitimate nature of the revolutionary government. In short, both
sides attacked each other's linguistic sources through an argument of
origins that established a pedigree of legitimacy predating the other's
sources: both sides attempted to legitimize their own "sources" while
they bastardized each other's "origins."

IV

Besides explaining the origins and consequences of the Revolution,
Burke also explored its nature, concluding that the Revolution was
essentially a new form of unprecedented power: "It is not a new power
of an old kind. It is a new power of a new species" (*Reg.* 5: 360). *Power*
is a thematic word, appearing frequently in his antirevolutionary writings, and Burke contended that while the revolutionaries did not initially
understand the nature of power and its physical consequences, they
soon comprehended both completely. For Burke, revolutionary power
was a new species of expansive energy; it was a combination of physical
and ideological forces for oppressive ends. Revolutionary power was
dangerous because it violently distorted the nature of things, turning
the French state into a "tyrannical democracy" (*Refl.* 218), a Catholic
nation into a secular messianic state.[35] To Burke, this new radical power
affected everything, transforming society and the French mind. His
metaphors of fragmentation and chaos depict this new power sundering
the European world—shattering states, splintering men's minds, sev-
ering man's allegiance to the legitimate prescriptive powers of Europe.
It is not only the power of French armies that alarms Burke, it is the
new revolutionary ideology and its power to expunge the past from
men's minds.

According to Burke, mental exertion is a form of power producing many of the institutions (another form of power) that previously benefited society (such as the eleemosynary monastic institutions). The metaphor he uses for both forms of power (the power mentally to conceive and the power physically to create) is "what our workmen call a *purchase*" (*Refl.* 440), that is "a 'hold,' 'fulcrum,' or position of advantage for accomplishing something; a means by which one's power or influence is increased."[36] In this sense, the new revolutionary power destroys not only the institutions but the ideas that produced them and hence destroys a form of power Burke insists was both natural and congenial to the human mind: "To destroy any power, growing wild from the rank productive force of the human mind, is almost tantamount, in the moral world, to the destruction of the apparently active properties of bodies in the material" (*Refl.* 441). Burke equates the mental exertion that conceived the traditional European institutions with a natural physical power, and he suggests that the suppression or annihilation of these ideas is analogously tantamount to the destruction of "the power of steam, or of electricity, or of magnetism" in the physical world (*Refl.* 441). He suggests the Revolution is engaged in the suppression and murder of the seminal ideas that helped create the traditional political order, but he seemingly contradicts his own argument by advocating the suppression or abolition of revolutionary ideas and institutions also "growing wild from the rank productive force of the human mind." Burke is, nevertheless, concerned with identifying the unnatural nature of the revolutionary power that pulverizes the world, splintering the traditional European order.

He maintains that the Revolution is unprecedented in three ways. First, he contends that its power transcends in scope any previous revolution; it is a "total revolution" that radically transforms everything, including the mind of man. Second, the Revolution is aggressively expansionist, intending not only the conquest of France but the conversion of European states into revolutionary clones.[37] The Revolution proliferates by converting ideological force into physical power: French armies pouring into Europe are prepared in advance by revolutionary ideas subverting the soft tissue of European discourse, the traditional but vulnerable values imbuing European thought.[38] The two forms of revolutionary power complement each other, for the Revolution is, above all, a militant, expansionist ideology. It is "a Revolution of doctrine and theoretic dogma," a "philosophical revolution," an aggressive "empire of doctrine"; in short, an "armed doctrine" that assaults with "epidemical fanaticism" the established order of Europe.[39] Burke therefore sees the military battle for Europe as an extension of the ideological battle for European hearts and minds. Third, he contends that the fatal combination of unprecedented physical and ideological power ensures that the Revolution will perpetuate itself solely through terror and force.[40] This is, indeed, Burke's central thesis throughout his antirevolutionary oeuvre: the Revolution is an unprecedented extension of tyrannical power by a militant ideological state. In *Letters on a Regicide Peace*, he contends that the individual in France has been subsumed into the war state and that the revolutionaries have totally militarized society: "Individuality is left out of their scheme of government. The state is all in all. Everything is referred to the production of force; afterwards, everything is trusted to the use of it. It is military in its principle, in its maxims, in its spirit, and in all its movements. The state has dominion and conquest for its sole objects—dominion over minds by proselytism, over bodies by arms" (*Reg.* 5: 375, Letter 2). In these haunting lines, Burke is arguably adumbrating for the first time the specter of the modern totalitarian state, the expansionist ideological state of the twentieth century.

This thesis, of course, has been resisted on various grounds, but Burke insists that the Revolution is totally unprecedented, and he struggles to explain a phenomena for which he lacks a correspondent political vocabulary. In his *Remarks on the Policy of the Allies* (1793), he contends that the nationalization of power results in a new assault on private thought and individual liberty: "Committees, called of vigilance and safety, are everywhere formed: a most severe and scrutinizing inquisition, far more rigid than anything ever known or imagined. Two persons cannot meet and confer without hazard to their liberty, and even to their lives. Numbers scarcely credible have been executed, and their property confiscated. At Paris, and in most other towns, the bread they buy is a daily dole—which they cannot obtain without a daily ticket delivered to them by their masters."[41] Burke thus warns against a Revolution waged in the name of "the people" against "enemies of the people" (a catchall phrase originating with the Revolution), a Revolution that, to him, promises liberation but establishes instead a revolutionary vanguard that governs in the "people's" name, a vanguard enforced by committees of security and surveillance and the concentrated power of the state. This, of course, retrospectively echoes J. L. Talmon's thesis that modern totalitarianism has its roots in doctrines and practices central to the French Revolution.[42] The thesis and its antitheses usually take three forms: Burke was correct about the totalitarian nature of the Revolution; Burke was wrong, in that the Revolution was in no sense "totalitarian"; Burke opposed the Revolution, but to characterize it as "totalitarian" is to use Burke anachronistically for political ends usually associated with anticommunism.

Various issues come into play here. First, it is arguable that Burke was wrong about the nature of the Revolution: that, in fact, the Revolution broke the power of the old oppressive order, instituted the "rights of man," and contributed to the development of Western political democracy. In this reading, the Revolution was republican, not totalitarian, and Burke was fundamentally wrong with both his "facts" and conclusions.

While this is arguable, it seems to me that the other antithesis is incorrect: Burke opposed the Revolution but did not see it as anachronistically "totalitarian." For despite his lack of a correspondent political vocabulary, Burke insists throughout his antirevolutionary works that the Revolution is unprecedented in its oppressive scope, its militarization of society, and its hostile, interventionist nature. He also laments that he lacks the language to describe it adequately. He describes the nationalization of the country into a war economy, the state's intrusive regimentation of individual life, and its promotion of an "armed doctrine"—a hostile, alien ideology that propels invading Jacobin armies into Europe's Christian commonwealths. Whether Burke was right or wrong, whether he was prescient, lucky, or an inspired exaggerator, his analyses of revolutionary France approximate what is suggested by the adjective "totalitarian."

The next part of the antithesis is more tricky, even though it illustrates ironically Burke's continuing relevance to twentieth-century thought. Baldly put, it is that so-called cold-war scholars have used Burke's critique of the Revolution to legitimize their own critique of Marxism-Leninism. In this reading, anti-communist proponents produce superficial, anachronistic parallels between revolutionary France and Marxist-Leninist states. They, in effect, sever Burke's comments from their historical context in order to advance a partisan thesis.

It is true, of course, that the subject of Burke and the Revolution lends itself to polemical discourse, and this often results in unkind name calling on both sides.[43] This does not mean that Burke and the French

Revolution should be explained by reductive "left-right" positions, but it does suggest that Burke and his opponents consummated a preexistent cleavage in Western political thought and that this cleavage continues to constitute and color our historical understanding of the Revolution. Even rejections of "ideological" positions and the promotion of a "neutral" *tertium quid* are, inter alia, responses to this cleavage. In this context, Burke's totalitarian thesis and its applications need to be confronted head on rather than dismissed out of hand. It is pertinent, for instance, to consider whether or not Burke's critique applies to the modern totalitarian state, regardless of ideology. Although the issue here is that of tendentious selectivity, it is curious that with a few exceptions, neither opponents nor defenders of the Revolution have applied Burke's critique to Fascist totalitarian regimes. For instance, although Nazi Germany's ideology of a *volk* was racially more exclusive than the vague but more inclusive *peuple,* it was a terrorist ideology that produced massacres and rationalizations of expansionist Nazi power. Does Burke's critique apply, à la Talmon, only to left-wing totalitarian states or is his critique also pertinent to right-wing totalitarian states?[44]

One of the reasons that the last connection has been resisted is the Left's historical identification with the French Revolution as "the Mother of us all," and hence some of its implicit premises have been incorporated in standard critiques of Burke's position.[45] For instance, the thesis that ideas influence or cause events such as the French Revolution has been questioned by both American and European scholars: Burke and his admirers impose an idea on a historical event to explain and to provide it with an intellectual foundation it lacks. They demonize the Revolution, ignoring the complicated "material" factors that created it. In short, they resort to tendentious ideological interpretations.

There is some salient truth to this criticism, but the denigration of ideas as a contributory cause or factor in the Revolution and the unilateral elevation of material explanations also result in a distorted, reductionist caricature of the Revolution. The implicit premise that material conditions produce social ideas is itself an idea that was classically formulated by Marx and Engels in the nineteenth century. Indeed, the power of this idea has dominated twentieth-century French historiography, especially the works of Jean Jaurès, Georges Lefebvre, Albert Mathiez, and Albert Soboul.

Burke undoubtedly overemphasized the role of ideas in the Revolution, but recent scholarship is returning to a reconsideration of the nexus between ideas and praxis.[46] In this context, Burke's thesis is valuable if it directs our attention to the function of ideas in the formation of a revolutionary *mentalité* interacting with the given "world"—especially expressions of this *mentalité* in the action and language of the time. Thus Enlightenment ideas become not so much the cause of the Revolution as an essential "constituent of the event itself."[47]

Finally, and perhaps appropriately, the debate over the Revolution's nature is being refought in France, where a group of historians is waging a revolution (or counterrevolution) against orthodox defenses of the Revolution advanced by leading French historians in this century. This, in turn, has led to vigorous counterattacks—all of which constitutes the continuing "meaning" of the French Revolution and which brings us back to Burke.[48] In one sense, discussions of the French Revolution's significance are still expressed in terms Burke crystallized in the 1790s. And Burke's critique provoked the respondent political terms that still resonate in aggressive celebrations of the Revolution. It is perhaps here in the jagged juncture, where antithetical words diverge into discrepancies, in the interstices of warring and wounded language—the language that is our principal historical repository of what Burke and the Revolution "are"—that we can begin to understand the ways in which they both continue to tincture our world, even as they war in our language.

Notes

1. See, for instance, Conor Cruise O'Brien's Introduction to Edmund Burke, *Reflections on the Revolution in France*, ed. Conor Cruise O'Brien (Harmondsworth: Penguin, 1968).

2. According to Elizabeth Lambert, commenting at a Liberty Fund seminar on Burke's significance (Chicago, 21 May 1988). Lambert also notes that Burke helped create various institutions to provide for the poor and elderly in Beaconsfield, becoming a patron member who attended the meetings and visited those who needed assistance. In 1795 and 1796, when the price of corn was high, he had a windmill grind corn for the poor and sold them bread made in his house at a reduced rate. Burke was always providing or lending money to the needy, and his house was often filled with sickly Irish kinfolk, refugees, and French émigrés. With a government subsidy, he directed, near his home, a school for the children of émigré families.

3. Edmund Burke, *Reflections on the Revolution in France* (hereafter cited as

Refl.), in *The Works of Edmund Burke*, 12 vols. (St. Clair Shores, Mich.: Scholarly P, 1965) 3: 364 (hereafter cited as *Works*).

4. Edmund Burke, *Letters on a Regicide Peace* (hereafter cited as *Reg.*), in *Works* 5: 317; cf. fourth letter, *Reg.* 6: 61.

5. Cf. Edmund Burke, *An Essay towards an Abridgment of English History*, in *Works*, vol. 7.

6. Edmund Burke, *Observations on the Conduct of the Minority*, in *Works* 5: 62.

7. Edmund Burke, *Preface to the Address of M. Brissot to his Constituents*, in *Works* 5: 102.

8. J. M. Roberts, *The French Revolution* (London: Oxford UP, 1978) 139.

9. *Corpus mysticum* imagery permeated British common-law thought. See Ernst Kantorowicz, *The King's Two Bodies: A Study in Medieval Political Theology* (Princeton: Princeton UP, 1957) 405.

10. As early as 1769, Burke had criticized feudal vestiges in France's system of taxation (see his *On the Present State of the Nation*, in *Works* 1: 332). On 26 Sept. 1791, he wrote his son, Richard, that Europe's princes, nobles, and magistrates should issue a Bill of Rights guaranteeing, among other things, the abolishment of "all *Lettres de Cachet* and other means of arbitrary imprisonment" as well as the economic and ecclesiastical "abuses" of the Old Regime. He concluded that while he opposed France's revolutionary government, he could not "with a good heart and clear conscience" support the "establishment of monarchical despotism" in place of the Revolution's "system of Anarchy" (*The Correspondence of Edmund Burke*, ed. Thomas W. Copeland et al., 10 vols. [Chicago: U of Chicago P, 1958–78] 6: 413–14 [hereafter cited as *Corr.*]).

11. Many have noted that the Revolution's violent phase occurred after Burke had written the *Reflections* and have consequently accused him of hysterical overreaction. Burke probably started the *Reflections* in Jan. 1790, and by the time he completed it, the following events had already transpired: in July 1789, the worst phase of the "Great Fear" had begun; at the end of July, the National Assembly created the Comité des Recherches, which, according to Simon Schama "was, in effect, the first organ of a revolutionary police state"—arrogating "to itself all the powers which had been deemed so obnoxious under the old regime: opening letters, creating networks of informers and spies, searching houses without warrant, providing machinery for denunciation and encouraging patriots to bring any of their suspicions to the attention of the authorities. This committee of twelve members (the same size of the future Committee of Public Safety) was even empowered to imprison suspects without trial for as long as they were deemed a danger to the *patrie*" (Simon Schama, *Citizens: A Chronicle of the French Revolution* [New York: Knopf, 1989], 448–49; cf. *Refl.* 511]); in August (5–11), the National Assembly abolished "feudalism" (some vestiges of which Burke also opposed, but he believed that this unhistorical catchall

also affected France's inherited historical structures); on 26 Aug., the National Assembly approved the text of a *Declaration of the Rights of Man and Citizen* (a text Burke perceived as an indulgent exercise in metaphysical abstraction); on 6 Oct. the royal family was removed forcibly from Versailles to Paris; on 29 Oct. the Assembly passed a decree distinguishing between "active" and "passive" citizens—a distinction Burke ridiculed as a hypocritical example of revolutionary "democracy"; on 2 Nov. the National Assembly appropriated the church's property—an appropriation that he believed violated a fundamental part of the traditional constitution; on 19 Dec. the first *assignats* were issued, which became in the *Reflections* a metaphor for the economic, political, and moral bankruptcy of France; on 13 Feb. 1790 the religious orders were suppressed (unless engaged in charitable work or teaching) and the taking of monastic vows was prohibited; on 12 July the State's Civil Constitution of the Clergy was instituted; and on 19 July the titles and honors of the hereditary nobility were abolished. Since Burke contended that the Revolution was transforming the essential historical structure of France's constitution and hence, to him, an essential part of the inherited European commonwealth, he was concerned with the new forces transforming the traditional eighteenth-century world.

12. See, for instance, Burke's *Appeal from the New to the Old Whigs*, in *Works*, vol. 4: "the Author of our being is the Author of our place in the order of existence" (165).

13. Edmund Burke, *Speech on Army Estimates*, in *Works* 3: 221, 223.

14. Edmund Burke, *Letter to a Noble Lord*, in *Works* 5: 224–25.

15. Burke, *Observations on the Conduct of the Minority* 49.

16. See, for instance, the second letter in *Letters on a Regicide Peace*: the Revolution's "spirit lies deep in the corruptions of our common nature" (*Reg.* 5: 343).

17. Cf. Burke's letter of Jan. 1790—"the incurable ignorance of this most unenlightened age"—and his letter of 26 Feb., "I had rather remain in ignorance and superstition than be enlightened . . . out of the first principles of law and natural justice" (*Corr.*, 6: 80, 95). Burke continually ridicules Enlightenment ideology and its favorite self-descriptive adjective by suggesting that in practice it really means darkness and savagery. Pierre Bayle is representative of what Burke was ridiculing. In Apr. 1684 he had written: "We are now in an age which bids fair to become more and more enlightened, so much so that all preceding ages when compared with this will seem plunged into darkness" (*Nouvelles de la republique des lettres* [art. 11]). While it is true that only the Germans in the eighteenth century referred to the *Aufklärung* (in 1784, Kant had written his famous essay "What Is Enlightenment?") and the English did not import the word's meaning until the nineteenth century, the noun and adjective had a special significance for revolutionaries, who identified with previous struggles against the errors of the past. Throughout the seventeenth century,

"enlightened" meant "free from prejudices or superstition" (*Oxford English Dictionary*, def. 3)—an acceptation used frequently by Thomas Paine and Mary Wollstonecraft, for instance, in their celebration of a revolutionary age free from the very "prejudices" Burke defended.

18. Because Burke, Hippolyte Taine, and others have emphasized the nexus between Enlightenment ideas and the Revolution, it is often forgotten that the revolutionaries and their supporters were proclaiming the same connection, mutatis mutandis. Indeed, it was a cultural commonplace proclaimed by both sides. Mary Wollstonecraft is representative of the "revolutionary" side: Voltaire and Rousseau effected a "change in the sentiments of the French"; it "was a revolution in the minds of men, and only demanded a new system of government to be adapted to that change"; "Ideas so new . . . could not fail to produce a great effect on the minds of Frenchmen" (Wollstonecraft, *An Historical and Moral View of the French Revolution* [London, 1795] 7, 289, 363).

19. See *Refl.* 376–80; *Reg.* 5: 380. Cf. Burke's *Thoughts on French Affairs*, in *Works* 4: 325; on men of letters, see Burke's *Remarks on the Policy of the Allies*, in *Works* 4: 469. Burke recognized that men of talent were prevented from rising socially and that this contributed to their resentment of the Old Regime. By 1791, however, he thought this resentment had been exaggerated because many had been previously able to buy their way into the nobility. See *Thoughts on French Affairs* 326. Cf. Schama 116–18.

20. On the role of newspapers in spreading subversive ideas, see Burke, *Thoughts on French Affairs* 327–28, and *Corr.* 6: 229. Cf. Robert Darnton and Daniel Roche, eds., *Revolution in Print: The Press in France, 1775–1800* (Berkeley: U of California P, 1989); Emmet Kennedy, *A Cultural History of the French Revolution* (New Haven: Yale UP, 1989) 325.

21. Edmund Burke, *Letter to William Elliot*, in *Works* 5: 122. Cf. *Refl.* 414–15. This is Burke's radical-chic thesis. For its most vigorous expression, see his *Letter to a Noble Lord*.

22. Burke, *Letter to William Elliot* 122.

23. "The present war is, above all others of which we have heard or read, a war against landed property" (*Reg.* 5: 491, Letter 3); Burke, *Letter to William Elliot* 122.

24. Cf. Edmund Burke, *A Letter to William Smith on the Subject of Catholic Emancipation*, in *Works*, vol. 6, where Jacobinism is additionally an attempt "to eradicate prejudice out of the minds of men" in order to empower an ideological vanguard "capable of occasionally enlightening the minds of the people" (367).

25. Although it is now a commonplace that Robespierre and the Committee of Public Safety opposed the Dechristianization campaign, Fred Hembree has convincingly demonstrated, through an exhaustive examination of correspondence between the committee and representatives-on-mission, that Robespierre and his colleagues, in fact, intentionally accelerated the process of Dechristian-

ization while simultaneously issuing statements and decrees which proclaimed their adherence to the principle of religious toleration. See Fred Hembree, "Robespierre and Dechristianization in the Year II: Ideology and Religion during the French Revolution" (Ph.D. diss., U of South Carolina, 1986). Cf. Richard Cobb, *The People's Armies*, trans. Marianne Elliott (New Haven: Yale UP, 1987) 722 n. 1.

26. Cf. *Refl.* 324 and Olivier Bernier, *Words of Fire, Deeds of Blood: The Mob, the Monarchy, and the French Revolution* (Boston: Little, Brown, 1989) 105–106.

27. Burke, *Letter to a Noble Lord* 175.

28. Burke's formal response was, of course, due to a letter from Charles-Jean François Depont that arrived 4 Nov. 1789. For the chronological origins of the *Reflections*, see F. P. Lock, *Burke's Reflections on the Revolution in France* (London: Allen and Unwin, 1985) 52–57; Stanley Ayling, *Edmund Burke: His Life and Opinions* (New York: St. Martin's, 1988) 194–97.

29. Although Burke argues in the *Reflections* that Enlightenment and revolutionary books were not widely read in England, he later became more pessimistic about their influence. In France, Enlightenment literature was, despite beleaguered censorship, both popular and available twenty years before the Revolution, when illegal books sold best. See Robert Darnton, "Sounding the Literary Market in Prerevolutionary France," *Eighteenth-Century Studies* 17 (Spring 1984): 284–307, and *The Literary Underground of the Old Regime* (Cambridge: Harvard UP, 1982).

30. Edmund Burke, *A Letter to a Member of the National Assembly*, in *Works* 4: 31. For an examination of the authoritarian tendencies in Rousseau's thought and their reproduction in the revolutionary thought of Robespierre and Saint-Just, see Carol Blum, *Rousseau and the Republic of Virtue: The Language of Politics in the French Revolution* (Ithaca: Cornell UP, 1986).

31. Burke, *Thoughts on French Affairs* 376.

32. Burke, *Observations on the Conduct of the Minority* 18–19.

33. "It is remarkable that they never see any way to their projected good but by the road of some evil. Their imagination is not fatigued with the contemplation of human suffering through the wild waste of centuries" (Burke, *Letter to a Noble Lord* 207). Cf. Burke's letter to Adrien-Jean-François Duport (29 Mar. 1790): "I confess to you that I have no great opinion of that sublime abstract, metaphysic reversionary, contingent humanity, which in *cold blood* can subject the *present time,* and those whom we *daily see and converse with,* to *immediate* calamaties in favour of the *future and uncertain* benefit of persons who *only exist in idea*" (*Corr.* 6: 109).

34. See Steven Blakemore, *Burke and the Fall of Language: The French Revolution as Linguistic Event* (Hanover, N.H.: UP of New England, 1988), for a discussion of these matters.

35. Cf. *Refl.* 514: the new French state is a "military democracy."

36. *Oxford English Dictionary*, s.v. "purchase," def. 15.

37. See Burke, *Thoughts on French Affairs* 319–21.

38. This was a common counterrevolutionary charge. Cf. Daniel Dolfin, the Venetian ambassador at Vienna, reporting to the government of Venice in 1793: "The arms of the French are all the more dangerous since the poison of their maxims is diffused everywhere, and by preceding their armies contributes to their success. . . . The French Revolution is gradually bringing another equally dangerous revolution in the universal way of thinking" (quoted in R. R. Palmer, *The Age of the Democratic Revolution*, 2 vols. [Princeton: Princeton UP, 1964] 2: 34).

39. Burke, *Thoughts on French Affairs* 319; *Refl.* 147, 159; *Reg.* 5: 290, 168. Napoleon called the Revolution "an idea that has found bayonets."

40. Edmund Burke, *Remarks on the Policy of the Allies* 469–70.

41. Burke, *Remarks on the Policy of the Allies* 419; cf. Burke's comments on the Comité des Recherches in *Refl.* 511 and in *Thoughts on French Affairs* 352.

42. J. L. Talmon, *The Origins of Totalitarian Democracy* (New York: Praeger, 1960).

43. As François Furet points out, to take a position on the French Revolution is to risk being immediately assigned a political label, and then the person's comments can be either rejected or accepted based on the "correctness" of his "political" position (François Furet, *Interpreting the French Revolution* [Cambridge: Cambridge UP, 1981] 1).

44. The question is relevant not only if Burke is correct about the Revolution's inherent, repressive nature. Since his critique apparently delineates for the first time in Western political thought the nascent totalitarian state, it is pertinent to our own historical position. The obvious rejoinder is that in terms of scale and scope there can be no telling comparison between the Revolution and, for example, National Socialism. This is undoubtedly true, but it is also true that the modern state had 150 years to perfect the technology of repression and that while the comparatively miniature massacres in the Vendée and the federal cities, the forced drownings at Nantes, and the other political executions constitute the consummation of the Terror—the Terror also arguably had a genocidal component (see, for instance, Reynald Sécher's *Le Génocide franco-français: La Vendée-vengé* [Paris: Presses Universitaires de France, 1986]). Once the Jacobin state enshrined an abstract *peuple* as an even abstracter "general will" or Nazi Germany celebrated a mythical *volk,* then all enemies of the "people"—aristocrats, royalists, traitors, hoarders, Jews, and counterrevolutionary schemers—all *concrete* "enemies" could be isolated Manichaeistically and then targeted for detention or extermination. As the Revolution progressed, the crucial distinction between reprisals against real rebellions, in the Vendée and the federal cities, and the terror directed against fantasied "enemies of the people" became increasingly blurred.

45. See Robert Darnton, "The History of *Mentalités:* Recent Writings on Revolution, Criminality, and Death in France," in *Structure, Consciousness, and History*, ed. Richard Harvey Brown and Stanford M. Lyman (Cambridge: Cambridge UP, 1978) 107–108. Lenin, of course, identified strongly with the Revolution, and Bolsheviks like Trotsky were obsessed with historical parallels, fearing the possibility of a "Thermidor" reaction that would destroy the Russian Revolution. In *Interpreting the French Revolution*, François Furet explains how left-wing historiography incorporated the French Revolution into the macrocosmic Russian Revolution, making the former "the mother of a real, dated, and duly registered event—October 1917": "The Russian Bolsheviks never—before, during or after the Russian Revolution—lost sight of that filiation. But by the same token the historians of the French Revolution projected into the past their feelings or their judgements about 1917, and tended to highlight those features of the first revolution that seemed to presage or indeed anticipate those of the second. At the very moment when Russia—for better or worse—took the place of France as the nation in the vanguard of history, because it had inherited from France and from nineteenth-century thought the idea that a nation is *chosen* for revolution, the historiographical discourses about the two revolutions became fused and infected each other. The Bolsheviks were given Jacobin ancestors, and the Jacobins were made to anticipate the communists" (6). Note that, mutatis mutandis, "left-wing" historiography connects both revolutions, just as "right-wing" historiography does. (In his address to the United Nations [7 Dec. 1988], Mikhail Gorbachev commented that "the French Revolution of 1789 and the Russian Revolution of 1917 exerted a powerful impact on the very nature of history and radically changed the course of world development. . . . To a large extent, those two Revolutions shaped the way of thinking that is still prevalent in social consciousness" [*Time* 9 Dec. 1988: 18]).

46. See, for instance, Trygve R. Tholfsen, *Ideology and Revolution in Modern Europe: An Essay on the Role of Ideas in History* (New York: Columbia UP, 1984); William H. Sewell, Jr., "Ideologies and Social Revolutions: Reflections on the French Case," *Journal of Modern History* 57 (Mar. 1985) 57–85.

47. Tholfsen xi.

48. See David A. Bell, "All the King's Men," *New Republic* 18 Jan. 1988: 36–40; Richard Bernstein, "The French Revolution: Right or Wrong?" *New York Times Book Review* 10 July 1988: 1, 26–28.

Contributors

STEVEN BLAKEMORE, an associate professor of English at Palm Beach Atlantic College, has published on a variety of subjects in English and American literature. He is the author of *Burke and the Fall of Language: The French Revolution as Linguistic Event* (1988).

FRANS DE BRUYN is an associate professor of English at the University of Ottawa, Ontario, Canada. He completed his dissertation on Edmund Burke at the University of Virginia and has published numerous articles on Restoration and eighteenth-century writers and subjects.

TOM FURNISS wrote his dissertation on Burke at the University of Southampton. He is a lecturer in the Department of English Studies at the University of Strathclyde, Glasgow, Scotland. He has written on political language and has published various articles on Edmund Burke, Thomas Paine, and Mary Wollstonecraft.

CHRISTOPHER REID is a lecturer in English, specializing in eighteenth-century studies, at Queen Mary College, London. Among his publications is *Edmund Burke and the Practice of Political Writing* (1987).

DANIEL E. RITCHIE was educated at Amherst and Rutgers, where he wrote his dissertation on Burke. He is an associate professor of English at Bethel College. The editor of *Edmund Burke: Appraisals and Applications* (1990), he has published articles on various other subjects in eighteenth-century literature.

PETER J. STANLIS is Distinguished Professor of Humanities emeritus at Rockford College. From 1982 to 1986 he was on the National Council for the Humanities and is a British Academy Fellow. For thirteen years he was the editor of *Studies in Burke and His Time*, and his voluminous articles and books include *Edmund Burke and the Natural Law* (1958), *Edmund Burke: A Bibliography of Secondary Studies to 1982* (1983), which he edited with Clara I. Gandy, and *Edmund Burke: The Enlightenment and Revolution* (1991).

Index